W9-BMN-064

Jesus and Muhammad

JESUS
AND
MUHAMMAD

Parallel Tracks, Parallel Lives

F. E. PETERS

OXFORD
UNIVERSITY PRESS
2011

OXFORD
UNIVERSITY PRESS

Oxford University Press, Inc., publishes works that further
Oxford University's objective of excellence
in research, scholarship, and education.

Oxford   New York
Auckland   Cape Town   Dar es Salaam   Hong Kong   Karachi
Kuala Lumpur   Madrid   Melbourne   Mexico City   Nairobi
New Delhi   Shanghai   Taipei   Toronto

With offices in
Argentina   Austria   Brazil   Chile   Czech Republic   France   Greece
Guatemala   Hungary   Italy   Japan Poland   Portugal   Singapore
South Korea   Switzerland   Thailand   Turkey   Ukraine   Vietnam

Copyright © 2011 by Oxford University Press, Inc.

Published by Oxford University Press, Inc.
198 Madison Avenue, New York, NY 10016

www.oup.com

Oxford is a registered trademark of Oxford University Press

Library of Congress Cataloging-in-Publication Data
Peters, F. E. (Francis E.)
Jesus and Muhammad : parallel tracks, parallel lives / F. E. Peters.
p.   cm.
Includes bibliographical references and index.
ISBN 978-0-19-974746-7
1. Jesus Christ—Biography.
2. Muhammad, Prophet, d. 632—Biography.
3. Christianity and other religions—Islam.
4. Islam—Relations—Christianity. I. Title.
BT301.3.P43   2010
200.92′2—dc22
[B] 2010006017

3 5 7 9 8 6 4 2

Printed in the United States of America
on acid-free paper

For
Christine Goettsche Peters
a pluperfect II, truly

Contents

Introduction: Clearing the Ground

"CHRISTIANITY" AND "ISLAM" are notions of enormous complexity, complex enough to give considerable pause to anyone tempted to define, or even merely to describe, either of them. And yet they are apparently embraced in their totality by the millions of believers who solemnly assert, "I am a Christian" or "I am a Muslim." The average Christian or Muslim probably does not much advert to all the details of those constructs, and, indeed, when presented with this or that particular feature of Christianity or Islam, might well say, "No, that's not what I believe. I do not believe that hell will last for eternity" or "No, I do not believe that our every act is determined by God."

This rejection of parts of what has been held to be an integral tradition is not new nor has it been confined to the ill-instructed or casual believer. Christianity and Islam have been evolving from their very inception, and not merely in incidentals but in their core components. What are called "heresy" by Christians and "innovation" by Muslims are in effect divergent opinions on this or another content of the faith. If they fail to attract support, they are consigned to the believers' popular catalogs of failed ideas and their adherents may even linger on at the margins of the community. But when and if these novel points of view eventually prevail, the earlier offensive labeling is removed and Christianity itself, or Islam, is quietly altered—the notion of immutability must be preserved—as when Christians began to hold that Mary was conceived without sin or Muslims that Muhammad was incapable of sin.

Though both religious systems are deeply committed to the proposition that God's will and God's revelation are eternal and immutable or, to put it in historical terms, that what the Christian or the Muslim now believes is what Jesus or Muhammad originally preached, and intended, the content, shape, and concerns of both Christianity and Islam have in fact changed over the centuries. Not essentially, the believer may insist. We set that issue aside; its resolution is the burden of the believer, not the historian. Here it is rather the fact of change that is being looked at and, more specifically, change as it affects the founding figures of the two communities, Jesus and Muhammad.

The Art of Portraiture

The portraits of Jesus and Muhammad are central to Christianity and Islam respectively. And not simply as sketches but as portraits drawn from life, as verifiable accounts of two historical personages and what happened to and around them. For the believer, that portrait is richly figured from its bold outlines down to its fine details and with nuanced color and shadings. It is a complex package indeed that the believer accepts when he or she affirms, as each Christian must, "I believe in Jesus Christ, the only Son of God," or the Muslim, "I bear witness . . . that Muhammad is the Envoy of God." Complex and evolving. The portrait of Jesus, which was substantially redrawn in boldly different colors in the fourth century, was refigured for many in the mid-nineteenth and mid-twentieth centuries and again in the final decades of the twentieth. That of Muhammad, though arguably more stable than that of Jesus, has been turned this way or that by Sufis and socialists, modernists and fundamentalists.

Historians can look at the current portraits of the two men and detect many of the various overcoats (though not necessarily their own!) that have been laid down on the original. What they attempt to discern is not the actual man, to be sure, who may be lost to us, but the original *portrait*, the one that the earliest generation of believers began to figure for themselves. We must remind ourselves throughout that, for all the stripping away of accretions and for all the deconstructions of the texts before us, we are still dealing with portraiture, with artists' renderings of a subject who was Jesus or who was Muhammad. We can conjecture about the men who sat for those portraits, but we nonetheless see them only through the eyes of the committed artists who set them down in writing.

Our only relief from the constriction of authorship is the knowledge that the Jesus and the Muhammad who were originally presented to us were not the products of an overly idiosyncratic or individualistic act of creation. Each of the Gospels, even if it was produced by the individual named, represents a *social* portrait of Jesus. Ibn Ishaq was a craftsman-auteur, not a Francis Bacon throwing off his own personally incandescent vision of Muhammad; and even John, the most particular of the evangelists, was writing to and for a community, confirming, and perhaps tweaking, a Jesus they already knew. Among them all, Paul alone warns us that we are in the presence of an original artist, but his portrait of Jesus is theological-impressionistic rather than biographical-realistic. Paul's Jesus Christ is a bold figure, but Paul was not working from life but rather from an already conceived sketch of the actual Jesus of Nazareth whose bare outlines alone we can occasionally discern there (1 Cor 15:3–5).

The Long Quests

This is not, of course, the first attempt to retrieve the original take on either Jesus or Muhammad. Quite the contrary: the "quest for the historical Jesus," as it was called in one famous book on the subject, has been going on at least since David Friedrich Strauss' *The Life of Jesus Critically Examined* (German original, 1835), and that for Muhammad since two decades later with the 1851 publication, likewise in German, of the first volume of Aloys Sprenger's *The Life and Teaching of Muhammad*. Since then, many have followed in their tracks.[1] The Jesus quest in particular has become not a path but a crowded highway, while the search for the historical Muhammad has been transformed for some into a dangerous passage, not because it is crowded but by reason of certain outraged bystanders who resent any traffic along this particular road.

Following back along the historians' footsteps will inevitably lead us to fashion our own portraits of Jesus and Muhammad, as many others have already done, and on the same evidence. As we shall see in detail, that evidence is, for both men, of two sorts. The first is documentary: we have at hand what are purported to be the very words uttered by Jesus and Muhammad. Muhammad's are freestanding as a work called the Quran, but in the Christian instance, Jesus' words are embedded in our second type of evidence, four biographical portraits whose quite unhistorical point is made in the very titles of the works. "This is," the Gospels announce, "the Good News of Jesus Christ, the Son of God." And the *Sira* or *Life* of the Prophet is no less forthcoming: it is, it tells us, nothing less than "The Life of the Envoy of God." The Christians prefer the portrait: it is not the sayings source but the biographical Gospels that are incorporated into the liturgy. Muslims favor the words: the faithful pray the Quran, not the *Sira*. The Quran is the stuff of liturgy; the *Sira*, of piety. But Muslims venerate the Quran not because it reveals Muhammad, but rather because it reveals God, whose very words, they believe, it records.

History and Revelation

What I have just called preferences are in fact determinations imposed by two different views of revelation. For the Muslim, revelation is *circumstantially historical.* God's final message to humankind was delivered through a middle-aged Arab at a given time and a given place: Muhammad ibn Abdullah, first at Mecca and then at Medina, between AD 610 and 632. For Christians, revelation is *history itself:* what was said and done by and to Jesus of Nazareth in Palestine between 4 BC and AD 30.

Islam springs from a revelation in history, while Christianity rests upon history as revelation. The latter leads directly back to and focuses on the man Jesus, while the Muslim view directs us through but beyond Muhammad to the Word of God. This is not a place where the historian wants to go. Christians present the Jesus evidence of the Gospels as divinely guaranteed history, and the historian is both willing and capable of ignoring the guarantee, which is underwritten by one or another theory of inspiration, and proceeds to confront the portraits of Jesus as admittedly tendentious documents. The *Sira* is put forward in much the same evangelical manner by Muslims, and if they rely less than the Christians on divine inspiration to validate the *Sira*'s contents, the Muslims are no less convinced than the Christians that the biographical document they have before them, which is as openly tendentious as the Gospels, represents the truth of the matter with regard to the life of Muhammad.

The Quran is not, however, represented by Muslims or the Muslim tradition as anything remotely resembling what we think of as history. It is not in their eyes a record, accurate or otherwise, of the sayings of Muhammad. Rather, it is a collection of the *sayings of God* and any attempt to treat it otherwise, as simply a *document*, for example, that conceptual touchstone of nineteenth-century historicism, is strenuously resisted and summarily dismissed. So the historian approaches the Quran document without Muslim consent, which is not crucial, but also without valuable Muslim assistance. Muslims have been copiously helpful on matters of content and even, more recently, on style, where the dogma of the inimitability of the Quran long inhibited analytical criticism, but they are still notably and understandably reticent on both the sources and composition of the Quran.

Saints and Their Lives

If we look to the narrative sources for Jesus and Muhammad, we immediately recognize the familiar genre of biography. We can be more specific, however. This is not only biography; the Gospels and the *Sira* belong to that specialized type of biography called hagiography, the life of a saint. Unfortunately, the lives of saints make good reading but very bad history. We observe from countless examples that the charisma of holy men or women, the quality that attracted followers during their lifetime, often grows stronger after death. Long after saints have departed life, their memories and their continuing ability to perform wondrous deeds draw people to their tombs and shrines. But if their reputation grows larger, so too does their legend. Memories expand, stories are enlarged as they are retold. And the retellings of saints' stories become literary shrines on the same scale, and often with similar ornament, as the buildings that enclose their remains or commemorate their holiness. Hagiography is not the history of the saint; it is his or her monument.

This is a book about two holy men. They are not, however, the familiar saints, men and women earmarked by themselves or others, or even by the deity, as possessing a high degree of sanctity and so too special powers. The holy men in question here, Jesus and Muhammad, are of course saints by any definition of that word. They were understood during their lifetime and after to possess an extraordinary degree of holiness. But that sanctity arose not from their powers or their persuasiveness but from their office. In the simplest terms, both men were regarded in the first instance as prophets, individuals chosen to be the mouthpieces of God, men sent to warn and to instruct. Other saints earn their authority by their personal holiness, that famous "odor of sanctity" that exudes from their persons. Jesus and Muhammad doubtless possessed that, but their authority derived from elsewhere, as they claimed and as their followers believed: they were the chosen of God. And they spoke with an authority higher than themselves.

But there is much more. The public instruction put forth by Jesus and Muhammad was not mere wisdom. Many prophets have given counsel or warning and many saints have preached reform or renewal, but what proceeded from the mouths of these two was radical and foundational: radical in that it represented a break with the current religious tradition and foundational in that it marked the beginning of a new "way" that was, on God's own authority, necessary for salvation. The words of these prophet saints would be ignored at the explicit price of eternity.

Saints are optional. If many are difficult to ignore, in the end the faithful make their own choices: cults wax and wane; saints slide or tumble, or indeed are occasionally cast, into oblivion. On the record at least, both Judaism and Islam do not much approve of saints or, to be more precise, the *cult* of saints, the public veneration accorded to the remains or the memory of holy men and women, which is thought to demean the divine. The Saudis, for example, are notorious, even among Muslims, for their demolition of the tomb shrines of saints. Jesus and Muhammad—whose tomb remains untouched, indeed, extravagantly enlarged, in Saudi Medina—are not optional holy men. The Christian creed offers no alternatives to the affirmation that Jesus Christ is in fact the only Son of God. Its Muslim counterpart is likewise insistent. It has only two members. The first is an affirmation of monotheism, "There is no god but The God," and the second memorably and unmistakably announces that "Muhammad is the Sent One of God." Here too no alternatives are offered. Unlike David or Isaiah, but quite like Moses, these two prophets are *essential* saints, objects of respect, veneration, and, what is crucial, perfect obedience.

In the Eyes of the Believers

The two men are by no means equivalent in the eyes of their followers. For Muslims, the Meccan Arab Muhammad ibn Abdullah was a prophet; indeed, the "seal of the prophets," the end of the prophetic line of monotheistic prophets that began with Abraham and included Jesus in its number.[2] But, for all that, Muhammad was a mortal; he was born, lived, and died in Western Arabia at the turn into the seventh Christian century. As just remarked, his remains are believed to be in a tomb inside a mosque in Medina, where he died.

The Galilean Jew Jesus, or Jesus Christ, as the Christians call him, was often taken for a prophet by his contemporaries, but in his followers' eyes he was and is the Messiah, the promised Savior of Israel. He was born, lived, and died in Roman Palestine at the turn into the first Christian century. But, Christians avow, he was subsequently raised from the dead, as many witnesses testified, and so demonstrated that he was truly the Son of God and the Savior and Redeemer of all humankind.

Jesus and Muhammad are, then, considerably more than saints, and the historical recollections of their lives, as there surely must have been, have naturally become magnets for a great mass not only of myth and legend but of argument and even polemic. And they are objects of faith. Myths and legends are accretions on history and can be removed, not entirely without pain, by paring with the critical scalpel. But the creeds or statements of faith take us into a different place. "I believe" or "I bear witness" is quite different from "I know as a fact." Faith, it is said, leads to understanding—*Credo ut intelligam*, as one of the believers elegantly put it—which may even be true. But the historian is seeking a different, perhaps even a lesser, result: demonstrated knowledge. Faith does not supply such. It can *assert* which sayings of Jesus or Muhammad are authentic, but it cannot demonstrate that they are such. The historian thinks he can, and if the results are at times tentative and always subject to rebuttal, they have a claim to be verifiably true.

For many centuries Christians and Muslim historians were content to accept faith's assertions on the subjects of Jesus and Muhammad, but in the nineteenth century, at the term of intellectual and religious developments that had been going on in the West since at least the sixteenth-century Reformation and the eighteenth-century Enlightenment, historians began to address afresh the lives of these two transcendental holy men, to disregard the assertions of faith and to pose the questions of history.

One of the critical moments in the passage of Jesus and Muhammad from the hands of believers into those of historians was the 1906 book by Albert Schweitzer titled *The Quest for the Historical Jesus*, and that characterization has often been appropriated to describe the historians' inquiries concerning both men. Muhammad in fact quickly followed Jesus into the historians' dock in the nineteenth century, and was subjected to the same critical scrutiny. And, it is worth noting, in both instances the inquiry was conducted by Western Protestant Christian scholars, where each of those qualifiers carried its own considerable baggage.

Polemic and History

No historical search begins from scratch, and certainly not the one being proposed here: no one comes to the investigation into the lives of Jesus and Muhammad without prior information and, even more consequentially, with no opinions regarding these two extraordinary, and extraordinarily famous, individuals. Indeed, with the possible exception of one or two Asian surnames, "Muhammad" has been given to more living individuals than any other name on the planet.[3] But if Christians know a great deal about Jesus, and Muslims about Muhammad, the knowledge that passes between the two communities is subject to intense screening. Christians' knowledge of Muhammad was long grounded in argument rather than evidence, and even now polemic remains a discernible ingredient in Western writing about the Prophet of Islam. Muslims for their part do not indulge in polemic against Jesus: the Quran instructs them that "Isa," as he is called in Arabic, is among the most esteemed of the prophets, a human who has not yet experienced death, as most Muslims believe, and who must one day return and suffer the fate common to all mortal humankind.

But if Muslims' appreciation of Jesus is grounded in the Quran, their knowledge of Jesus is also limited to the Quran and to what later Muslim commentators made of what they found there. Which was not a great deal. The Quran gives no signs of being acquainted with the actual Christian

Gospels, which are our earliest and best source of information about Jesus. Rather, the Quranic information about Jesus seems late, derivative, and legendary.[4] And since the Quran is the authoritative word of God, the Muslim has little incentive to consult the Gospels, which are, in any event, unreliable since they were tampered with by the Christians, according to a well-established Muslim article of faith.

If Muslims are instructed by their Scripture to venerate Jesus, Christians are warned by their religious tradition that Muhammad was a false prophet. In Christian eyes, Jesus is a unique event, without predecessors (there were those who foresaw his coming, however) and certainly without successors. The Jews divide the world into *Benei Israel*, themselves, and the *goyyim*, or Gentiles; and Christians, though they have carved out a special—and highly ambivalent—social and theological category for Jews, have generally followed the Jewish example and categorized all non-Christians as pagans, heathens, or infidels. Such are the Muslims.

Some Christians knew better, early and late. At its first appearance, Islam appeared to Christians too similar to their own faith to be a species of the familiar paganism. Islam looked and sounded like a Christian heresy[5]—early on Arabia was described by a Christian authority as "teeming with heresies"—and Muhammad, it was surmised, must have gotten his information from some malicious and disgruntled Christian monk; a charlatan, yes, but on the Christian model.

As Christians became better informed and, more to the point, as more and more Christians were swept under Muslim sovereignty, heresy was discarded as too benign a characterization of Islam. And the portrait of Muhammad turned darker and coarser as well. The Muslim sources began to be translated in the West and the information they provided became fodder for Christian polemicists. The much-married Prophet was portrayed as the epitome of an uncontrolled sexuality, his lifestyle was the archetype of *luxuria*, and Muhammad the military commander the antithesis of the pacifist Jesus. Prophets were not made of such stuff. The portrait has softened somewhat among more self-conscious moderns, but the polemical undertone still lingers in contemporary Western presentations of the Prophet of Islam.

Two Foreign Countries

An awareness of the theological rivalry that has turned sour with polemic in much of what passes as history in Christian and Muslim circles is only one step toward objectivity in writing simultaneously about these two surpassingly important religious figures. There is also the less discernible hobble of cultural bias for a Western historian approaching a figure in a different, and alien, culture. It was once famously remarked that "the past is a foreign country." In this instance we have not one but two quite different foreign countries.

The literary sources on Jesus and Muhammad are markedly divergent. The naked sayings of Jesus are couched in discourse that is relatively familiar to the Western historian because his own discourse has been modeled in part on it, and its style, content, and even its tropes have become embedded in Western modes of expression. Muhammad's words in the Quran are in a different register. They are in a Semitic language whose expressions and expressive intentions are different from our own Indo-European tongues.

That same linguistic dislocation took place in the passage of Jesus' words from his own native Aramaic into the evangelists' Greek, but in that instance their passage was eased by the fact that the Gospels' original reporters were contemporary aural witnesses to Jesus' words and had ears firmly fixed in both the Semitic and Indo-European Greek cultural milieus. We hear the Quran, or rather, in the case of the Western historian, we read the Quran across a profound linguistic and cultural divide and the yawning chasm of nearly a millennium and a half.

But on its own evidence, the Quran was apparently opaque to some of its own first audience—"How can I explain to you what X means?" is a frequent Quranic refrain—and it was certainly so to many of its medieval commentators for whom Arabic, though not necessarily its artificial art-speech, the Quran's very specialized poetic idiom, was a mother tongue. And it is assuredly such to us, and particularly to non-Muslims who are reluctant to accept the *communis opinio Islamica* on what the text means.

The other pieces of evidence, the Gospels and the classical *Sira* or *Life* of the Prophet, are both cast in a familiar biographical form. They display, in chronological order, the sayings and deeds of Jesus or Muhammad from the cradle to the grave, and beyond. In each the content has been collected from earlier sources, and it is there, in the collection and choice of material for inclusion and its subsequent presentation to the reader, that the two biographical traditions chiefly diverge. Both had their theological agenda, of course, and that was a powerful determinant of what went into the work and what did not. But there are further determinations that confront the reader who takes up the texts looking not for conviction but for intelligibility. The historiographical compass of the Hellenized Christians who wrote the Gospels and that of the Arab Muslims behind the *Sira* have very different settings.

Western readers are products of the same cultural tradition that lies, however imperfectly, behind the form if not the content of the Gospels. Though our comprehension has been broadened somewhat by the Semitic rhythms that shine through even translations of the Bible, we are entirely at home with the writer called Luke who composed the Gospel and the Acts of the Apostles. Not so with the Quran. The Gospels were written in the popular, almost demotic Koine Greek of the Mediterranean world. The Quran, in contrast, was orally composed in an improvisational and artisanal Arabic *Kunstsprache* that was the poetic medium of the day and whose intricacies were in this particular case thought to be God-given. Our Quran is an earthly representation, a "copy" (*mushaf*) of an eternal heavenly prototype, the "Mother of the Book" (43:3–4), and so the Muslim appreciation of their Scripture is in the first instance theological: the Quran is made up of the words—and the diction— of God Himself and hence its style is miraculously inimitable, a quality not shared by the Sacred Books of the Jews and Christians.

If the theological dogma of the "inimitability of the Quran" effectively dislocated serious *historical* analysis of Quranic style and diction on the part of Muslims, it has not prevented Westerners from making their own assessments of the text. Generally speaking, they have found it difficult to share the Muslims', and particularly the Arab Muslims', appreciation of it as a product of art, a judgment that is not particularly germane in this context.[6] What is at issue here is the validity and use of the Quran as a document, and most particularly as documentary evidence not for the divine *economia* but for Muhammad, the man from whose mouth it reportedly issued in the opening decades of the seventh century.

These and other evidence issues will be addressed in due course; here it is enough to signal the tangled landscape across which this quest is and has been conducted and to attempt to clear some of the ground before us. Here we have to confront not only our own ignorance but centuries of misunderstanding buttressed by ill will. Jesus and Muhammad, it is immediately clear, are not simply objects of study: they are the figures for whom millions upon millions have lived and died over the centuries. They are symbols of hope on one hand and, on the other, warners of God's terrible judgment on those who fail to heed their words. They are bringers of peace and the sword.

Parallel Tracks, Parallel Lives

Jesus and Muhammad have been the subject of the most sustained and detailed biographical inquiries in the Western tradition, and the quest for the historical

Jesus in particular has been almost a laboratory experiment in the historiography of the preindustrial era. And its successes and failures have seeped inevitably into the parallel inquiry into the life of Muhammad. The quest for both men will be retraced here, but *pari passu* and side by side in the hope that each of the parallel tracks might illuminate the other. In its course it will become increasingly clear what the two investigations have in common and how and why they differ. But it will reveal as well the parallels and differences in the persons and careers of the two men, each one of whom stands at the head of a religious tradition that divides much of the inhabited world and now claims, each of them, more than a billion adherents.

It hardly needs saying, but almost every sentence of what follows, or, more accurately, every word, has been the subject of both intense investigation and sustained and often acrimonious debate. We are intruding on privileged subjects whose followers have profound, indeed existential, commitments to their character, their teachings, and their significance. That condition imposes a limitation and a responsibility. The limitation is that it is impossible on this scale to support with the usual academic apparatus either my every statement of the facts of the matter or my own judgments as to their likelihood. I have tried to provide the appropriate authority when it comes to Scripture, but otherwise I can only offer a Guide to Further Reading where the reader will be invited to enter deeper and more opaque waters. The responsibility is more complex: to understand and accept the fact that these two are not simply figures of history and to respect what each stands for without allowing that respect to prejudice my historical judgment. It is simple in the saying but daunting indeed in the doing. The reader will judge.

I have been writing this book, or something like it, for most of my adult life, putting Jews, Christians, and Muslims face to face and interrogating them on their beliefs and practices. The questions, I hope, have been rigorous but not hostile. The answers have come at times from the principals themselves and at times from me when I have made bold to speak for them. But on this occasion the principals really *are* the principals, at least in the case of the Christians and Muslims. We are back at the beginning.

What I have written in the past has not been to everyone's liking. There is no surprise there: this may be the most inflammable matter devised by humankind, the same ingenious species that has delivered itself of gunpowder, dynamite, and the atom bomb. And there was not only the matter; there was also me, laboring under every current misconception since Prohibition. But I crave no indulgence: I have been at this so long that I have by now run out of any conceivable excuse for not getting it right. So this time I did.

Jesus and Muhammad

I

The Settings

IN THE COURSE of the almost two-century-long critical inquiry into their lives, the very existence of both Jesus and Muhammad has been denied by some. Such radical denials are generally prompted not so much by the evidence as by polemic, or perhaps wishful thinking. It is the believers who chiefly bother the skeptics, those devotees so committed to their faith, it is suspected, that they might well be willing to invent anything, including its founder. There are others who in greater numbers judge the testimony of the so-called witnesses so tendentious that they find it difficult to accept any of it, even on the most fundamental points. And some doubters simply misunderstand the nature of history, particularly the history of the premodern world. The evidence for the existence of Jesus and Muhammad is far better than that for most of their contemporaries, even the most famous. We do not always know what to make of the evidence for them, but the evidence itself is relatively plentiful, coming as it does from a world whose archives have not survived. We have no baptismal records from first-century Judea or the seventh-century Hijaz, no marriage registers or tax receipts. There are no autographs, no photos.[1]

Even though we lack these reassuring direct connections to the two men—and to all of their contemporaries—there is a great deal of other material to sift through. The best and most useful of the available evidence for the careers of Jesus and Muhammad is literary, that is, written accounts about them, many from apparent eyewitnesses, and some even purport to have preserved our subjects' very words. All of these are addressed in the next chapter; here we must first take a broader look around, a horizon tour of the landscape where the two men spent their lives.

Their followers regard each as divinely inspired, but we have no instruments for hearing that voice from on high. We can attempt to pry somewhat into the unconscious of each, but we cannot eavesdrop on the converse between Jesus and his "Father who is in heaven" or hear what transpired between Muhammad and the Angel Gabriel. Our crude antenna settings are for the grosser stuff of human portraits and physical, social, and political landscapes and, above all, the religious environment from which each came and to which each addressed himself. This is not to suggest that either Jesus or Muhammad was simply the product of that environment; but even if the preaching of each came from on high, how it was delivered and how it was received was a function of the atmospherics in first-century Palestine and the seventh-century Hijaz. We begin, then, with a weather report.

Jesus and First-Century Palestine

The Romans were not always careful about names: they called the august Hellenes "Graeci" after the name of one of the less significant Hellenic tribes they happened to encounter. So it is no surprise that they called the land of Canaan, which the Jews thought of as the Kingdom of Israel, "Palestine," after the long-disappeared Philistines. Eventually it became "the Palestines," since the onetime Kingdom of Israel had long since splintered into three smaller domains: Judea, the territory around sacred Jerusalem, east to the Jordan and west to the Mediterranean; in the north, rural and agricultural Galilee around the sea of the same name and up to the sources of the Jordan River; and in between, loudly schismatic Samaria, with a population who were genuine Hebrews in their own eyes but hybrid aliens and illegitimate pretenders in the view of the Jews who surrounded them.

The people in Judea and Galilee were both called, somewhat confusingly, "Judeans," even though they did not all live in the area called Judea. The Romans decided that these troublesome people constituted both a religious and an ethnic community and so they were all *Ioudaei*, the linguistic ancestors of our "Jews." Almost all the population of Judea were in fact Jews in that sense, but the population of Galilee was somewhat more hybrid: Iturean Arabs and the residue of the old Syro-Canaanite population there worshiped gods other than Yahweh, the tribal and ethnic God of Israel, whose temple was in Judean Jerusalem.[2]

The territory under "Judean" control waxed and waned over the centuries, as did the places where Jews were found. Since their sixth-century BC exile in Babylonia had led to the first Jewish *diaspora*, or "dispersal," Jews had slowly spread around the Mediterranean and eventually into most of the port cities ringing that sea. By the first century there were also Jewish settlements on the east bank of the Jordan and up onto the Golan Heights east of the Sea of Galilee. Jewish sovereignty extended there as well, particularly under Herod, a half-Jewish puppet king who ruled (37–4 BC) over a simulacrum of the Kingdom of Israel on behalf of the Romans, who were the real masters of the Mediterranean basin.

We know a great deal about Herod, and about his kingdom, thanks to Josephus, the Jewish historian who, between AD 75 and 95, published two major histories of Jewish affairs, the *Jewish War* and the *Antiquities of the Jews*, which not only take notice of Jesus, John the Baptist, and James, the brother of Jesus,[3] but constitute a major element in our understanding of the Palestinian milieu into which Jesus was born and out of which his movement evolved. Religion and politics, social and economic issues are all part of Josephus' attempt to explain Judaism to a not very sympathetic audience of Gentile readers as well as to his fellow Jews, who were also expected to read his work. And both groups read it, it should be noted, not in imperial Latin or the vernacular Aramaic of Palestine, but in Greek, the lingua franca of the literate Mediterranean.

It is Josephus, himself a Galilean, who alerts us to the social and political unrest in that province. And it is thanks to him that we have some understanding of the Jewish king Herod and the Roman procurator Pontius Pilate, Herod Antipas, the tetrarch (a vanity title) of Galilee, and the high priest Caiaphas, all major players in the life of Jesus of Nazareth. It is also Josephus, a Pharisee as well as a historian, who is our instructor on the parties and sects of Palestinian Judaism in the run-up to the great war with Rome (AD 66–70).

What has more recently attracted the interest of Jesus historians are Josephus' remarks on Moses and Elijah, who were also prominent paradigms in the Gospels, and his considerable attention to the phenomenon of charismatic prophecy, itself often linked to insurgency, in the Palestine of that era. There was Theudas (ca. AD 44–46)—Josephus calls him a "charlatan"—who cast himself as a new Moses who would part the waters of the Jordan. The Romans intervened: they killed or arrested his followers and Theudas himself was beheaded. The Christians remembered him very well (Acts 5:36) and they remembered the Egyptian insurgent (Acts 21:38), a "false prophet" to Josephus, who led a large force of armed men against Jerusalem, and Judah the Galilean (Acts 5:37), a probably messianic insurgent, and the father and grandfather of insurgents, whose family bravado—ill-considered according to Josephus—spills across many of the Jewish historian's pages. And finally there is the odd shouting Jesus who, as Josephus tells it, got under the skin of Jews and Romans alike in the late 50s in Jerusalem. Roman Palestine was not a very quiet place in the first half of the first century.

The political and sectarian issues that dominate Josephus' account of con-temporary Palestine do occasionally arise in Jesus' followers' accounts of his life—he is confronted, for example, with questions regarding taxation (Mk 12:13–17 and parallels)—but they seem remarkably marginal when viewed through the prism of the Gospels. The Romans are hardly present in evangel-ical Galilee and appear center stage only in the last days of Jesus' life, when they are the agents of his trial and execution. The Gospels are not about the Romans, nor is the Acts of the Apostles. There is, of course, the pious centu-rion Cornelius, whom Peter converts in Acts 10 and 11, and the various offi-cials who had to deal with the troublesome Paul, but in the Acts of the Apostles, no less than in the Gospels, the Romans are the agents of a criminal and not a political process.

What Was on Jewish Minds in the First Century?

Surrounding the historian Josephus is a body of Jewish religious writing that was not in the end included in the Bible.[4] These are the "apocryphal" or "restricted" books eventually considered, for sectarian or other reasons, as unworthy of being included among the authentic witnesses to God's covenant with Israel, but they were being read by Jesus and his contemporaries and form part of the spiritual landscape of that era. The nonbiblical works that interest us here are precisely those in circulation in Jesus' day. They cover a broad spec-trum of genres and subjects: rewritings, often for sectarian purposes, of older biblical books; wisdom literature, freestanding moral exhortations where Hellenic influence is apparent in the exaltation of "Sophia" and her effects; and finally, the abundant apocalypses ("unveilings") that described, in a highly imaginative and emotive fashion, the anticipated events of the Last Days.

The biblical apocrypha are a mixed bag. Many of the works were originally composed in Greek, the chief language of the Jewish Diaspora; many are com-posites of different works lumped together under a single (spurious) name like that of Abraham and Moses, Ezra and Baruch; and many too display trans-parent Christian interpolations. The reason why the Christians tampered with the texts is the same that promotes our own interest. These writings at their broadest show what was on the minds of many Jews in that era, including Jesus' own followers. More narrowly, they provide a conceptual matrix into which both Jesus and his followers placed him, namely, as a messianic figure both announcing and destined to play a role in the *Eschaton*, the End Time.

The Bible as we know it, a firmly defined collection of sacred books, did not yet exist in Jesus' day. There was already a broad unanimity on "the Law and the Prophets," that is, what constituted the Torah and who should be included among the Prophets. But the third of the traditional Jewish divisions of the Bible, the ambiguously titled "Writings," was an open category and its contents were still being debated two centuries or more after Jesus' death.

Jesus and his followers were avid students of the Bible. Isaiah and Daniel were among their favorite reading, but they were equally interested in what we—but not they—have called the apocrypha, the various works attributed to Ezra and Baruch, the Assumption of Moses, the Testament of Abraham. It was from them that both Jesus and his audience were drawing their understanding of the past, and the future, of the Covenant. And we must attempt to do the same. It is not only in "the Law and the Prophets," as the New Testament calls the Bible, that we can expect to find the spiritual core of Jesus and his movement, but also in the mélange of both biblical and apocryphal "Writings" that were circulating in the first century AD.

Sectarian Signals

The authors, editors, or entire communities that produced what we now call the biblical apocrypha sometimes appear to represent divergent strains of contemporary Judaism, what might now be called "sects" or "parties." That classification might be somewhat misleading since there was in that era nothing that can be described as "normative Judaism" against which a sectarian variant might be measured. But Josephus used the term *hairesis* in his very schematic presentation of the major ideological divisions among the Jews of his day, so it will have to serve. Literally *haireseis* means "choices" but it was generally understood as "schools," a sense that was more comfortably intelligible to Josephus' Gentile readers. To our ears, however, "schools" seems far too academic, while the alternative "parties" has too many political overtones and "sects" is, well, too sectarian.

There is in fact a good deal of sectarianism in the apocrypha, special pleading on behalf of some self-privileged view of Judaism, just as there is in the parallel writings of that other Jewish sect that sprang from the teachings of Jesus of Nazareth. As already remarked, Josephus is our chief informant on the various Jewish groupings and parties that come into view after the Jews' return from the sixth-century Babylonian exile. But Josephus' uniquely privileged position changed suddenly and radically with the 1947 discovery of what appears to be an entire sectarian library that had been hidden away, sealed and barely accessible, in caves high above the northwest corner of the Dead Sea.

The sect and its ruined settlement at Qumran below the caves and closer to shore was apparently the one characterized by Josephus and others as "Essenes," a highly organized, ascetic community whose chief issue was the Temple priesthood and whose emphasis was on strict ritual purity in the here and now—ritual bathing seems to have loomed large at Qumran—and validation in the approaching End Time. Almost immediately the importance of the find became manifest. Here was an extraordinary, in-their-own-words view of how some Jews understood their Jewishness in the exact years when Jesus lived and died not too far away.[5] Was Jesus in the Scrolls? Was Jesus an Essene? Was John the Baptist?

Jesus, it turned out, is not in the Scrolls—nor are the Essenes in the Gospels!—and he was certainly not himself an Essene. But there is much instruction at Qumran for the New Testament historian. The Essenes, or at least the Qumran branch,[6] were no less eschatological and messianic, though perhaps with somewhat less urgency, than the Jesus movement up the road in Galilee. There were, however, notable differences. Like some other groups, the Qumran Essenes expected at least two messiahs, a kingly Davidic one and a priestly one, the first representing a common theme in Jewish religious thought, the restoration of power and glory to the monarchical institution and through it to Israel; and the second reflecting the Essenes' own foundational issue of restoring legitimacy to the Temple priesthood.

If the Scrolls help focus the messianic claims of Jesus and his followers, they also present to us, in its own words, a Jewish sectarian movement, albeit one more highly organized and wardened than the Jesus movement. And it is not Jewish messianism alone that they illuminate. One of the most revealing aspects of the Scrolls is their manner of reading the Bible: their allegorical (and self-serving) understanding of Scripture is not very different from the Gospels' own.

What we have, then, for Jesus is a good deal of background information about the time and the place in which he lived, the varieties of Judaism that flourished there, and a sense of the hopes, fears, and expectations of his contemporaries. From the information provided by Josephus, the Dead Sea Scrolls, and the almost obsessive archaeological mining of Israel, we can put the admittedly sketchy foreground life of Jesus of Nazareth against both a Galilean and a Judean background that is very rich and very deep indeed.

Does that background also include the rabbinic writings like the Mishna (redacted ca. AD 200) or the two Talmuds (redacted ca. AD 400–600)? It was once thought so, but that conviction has grown progressively weaker in recent times. Jesus, it is clear, was not a product of the more institutionalized, more regulated, and progressively more uniform Rabbinic Judaism that is revealed to us in the writings of those industrious clerics who shaped the Jewish communities far and wide from their academies in "Babylonia," with one eye perhaps focused on what had already become a threatening "Christianity." Jesus and his movement belonged rather to the more open, fluid, and chaotic first-century Judaisms whose heart still beat vibrantly in a troubled *Eretz Israel*.

The Context for Muhammad

Muhammad's Hijaz, the stretch of Western Arabia, coast and rising upland, from Rome's borders on the north (near those of today's Jordan) to the frontiers of the Yemen on the south, is for us an Empty Quarter. It is a stretch of the Arabian Peninsula that was not devoid of life in the sixth and early seventh centuries of the Christian era, but is unhappily devoid of evidence, not only for Muhammad, as we might expect, but even for Mecca. Between the last monumental northern remains of the Nabatean Arabs, whose regime was extinguished in the first century AD, and the first eighth- and ninth-century traces of Muslim activity here and there in the area, the Hijaz has yielded little more than the scratched graffiti left behind by bored and barely literate Bedouin more interested in cursing Harith or scaring off the desert goblins than in contemplating the End Time.

The Silence of the Sources

This dearth is not unexpected perhaps. The area was entirely unurbanized—perennial monuments are a city phenomenon—and its population mostly illiterate. What is not expected is the silence of the outside observers. In the sixth century the Hijaz was bordered by highly literate societies to the north, south, and east and even in Abyssinia westward across the Red Sea. And those neighbors were interested in Western Arabia, whose Arab tribesmen could be useful as transit carriers in trade or even dangerous either as frontier raiders in the pay of others or as greedy plunderers of the settled lands on the margins of the steppe. And while their neighbors were well acquainted with the Arabs as a nation and with nomads as an untidy security problem, no Byzantine, Sasanian, or Yemeni who put stylus to parchment or chisel to stone professed to know anything of Mecca and its shrine. The Byzantine historian Procopius in particular, who sometime about the middle of the sixth century did a careful and systematic intelligence survey of Western Arabia, has only a silent hole

8

where Mecca should have been. Our Arab sources make a great deal of the commercial activity of Mecca in that same era, but neither Procopius, who had looked, nor anyone else had apparently ever heard of the place.

Today we possess no sixth- or seventh-century documentation from the Hijaz, and if our extant sources had such, it could not have been a great deal, and certainly not so much as some of them would have us believe.[7] Mecca and Medina had no archives in Muhammad's day, nor any, it appears, for a long time thereafter. In the sixth and seventh centuries they were centers of an oral society where writing, if it existed at all, was of an extremely limited and specialized use.

We have, then, few resources for reconstructing the society of Muhammad's Mecca and Medina from contemporary written sources, or even archaeological ones, since formal archaeological investigation has never been permitted within those sacred precincts.[8] If such a reconstruction is to be done at all, it must be accomplished from the redacted work of tribal poets of the steppe and later Muslim histories of that time and those places, and, in either case, by authors not much interested in the political economy of the pre-Islamic Hijaz, and even less concerned with the pagan religious practices of those unholy and "barbarous" (*jahili*) days.

Reconstructions

The social, political, and religious systems of the pre-Islamic environment of Western Arabia have thus to be *extracted* from highly resistant material. It was first attempted at the end of the nineteenth century by the celebrated biblical scholar Julius Wellhausen, and completed, in a remarkably virtuoso manner, by two scholars, the Italian prince Leone Caetani and the Belgian Jesuit Henri Lammens. Ironically, both men were highly skeptical of the Arab sources with which they were dealing, but Lammens' portrait of Mecca in particular, a highly seductive and self-serving construct, has provided, and continues to provide, the background of many of the modern Western lives of Muhammad. Henri Lammens, S. J., is, in effect, the Josephus of Muhammad research, and that fact marks with great precision one of the principal differences between the study of Muhammad's life and that of Jesus.

Extraction

There is no lack of evidence for Muhammad's Mecca. It is, however, entirely literary, and it dates from more than a century after the Prophet's death. And it is the product of a different society living in a place very different from the pagan and tribal Mecca of the sixth and early seventh centuries.

The passage of Christianity out of its Jewish matrix into a predominantly Gentile milieu dulled the sensibilities of later Christians regarding the Jewishness of Jesus and his first followers in the nascent "Church." But those Christians still had the Jewish Scriptures, their "Old Testament," as they came to call it, as well as the Jewish background "noise" in the Gospels to guide them back to at least a general sense of Jesus' historical position.[9] Our Muslim sources on the origins of Islam had no such help. They were far more remote from Meccan paganism than were the early Gentile Christians from Judaism. The Christians, following Paul, had declined Judaism; the Muslims, following the Quran, had absolutely rejected and repudiated Meccan paganism and destroyed it. Nor had they an Old Testament to remind them of what it once was, and the Quran gives only glimmering hints of Muhammad's religious setting, his *Sitz im Leben*.

From this unpromising body of material some rare and precious information has been extracted. The body of pre-Islamic poetry has been thoroughly sifted to good effect, and the Quran has been wrung dry of contemporary allusion. The one surviving work on "The Gods of Mecca" by Ibn al-Kalbi (d. 820) has been dissected and analyzed, and the often random remarks of later historians and chroniclers have all been collected and some cohesive semblance of pre-Islamic Mecca and the Hijaz constructed from them. But in the end it remains a reconstruction, a building with no material foundation and no independent confirmation.

Finally, there is the matter of the Quran itself. We have no precise examples of works called "Good News" (*euangelion*) in Jewish, Greek, or Roman literature, but we can recognize the parents of this literary hybrid in the *Bios* or *Life* of Greco-Roman antiquity and in the logoi or sayings collections of Mediterranean sages. As literary artifacts, the Gospels nestle not entirely uncomfortably in a rich tradition of writings, Greek and Hebrew, pagan and Jewish, and in a place where all those traditions met and mingled.

The Quran is far more baffling. It is the earliest preserved work in Arabic, preceded only by four or five brief inscriptions scattered across the remote fringes of the Syrian steppe. First, it should be remarked that it is not a literary composition at all. Like the New Testament, our Quran is an editorially assembled and arranged collection whose unity resides in the fact that its contents are the revealed word of God.[10] Muhammad's own Quran was in fact what are now the constitutive parts of our book, those stanza-like units (*suras*) whose original contours are no longer easy to discern.[11] But where we can isolate the original elements of the work, we must affirm that, if it is primary, the Quran is not primitive. Like the Homeric poems, its sophistication seems to signal the prior existence of a religio-poetic tradition. There is no trace of such, however; the Quran appears to be a virginal conception. And if it is mysterious what kind of prior tradition could produce the Quran, what is even more mysterious is who in that society barely emerging from illiteracy had the skills to write it down.

Afterthoughts: The Prophets in Place

Palestine and the Hijaz

We are now in a somewhat better position to step back and cast a comparative regard over the two men in their proper environments. Jesus was born and worked within a culturally and religiously pluralistic society. Israelite and Greek culture existed side by side in first-century Palestine, and a third, Latin Roman, was also present: in addition to Jesus' Roman trial and execution, Roman centurions are encountered in Galilee as well as Jews in Roman employ as tax collectors, the notorious *publicani*. And Jesus' Palestine was the home of one of the most literate populations in the entire Mediterranean basin—the Gospels are filled with "scribes" (*grammateis*).

Judaism was the religion of the mass of the people, but some of the larger cities of Palestine like the nearby cities of the Decapolis across the Jordan and Caesarea-by-the-Sea in Judea itself were pagan through and through, and one had but to step beyond the northern borders of Galilee, as Jesus occasionally did, to encounter a population that was neither Israelite in culture nor Jewish in religion. And schismatic Samaria too, where Jesus also traveled, was in many respects a foreign country to the Jews who lived around it.

Muhammad lived in a very different place, and we cannot be sure that he ever left it. The population of Mecca in the Hijaz was singularly Arab, relatively recent transplants from a tribal to an urban culture with the shared values of each, uniquely Arabophone and vastly illiterate. Religiously, the Meccans were idol-worshiping animists. There were Jews about in some of the northern oases like Medina and even more to the south in the Yemen, but none installed in Mecca. Nor were there any Christians there. The Yemen was officially Christian and so was Abyssinia across the Red Sea, and there were undoubtedly indirect contacts since Muhammad knew something of both faiths and defined Islam against both. But the Prophet seems never to have had direct encounters with Christians until the very end of his life.

Jesus spent almost all of his brief public career on his home soil of Lower Galilee with only an occasional foray beyond its fringes and brief liturgical visits to Jerusalem. Muhammad may have traveled more widely, even during his residence in Mecca, but his journeying would have taken place during his merchant days and before his call to prophecy. We do not know how far afield his commercial travels took him, but in the reduced view of Mecca's trading network, it seems unlikely that Muhammad ever left the Hijaz: Syria, the Yemen, and Iraq were beyond his personal horizon.[12] And once he took up his post as a "warner" in Mecca's sacred central space, the Haram, Muhammad seems to have stayed firmly fixed within the very narrow confines of his hometown. Jesus, who somewhat oddly refused to preach in his hometown because of the locals' lack of faith or, more pointedly, because he was unable to perform any miracles there (Mk 6:4–5 and parr.), was an itinerant; Muhammad was not, nor had he any need to be: the Meccan Haram stood at the epicenter at an expansive field of religious force, the catchment of the Arab pilgrimage network.

Galilee and Mecca

Jesus and Muhammad were both townsmen: Jesus a craftsman in a farming village in relatively densely populated Galilee, Muhammad a trader in a more important place in a less important area. The late sixth-century Hijaz, which was essentially a land-locked region with no Red Sea ports to speak of, was lightly inhabited, with few and very marginal settlements. Most of those were, like Medina, oases supporting a community of Arab date-palm growers and a few craft specialists—the carpenter Jesus would have fit in very comfortably in Medina, but the trader Muhammad would have had no employment in Nazareth. The date-palm groves cultivated in the oases could sustain a precarious subsistence-level living but the cultivators were subject to the same problems that brought Muhammad to Medina: the palm orchards could not expand with the population. Family and tribal rivalries over space and produce developed within their narrow confines: civil strife (*fitna*) was an endemic and dangerous condition in the Western Arabia palm groves.

Mecca was not an oasis, however. It had no agriculture and the people who lived there in Muhammad's day, and for long afterward, supported themselves on traffic: the traffic in pilgrims—the paramount tribes controlled both access to the shrines and the victualing and watering of the visitors—and the probably mostly local trade capitalized by the pilgrim traffic. Muhammad belonged to the latter category of Meccan: as best we can tell, he was a minor merchant, certainly not a magnate, in a clan of middling rank.

Mecca had its own social problems, not of space and population as was the case in Medina, but in the breakdown in tribal loyalties and kinship connections and their replacement by constantly shifting alliances of convenience and advantage. These were internally generated tensions. In Galilee, however, and in Palestine generally, the pressures came largely from without. Muhammad lived at Mecca in an autonomous and self-governing town and, in the last decade of his life, he was in fact the ruler first of his Medina community and then of a burgeoning "empire" that was rapidly extending out from it. Jesus spent his life under an occupation, virtual under Herod Antipas, Rome's puppet "tetrarch" in Galilee (r. 4 BC–AD 39) and then, after AD 6, under direct Roman rule in *Provincia Ioudaea*.

Rome's presence in Palestine was taxing in every sense of the word. Herod the Great had tax-burdened his subjects to pay for his lavish public works programs, including the rebuilding of the Jerusalem Temple (20 BC–AD 66), and the Romans simply added to the load, with the gall of a tax-farming system and the exaction of the tribute in Roman coin. Piled atop this was Roman interference in Temple affairs—the Jerusalem Temple was, irresistibly, the largest corporation and the largest bank in the land—and nowhere more painfully than in Rome's pushing upon the monotheistic Jews the most odious form of their own polytheism, emperor worship.

All of this tense and varied background is reflected and underlined in the Gospels. There is, to begin with, the emergence in that same milieu of the nucleus of both a *Greek* narration of the life and a collection *in Greek* of the sayings of the Aramaic-speaking Jesus. There is, of course, Jesus' Roman trial and execution on one hand and, on the other, his very Jewish involvement with both the Temple establishment and the Pharisees, the reigning religious ideologues of his day. The Gospels show us not only Rome's military and judicial systems in action but its tributary taxpayers and Roman tax collectors. We are shown cool and collected Jewish aristocrats like Nicodemus and Joseph of Arimathea and the psychically vexed; the sound and the grievously ill; the rich and the poor; day-laborers and owners; tenants and their landlords; the rulers and the ruled; and we are exposed to all the issues that those pairs had between them. We are taken inside homes, humble and grand, palaces, Roman tribunals, synagogues, the Temple.

There are issues in the Quran, to be sure, but they are chiefly transcendental, theological, perennial: submission or rejection, obedience or disbelief, eternal punishment or eternal reward. The quotidian is deeply submerged *sub specie aeternitatis*. On the evidence of the Quran alone we would know little or nothing of Mecca save that perhaps there was such a place—but was it called Becca (3:96)? We can perhaps deduce that the Quraysh were traders there and the evidence is quite direct that many Meccans were stubborn in their resistance to the preacher and his message of "Submission." There are no homes, no friends or families in our picture of that place. The Quran's mountains are archetypical, like Sinai or Olivet; its seas generic. As was once said of quite another place, there is no there there.

The *hicceity* of Mecca was a later construct of Muslim Arab authors writing in other, very urbanized places and across a very consequential century. As in the case of the Bible's editor-authors' Pentateuchal representation of Iron Age Israel, there may be some very old and quite authentic memories built into that Meccan edifice, though in the absence of outside confirmation we cannot very often make out what they are. The Iraqi compositors of the *Sira* did know the Muslim Hijaz firsthand and they filled in the spaces back to its pre-Islamic condition from reported memories, which they tried to authenticate, and by imagining the past from its shadowy presence behind the Quran. The medieval Muslims' intuitions as to what must have lain behind the Quran's often opaque complaints, commands, and prohibitions should not be too readily dismissed. We do the same through analogy: we infer from what we judge as parallel instances. And often with the same results, and with the same degree of certainty.

2

Opening the Files

We have taken a rapid overview of what we do and do not know about the political, social, and economic settings in which Jesus and Muhammad lived; we turn now to the evidence regarding the men themselves. We must not expect a great deal. There are no archives, no baptismal or marriage registers, none of the primary documents from which historians of a later era are accustomed to work. What we have is essentially literary remains, later writings about our two subjects. There is of course some contemporary material evidence, particularly in the case of Jesus, but it is merely confirmatory: it confirms that Pontius Pilate was the governor of Judea in the first century, that the agricultural life of Galilee was pretty much as Jesus described it in his parables, that there was a pool with five porticos located just north of the Temple area in Jerusalem and rather precisely what death by crucifixion might involve. But the basic fact remains: the surviving evidence for Jesus and Muhammad is overwhelmingly literary.

The Dossier on Jesus

The literary evidence for Jesus falls conveniently, though not symmetrically, into three categories: that produced by pagans, that by Jewish authors, and, finally and most substantially, that from Jesus' own followers.

The Pagan Sources

No one is quite sure what precisely paganism was, not even the pagans, who never thought of themselves as such. What is certain is that the term is derogatory: the adjective *paganus* was used by the Christians to describe the last outback holdouts against Christianity—it can be roughly and contemporaneously translated as "hillbilly"—all those who clung to their ancient cults and refused both monotheism and belief in Jesus as the Son of God. In any event, the classical pagans seem to have disappeared from the West, leaving only the more fastidious atheists and agnostics to man the barricades against faith communities.[1]

The pagan sources on Jesus of Nazareth are somewhat illusory as sources. They are chiefly about Christians rather than Jesus, who is never called by his Hebrew or Aramaic given name but is referred to as "Christus" or "Chrestos." Like the material evidence, the pagan authors simply confirm or, at best, enlarge our knowledge of the background. They fill in information about the career of Pontius Pilate, for example, or the system of tax collection under Roman auspices in Palestine. At their very best they confirm for us that in the 60s in Rome there was a group of religious fanatics who called themselves "Christers" and who caused problems—unspecified—for the Roman authorities in Rome and elsewhere.[2] Most pertinent is what the historian Tacitus wrote at the turn into the second century:

> Nero . . . inflicted the most cruel tortures upon a group of people detested for their abominations, and popularly known as "Christians." Their name came from one Christus, who was put to death in the principate of Tiberius by the Procurator Pontius Pilate. Though checked for a time, the destructive superstition broke out again, not in Judea only, where its mischief began, but even in Rome, where every abominable and shameful iniquity, from all the world, pours in and finds a welcome. (*Annals* 15:44)

That is the sum of it. There had been a Judean holy man named Christus whom the Romans had executed sometime between AD 26 and 36 and whose followers had already in the 60s of the first century constituted at Rome and elsewhere a discernible religious community called after him.

The Jewish Sources

Flavius Josephus

The Jewish sources are somewhat more helpful. Josephus has already been mentioned. In his *Antiquities* he not only provides abundant political and religious background for the era but also mentions in a paragraph or so John the Baptist (18:116–19), Jesus (18:63–64, 20:200), and Jesus' brother James (20:200–203). At first glance, this is an extraordinary stroke of good fortune for the historian. In the first passage Josephus says Jesus was a wonder-worker and teacher, that he was condemned to death by the Roman governor Pilate, and that his followers later claimed he had risen from the dead. But he also says "He was the Messiah" and that he had actually appeared to his followers after his death!

But this good fortune must immediately turn to a suspicion that the Christians later tampered with the text of Josephus or perhaps inserted this entire paragraph into his text. It may indeed be so, but in the tenth century an Arab Christian author quotes this same passage of Josephus without the Christianizing elements and thus in the form that many believe Josephus originally wrote it:

> At this time there was a wise man who was called Jesus. And his conduct was good, and (he) was known to be virtuous. And many people from among the Jews and the other nations became his disciples. Pilate condemned him to be crucified and to die. And those who had become his disciples did not desert his discipleship. They reported that he had appeared to them three days after his crucifixion and that he was alive; accordingly, he was perhaps the Messiah concerning whom the prophets have recounted wonders. (Agapius of Manbij, Kitab al-'Unwan)[3]

This passage in the *Antiquities* has generated a large and at times heated literature. But Josephus is illuminating in other respects, not least in the considerable attention he pays to the phenomenon of charismatic prophecy, often linked to insurgence, in the Palestine of that era. Jesus fits comfortably into the pattern of prophet-messiahs that appeared among the Jews before and during his own lifetime. They were charismatic wonder-workers who took their inspiration from Moses and were surrounded by bands of loyal followers. They were almost all involved in some type of political action, whether directly by taking up arms against the Romans or indirectly by demonstrating against or criticizing authority. And most of them came to a violent end.

The Dead Sea Scrolls

Josephus describes the religious currents of the day in terms of action. We can discern some of the atmospherics in the literature produced by various religious groups, whether identifiable, like the Essenes who produced the Dead Sea Scrolls, or anonymous, like the various shades of sectarians who stand behind the visionary and apocalyptic writings that never made it into the Bible but were popular in that era. An apocalypse is literally an unveiling, in this instance an unveiling of the events of the last days of human history. It would be God's conclusion to His creation and, it was piously hoped, the final vindication of Israel in the face of its enemies. A time of terror would yield to a time of triumph, and in the midst of the latter would stand a figure of Israel's liberation, the Anointed One, the Messiah. Not all Jews of Jesus' day believed in the imminence of the End Time nor in a Messiah; Jesus' followers obviously did, and the shape and color of their belief can be read off the pages of this apocalyptic literature. The Dead Sea Scrolls reveal just one such apocalyptic community in the grip of expectation of the End Time. The Jesus movement was another.

The Rabbinic Sources

The rabbis also weigh in on Jesus, though from distant Babylon, as they called Iraq, at an interval of four hundred to six hundred years after the event.[4] And, as has recently been observed, what they do say reveals far more about the status of the Jews in pre-Islamic Iraq than it does about the historical Jesus. According to the statements in the Talmud regarding Jesus, his birth was illegitimate: he was the son of Miriam (by one account a hairdresser) who had conceived of a certain Pantheros, a Roman soldier. By the same accounts Jesus was put to death by the Jews, either by crucifixion or by hanging, on the capital charge of having led the people astray. Jesus, then, in the standard—that is, rabbinic—accounts was arrested, tried, and executed by the Jewish authorities of his day on the charge of treasonous seduction.

The Christian Sources

Finally, we come to our chief evidence for Jesus, namely, the material contained in the collection known as the New Testament. The New Testament is in effect an argument, a brief assembled to demonstrate that the Abrahamic and the Mosaic covenant (Hebrew *berith;* Latin *testamentum*) had been redrawn in the person of Jesus, who was the Messiah promised by the prophets.

The documents collected there consist in the four works called Gospels or "Good News"; a work of history called, somewhat misleadingly, "The Acts of the Apostles"; a number of letters, chiefly those of Paul, a very early Jewish convert to the cause of Jesus, but also those attributed to the Apostles Peter and John and Jude, and to Jesus' brother, James; and finally an Apocalypse or Revelation, the Christian version of a familiar Jewish literary genre, a visionary unveiling of the End Time, now seen from a Christian perspective. These documents would all appear to date from the first century: the earliest are certainly Paul's letters written in the 50s and the latest the Apocalypse, which was probably written toward the very end of the century.

The Gospels

Even though Paul's letters are the earliest documents in the New Testament, they have, as we shall see, very little to say about the life and teachings of Jesus of Nazareth. Most of what we know about Jesus comes in fact from one set of books, the four so-called canonical Gospels of the New Testament. Canonicity is a theologian's, not a historian's, judgment, and the fact that the Christian churches have dubbed these four "canonical" does not, of course, make than any more (or less) authentic as historical documents. Indeed, one of the most strenuous current arguments over the sources for Jesus is how much evidentiary credit should be given to some of the materials, including gospels, that are *not* included in the New Testament. Most have remained unconvinced of their independent value, and most historians continue to operate on the premise that, if the historical Jesus is going to be extracted from any documents, they will most likely be the Gospels called after Matthew, Mark, Luke, and John and composed by Christian believers *sometime*—and that is the operative word—between AD 60 and 100, that is, thirty to seventy-odd years after the death of Jesus.[5]

Before addressing their dating, we must regard four New Testament Gospels as documents. They are cast in the form that we would identify as biography, even though they do not name themselves as such—the Greek word for biography is *bios*, or "Life"—but rather "The Good News," in Greek *euangelion*. This latter word had been in technical use earlier; it referred to a proclamation, usually of an official nature, of some important piece of information. It does not, however, appear as the denominative of a literary work.

The Gospels individually identify themselves, though not exactly by author. Each bears the title of "The Good News according to Matthew" or Mark or Luke or John. Thus we are told at the outset that we are getting four different versions of what is essentially the same Good News. Three of the four—those of Matthew, Mark, and Luke—are quite similar in their structure, their approach, what they include, and often even their very words. Since they cover the same ground in the same way, they are now termed "Synoptic." John, however, is quite different. He covers different incidents, in a different order, and according to a different chronology. In the Synoptics Jesus speaks generally in aphorisms or in homely parables; in John, in long discourses of considerable theological sophistication. The Fourth Gospel omits a great deal of what is in the Synoptics and adds a good deal that is not.

SEQUENCING AND SIFTING The three Synoptic Gospels are obviously related in some not very obvious way, and to understand that interrelationship, it is first necessary to attempt to sequence them. It is not a simple matter because there are no internal hooks on which to attach dates. Mark is the shortest of the three, its style is the most primitive and least polished, its narrative the most direct. For all these reasons there is a general consensus—which is the best one can hope for in this kind of inquiry; unanimity is a fugitive ideal—that Mark is the earliest of the Synoptic Gospels and, it was once thought, our best and truest source for the historical Jesus.

Once it is granted, as it generally is, that Mark was the first Gospel to be composed, it becomes apparent, from the two hundred or so verses identical in all three, that Matthew and Luke must have used Mark in composing their Gospels; that there was an unidentified written source, which we now call "Mark," lying before them when they composed their versions of the Good News. We are also in a position to observe, with great interest, exactly *how* Matthew and Luke each used Mark, how they modified or corrected or expanded the earlier Gospel.

But something else is apparent if we put the three Synoptics side by side. There are another two hundred-plus verses more or less identical in Matthew and Luke, but *not* found in Mark. The easiest explanation is that the two evangelists must have had another source they incorporated into their work. We do not know what it was; we only know what was in it, or some of what was in it, namely those 235 identical non-Markan verses that occur in Matthew and Luke. The nineteenth-century scholars who formed this convincing hypothesis named it "Q," for the German *Quelle*, or "source."

If we isolate and look more closely at what constitutes Q, it becomes apparent that Q was a collection of Jesus' sayings, or logoi, as they were called in his day. And only sayings. There is, oddly, no death by crucifixion, no resurrection in the hypothetically reconstructed Q. Who would make such a collection and why? Was it a kind of primitive catechism to serve as an introduction to the Jesus movement, leaving the hard parts till later? Was it conceivably a real Gospel? A quite different Good News, and perhaps about a quite different and, as some now suggest, even the *authentic* Jesus?

The Jesus questers of the nineteenth century thought they had uncovered in Q an interesting new source for Matthew and Luke. It added no new information, of course, since the Q material was there in those two Gospels from the very beginning. But historians of the second half of the twentieth century began to regard Q in a quite different way, as we shall later see in more detail.

One of the reasons was the 1945 discovery of a manuscript of a work that called itself "The Gospel of Thomas." This self-described Gospel was a collection of 114 sayings of Jesus, some of them echoed from the canonical Gospels, some of them not. But the important thing is that it was, formally, a Gospel. So it was possible to conceive of a sayings collection like Q as a genuine Gospel, a formal announcement of the Jesus message. And "Thomas" presents to us, exactly like Q, a Jesus who had not died on the cross and had not risen from the dead. The Jesus of both Thomas and Q was simply a teacher-preacher.

Q must have been early, at least as early as Mark's Gospel, but whence and when Thomas? The preserved Gospel of Thomas, which is a Coptic translation of a Greek original now known only in fragments, does not, in any event, have spotless credentials. It was part of a fourth-century sectarian library uncovered at Nag Hammadi in Egypt. The sectarians were known as Gnostics, an early Christian movement condemned by the mainstream churches, and their library included a number of works that bore the title of "Gospel" but do not appear in the New Testament. They came to be called "apocryphal."

THE APOCRYPHA   The word means "reserved" or "restricted," and "apocryphal" is a term used to describe works not included in the official collection. Thus there are both biblical apocrypha, like the already mentioned Jewish works attributed to Enoch and Baruch, that are not included in the Jewish Bible, and, as in this instance, New Testament apocrypha, works that make some claim to authenticity—in its simplest terms, by merely calling itself a "Gospel"—but are not part of the Christians' New Testament. Who made that important decision? Indeed, who made the "New Testament"? And who decided what was in it and what was not?

The New Testament is the scriptural canon or standard for the entire Christian Church, and if it is understood this way, the Scriptural canon is clearly a product of an age when the Universal or Catholic Church, as it styled itself, had come into existence. The institutional debut of that Universal Church was a solemn convocation of all its bishops at Nicea in AD 325 by order of the emperor Constantine. It was then and in the years following that a scriptural canon could be ratified and promulgated. But that is only the end of the story. On all the evidence, by the second century Christians were already using in their church services these four Gospels and these alone. So it appears that relatively early on there had developed a consensual Gospel canon among the individual congregations (*ekklesiai*) of Christians that had come into existence around the Mediterranean.

And why had they settled on these four? It is perfectly clear that in this context *canon* is a theological and a juridical term. It is a judgment that these works, like the New Testament as a whole, bear authentic witness to Jesus as the Messiah and the Son of God. This is the Church's standard, but it is of use to the historian only insofar as it reflects a judgment about the historicity of the Gospels. This it does in part—for Christians the "real" Jesus was and is undoubtedly the historical Jesus—but there was more than history at stake in the fashioning of this canon, and modern historians in particular are chary of overprivileging the churches' "canonical" Gospels. They want to dissolve the distinction between "canonical" and "apocryphal": each gospel should be judged on its own merits as a historical document.

What the historian is looking for is a source on Jesus that is both early and independent, that is, it is not simply repeating or paraphrasing what it has derived from other, earlier documents. Most of the apocryphal Gospels that are preserved—many of them we know only by their titles—fall into the derived category. The Gospel of Thomas, for example, is thought by many to be dependent on the Synoptic Gospels. Others are patently late creations devoted to spelling out or amplifying the Jesus story already known from the canonical Gospels. The best-known example of this is undoubtedly the so-called Proto-Gospel of James which retells the story of Jesus' birth as found in Matthew's and Luke's Infancy Narratives. It is filled with curious and novelistic details, but it is also vividly entertaining and the Proto-Gospel found a wide readership among Christians.

DATING THE GOSPELS   Lurking in the background of this discussion of the sources on Jesus is the critical issue of their date. If by looking for Friday Passovers in that era and plotting them against the known procuratorship of Pontius Pilate in Judea (AD 26–36), the death of Jesus can be located on or about the year AD 30, how much after it were our sources composed? There are no dates in the Gospels themselves, no direct internal clues as to when they were composed. Historians have again to rely on indirection. In the year 70, at the end of the Jews' failed insurrection, and some forty years after Jesus' death, the Romans took the city of Jerusalem after a savage siege. In the course of the battle for Jerusalem, Herod's great Temple, which had finally been completed only eight years before, was set afire and eventually razed to the ground. It meant the end of Jewish sacrificial worship of their God, which for centuries could be performed only by the priests in the great Scripturally authenticated Temple. By all accounts the siege and fall of Jerusalem and the destruction of its Temple was a dramatic and a traumatic event in the life of the Jews, including Jesus' emerging first generation of followers.

Was, then, this critical event mentioned in the Gospels? If so, they may be safely dated to after 70; but if not—it is inconceivable that such an event should not be mentioned in the life of someone whose fate was explicitly tied to that of the Temple—then it seems highly likely that such a work would have been composed before the event, that is, before 70. Q makes no mention of the destruction of the Temple, and if we turn to Mark, which has already been judged to be the oldest of the Synoptics, most critics seem to think there is some reflection of the events of 70 in Mark chapter 13, which professes to be Jesus' own apocalyptic vision of the End Time. Thus, Mark's Gospel is generally dated, with considerable wiggle room that reflects the uncertainty of the judgment, circa AD 60–70. Since Matthew and Luke, who have their own apocalyptic chapters (Mt 24:1–31; Lk 21:5–28) that are parallel to Mark's, both used Mark's Gospel as a source, time must be allowed for the latter to be in circulation. Hence the dating of Matthew and Luke is usually put at AD 80–90 and the destruction of the Jerusalem Temple is somehow recognized in their individual versions of the End Time.[6]

AND WHAT OF JOHN?   Was the Fourth Gospel composed independently of the Synoptics? And when was it composed? John's Gospel is a source of great complexity. It represents a finished literary composition (with a very probable tack-on at the end) of both great originality—John describes miracles and events in the life of Jesus unmentioned by the Synoptics—and at the same time an urgent historicity: the author seems to know more about the political and topographical details of Jesus' Palestine and Jerusalem than any of the other three. At the same time, he is less a reporter and more of an author than the others. John's Jesus has a very distinct point of view that is enunciated in a highly sophisticated language and imagery quite alien to the aphoristic and homely Jesus portrayed in Mark and Q, for example. The consensus opinion is first, that John in all likelihood knew the Synoptics but that he preferred to go his own way; and second, that in many instances John also represents a firsthand eyewitness tradition to the life of Jesus.

As for the dating of the work, John has no apocalyptic chapter and hence no formal forevision of the destruction of Jerusalem. Many critics have been persuaded by its sophisticated theology that it must be quite late, and that judgment is strengthened for others by John's apparent references to an existing community of Christians already at odds with their fellow Jews. On these grounds John has been dated circa 90–100. But both these criteria, the high theological view of Jesus and the presence of community tensions between Jesus' followers and their fellow Jews, are already present in Paul, whose letters can be dated with absolute certainty to the mid-50s. These misgivings have not much affected the usual dating of this Gospel, which is still felt by most to have been composed around the turn into the second century.

Paul

Paul, or Saul (Shaul), was a Diaspora Jew from Tarsus, in modern Turkey, who was born about 6 BC, and so two years older than Jesus, and who died in Rome, probably in AD 67. He is a valuable early witness to the Jesus tradition—by his own account, he never saw the historical Jesus—in that his name is authentically connected to a series of letters that are included in the New Testament; indeed, his is the only uncontested authorial voice in the entire corpus, and the inclusion of his letters there shows that the early Christians took that voice seriously indeed. The canonization of the Pauline body of correspondence not only guaranteed the Jesus information there transmitted, but more consequentially, since that information is available in more detail elsewhere, it guaranteed Paul's understanding of the significance of Jesus' life and, above all, his death. If the distinction between the Christ of history and the historical Jesus has any validity, then we have our very first glimpse of both in the letters of Paul.

Paul does more than offer scattered pieces of information about the historical Jesus and a bold sketch of the emerging Christ of history; the letters provide us with a valuable—and unique—autobiographical portrait of one of the earliest followers of Jesus and an insight into the beliefs about Jesus current in some circles in the 40s and 50s of the first century, ten to twenty years, no more, after his death.

It must immediately be conceded that the evidence is far stronger for what certain of his followers *thought* about Jesus a decade or so after his death than what was *known* about Jesus. The Pauline letters are, after all, about Christian beliefs and practices and not in the first instance about Jesus. But there is something even in this: on the evidence of Paul's letters, the events of Jesus' life were never at issue. To explain this, the historian must choose between the irrelevance of those events to the Christian faith or a prior knowledge and agreement on the particulars of Jesus' life and teachings, at least on those particulars that were considered important. If the agreement of the two parties, Paul and the addressees of his letters, seems the more plausible alternative, we are still well short of discovering, save in a few matters, what those particulars were.

Those few exceptions are interesting. Paul asserted (1 Cor 11:23–25)—and apparently no one contested the assertion—that Jesus, on the night before he died, had shared an extraordinary ritual meal with his followers in which he identified the bread and wine of the repast as (not *like*) his body and blood and commanded the ritual repetition of the event ("Do this in remembrance of me").[7]

Modern scholarship denies authenticity to some of the letters collected under Paul's name in the New Testament. 1 Thessalonians, 1 and 2 Corinthians, Galatians and Romans, and probably Philippians and Philemon, are all regarded as Paul's own work, while doubts have been raised about 2 Thessalonians, Colossians, and Ephesians. Hebrews and the pastoral letters, two of them to Timothy and one to Titus, are certainly from someone else's hand. The early Church canonized them all in the New Testament, perhaps on the understanding that they were all "Pauline" though not necessarily from Paul. Whatever the theological soundness of that decision, it is of no consequence to the historian: only the authentic Paul will do as a first-generation witness to Jesus.

The Christian Literary Sources in Sum

On the earliest, apparently underived level we have, then, on the strict view, two sources for the life of Jesus, the Gospel of Mark and the reconstructed Q; on a broader view, there should be added John; what can be gleaned from Paul; the "new" material in Matthew and Luke, that is, events and sayings not derived from either Mark or Q; and finally, perhaps Thomas or other bits and pieces from the apocrypha.[8]

Some think it is possible to get behind the two earliest sources. Attempts at deconstructing Mark's Gospel have been largely unsuccessful—there is no consensual *UrMark*—but recently there has been emerging what may be called an *UrQ*. This twice-removed hypothesis is achieved by positing a kind of single source, an original Jesus sayings collection that lies behind both Q and Thomas. The necessarily early dating of Q, which is before Matthew and Luke and arguably earlier than Mark as well, has undoubtedly exercised a kind of "gravitational pull" on the dating of Thomas. It is impossible to say precisely what was in this proposed earliest collection of Jesus sayings, but if one accepts the redactional paring down of both Q and Thomas, it is fairly clear what was not. In this earliest portrait of Jesus there was no eschatology, no passion narrative, and no resurrection or appearances account. Jesus was a wisdom teacher purely and simply and it merely remains to determine of what sort.

The Dossier on Muhammad

As we have already seen, there is little physical or material evidence for Muhammad. He lived in what was an ephemeral physical environment, where the settled population dwelled in buildings of mud brick—the Ka'ba was reportedly the only stone building in Mecca, which was nonetheless often taken down by flash floods—and the nomadic or Bedouin population left few if any traces behind them. The archaeology of Arabia is the excavation of memory.

The file on Muhammad is composed of two sets of documents. The first is a unified work called the Quran, venerated by Muslims as the Word of God delivered through His Prophet. Whatever its ultimate origin, human or divine, the Quran is regarded by all, Muslims and non-Muslims alike, as a collection of the pronouncements that came forth from Muhammad over the course of some twenty-two years until his death in AD 632.[9] It is of central importance for our purpose. "The primary source for the biography of Muhammad is the Quran." So begins Aloys Sprenger's *The Life and Teaching of Muhammad*, one of the first critical biographies of the Prophet in the modern era, and no evidence since discovered, or judgment subsequently rendered, has altered that fact. The second source on Muhammad, less certain but no less crucial, is a series of redactions, or editions, or in some cases, mere bits and snippets of information, most of which derive from a biography of Muhammad composed in Baghdad by Ibn Ishaq, a scholar who died sometime about AD 768, or from a work on Muhammad's armed raids across Arabia written by al-Waqidi (d. 823).

God Knows Best: The Quran

In the case of Jesus, the closest we can get to the actual person, where we can hear his own voice, is probably in the sayings source called "Q." We can do the same with the Muslims' own "Q," which in this instance is the Quran. But the Quran's verses, singly or in larger units, are, like Jesus' aphorisms in Q, sayings without context, utterances without a *Sitz im Leben*, a "life circumstance," or as the Muslims called them, an "occasion of revelation." To supply that context, to provide us with the narrative frame of Muhammad's life, the Muslim equivalent of the Gospels, we must turn to the Muslim biographical tradition. First, however, the Quran itself must be regarded more closely.

The Making of Our Quran

The Quran is the collection of Muhammad's reportedly inspired utterances that date from after his "call" to prophethood at Mecca, traditionally dated to 610, and that continued to his death in 632.[10] As the revelations, or better, "the recitation" (Arabic *al-qur'an*) emerged from his mouth, Muhammad's small band of believers, the *muslimun*, or "Submitters" (*islam* means "submission"), memorized and recited them as a form of worship under his own guidance. Then, shortly after Muhammad's death, the traditional account continues, his divinely inspired utterances began to be retrieved and collected from the memories of his contemporaries and from scraps and pieces of writing in that barely literate society. These early processes are not entirely clear to us, but the tradition insists that sometime about 650, some twenty-odd years after Muhammad's death, there was available, courtesy of a committee charged with its preparation by the third caliph, Uthman (r. 644–56), a standard written text of the Quran,[11] a book that is in essence our present Quran. The revelations had been collected and divided into 114 suras or chapters.

How Does It Help?

There is an almost universal consensus that the Quran is authentic, that the text that stands before us is the product of one man, Muhammad. It may not be all Muhammad pronounced—indeed there is good evidence that all his revelations are not in our Quran—but there is no indication of interpolation or tampering. But our "copy" (*mushaf*) is an edited text. The anonymous editors of the Quran created the suras, regrouped and even combined Muhammad's utterances, provided titles for the suras, and then arranged them in what is roughly—we are only guessing—the descending order of length.[12]

The way the Quran presents itself, it is generally God who is speaking, either threateningly to an audience of Meccan pagans in the earliest utterances or instructively to a community of "Submitters" at Medina in the later ones. If such is the case, God (or Muhammad speaking on His behalf) is interested in "submission" but not much interested in either local or contemporary history. The Quran's interest in the past is overwhelmingly in Sacred History, the story of Creation and the histories of the various prophets from Abraham to Jesus sent to humankind to keep them on the straight path. Of Mecca and the Meccans, even of Muhammad, we are told very little. It is not what the Quran is about.

One of the more remarkable things about the Quran is the history that is *not* revisited or revised. There is in it no visible reflection on Muhammad's unhappy Meccan experiences, no vindictiveness against the Quraysh who had sought to kill him, and, perhaps most surprisingly, no triumphalist gloating in the light of the increasing successes of Muslim armies and the ever wider spread of Islam. Unlike Jesus, Muhammad lived long enough to be his own Constantine, to see Islam established as the religion of most of Arabia and be the sovereign of an Islamic commonwealth. And he could have, if he had chosen, written his own *Laudes Constantini* into the Quran. He readily embraced the role of Constantine, the priest-emperor, and his mosque-domicile in Medina was at least in some respects a *sacrum palatium*. But Muhammad declined to play Eusebius. The Medina suras of the Quran do not lack for confidence, but they are not filled with either self-praise or self-congratulation. The Quran "ends"—a very imprecise notion—much as it "began," with its gaze focused on Salvation History and not on the contemporary events at Mecca and Medina that the historian is so eager to hear about.

The Circumstantiality of the Quran

Muhammad's followers were required to believe from the outset—they did not, as in the case of Jesus, have to come to a later conclusion—that what they were hearing from his lips were the very words of God. As originally delivered they seem profoundly obscure in places, heavily freighted with circumstance, with references to unnamed persons and places presumably known to his audience and to objections raised by largely unidentified critics.

Two editorial facts erased the circumstantiality of what was being recited. In the first instance it was Muhammad's own insistence that his recitations be memorized as liturgical chants, as a series of affirmations as timeless as the creed recited at a Catholic Mass, and without any reference to the grave theological event that set them in train. Their recitation dissolved, *ex opere operato*, the history of the words. The second erasure was effected by the editors responsible for our present Quran. It was they who reassembled the original "recitations" into the 114 new units called suras and so obliterated for Muslims the size and shape of the original revelations. Then, in a final act of dehistoricization, the editors reassembled the new suras in a quite mechanical fashion, generally, as just noted, from the longest to the shortest. Their only, perhaps reluctant, concession to context was the addition, at the head of each sura, of the laconic phrase "Mecca" or "Medina."

The divisions of our present Quran have no particular theological or historical significance. They were the product of a redaction and the precise reasons for their composition, length, and sequence are unknown. The significant unit has now become the verse, any one of which may be cited or produced with equal effect in a legal or theological context. The Quran is entirely and simultaneously true.

But there is an important exception to this flattening of historical context. According to His own testimony (2:106), God abrogated or canceled certain verses of the Quran and replaced them with others, while somewhat unaccountably leaving the canceled verses in the text. This explicit theory of abrogation is unknown to the Gospels, whose later exegetes had to solve contradictions among the four by harmonizing them. Muslim exegetes certainly knew how to harmonize discordant texts, but abrogation represented a special challenge, one for whose solution the redacted Quran provided them little evidence. An earlier verse had obviously to be canceled by a later verse, but the Quran gives no clue to which verse followed which in this fundamentally rearranged text. Muslims had then to attempt a chronological arrangement.

The Quran is thus caught up in its own self-referential system, with Muhammad often playing the role of little more than a bystanding *répétiteur*. We know this is not the whole story, however. There is a before and an after in the Quran, early and late, first thoughts and second thoughts, as there must be in any document formulated over the course of twenty-two years. We know too that the Quran, certainly the Meccan Quran, was addressed to an already existing religious tradition which was being in part repudiated and in part reformed but which nonetheless represented the current beliefs and practices of Muhammad's audience. We know *that* it was; our problem is, we do not have a very clear idea *what* the pre-Islamic religious tradition of Mecca was since we have few if any of its myths, rituals, or artifacts.

Restoring History to the Quran

If the secular historian believes, as he or she must, that what came forth from Muhammad's mouth is Muhammad's own product, then the Quran is all about Muhammad, an unparalleled authentic record of his religious thinking. And an evolutionary one as well, since the pronouncements are spread out over twenty-two years. Jesus' public career lasted barely two years; Muhammad's stretched over more than two decades.

That is what the Quran should be, but it can hardly serve as that in its present condition. The decontextualization of the Quran is not entirely irremediable, however, and both Muslims and non-Muslims alike have had strong motives for restoring a degree of history to the Quran by attempting to discern the chronological order of the revelations. There was, as we have seen, the matter of abrogation, of attempting to determine the earlier abrogated and the later abrogating verse. But Muslims had other historical and legal motives for attempting to recontextualize the Quran. Once they began to interest themselves in Muhammad's life, they took up the task of matching Quranic verses with remembered incidents of the Prophet's life. Or perhaps it was the other way around: the Quranic verses, repeated over and over again, promoted wonder at what was happening behind the naked revelation.

Finally, the matter of the revelations had also to be unpacked. The verses constituted a divine guidance and it was important to get it right, not only individually but also as a community, a congregation of believers. This provoked a search for what came to be called the "occasions of revelation," the collection of biographical anecdote and incident, the lost contexts of the Quran that make the task of both the Muslim moral theologian and the Muslim historian unspeakably easier.

So the Muslim and the Western historian have put their hands to the task of discovering the chronological order of the suras of the Quran. It has been done chiefly on internal evidence: changes of style and tone and audience that reflect changing settings, changing challenges, and changing objectives. Muslims and non-Muslims alike have come up with their chronological lists and they are not very different. The results are convincing, at least in their general categories, distinguishing Meccan and Medinan suras and dividing the former, where the changes are more rapid and obvious, into Early, Middle, and Late periods. But problems remain, most notoriously that of the combined suras, where ragged seams show that a number of revelations have been made into a single sura.

The Biographical Tradition

All peoples have memories, but memories are particularly tenacious in oral societies that do not have the written word to record the events and actors of the past. They remember important or remarkable things, deaths not births, prodigies of nature or achievement. But the records of memory carry no dates: events occur "long ago" or "during the famine" or "in the year of the flood."

Memories of Muhammad

We can be certain that the Muslims had memories of Muhammad. For many they must have begun with his rise to public consciousness as a preacher in Mecca and they became progressively stronger as his power and prominence increased at Medina. And his followers remembered his sayings, or rather God's own sayings, which they repeated and memorized. But a remembrance of the events of his life, like those of Jesus, was probably a function of his death, that memory was born when the reality died. Memories of Jesus' life and sayings were embedded in a narrative very soon after his death, when his followers began to preach the "Good News of Jesus," which was really the "Good News *about* Jesus." For Muslims the "Good News" was not Muhammad but the Quran, which calls itself (16:89) precisely that, *bushra*, "good news." Memories of Muhammad himself, of his ordinary talk, and of his doings at Medina floated free of the Quran and circulated, piecemeal, discretely, in Muslim circles.

It is difficult to know precisely when those personal recollections of the man and his words began to be written down since between the Quran and the earliest preserved writing by Muslims there is a gap of a century or more. The reasons are easy to surmise. The still-illiterate Arabian Muslims used their new literate subjects in Syria, Egypt, and Iraq as their scribes and record keepers—and even permitted them to keep the records in their own vernacular tongues—while the Muslim elite, which preferred to live in all-Arab cantonments rather than amid their alien rivals in the old cities of the Middle East, was engaged in the more attractive activity of conquest and tribute-taking. It took a century for the Arab Muslims to learn to write easily and perhaps even longer to fashion their primitive script into a facile instrument for writing.

Ibn Ishaq

Sometime around 750 appeared the "The Raids" of Ibn Ishaq (d. 768). It was not only a life of Muhammad but apparently—the work is now lost—a widely ranging "world history" as seen from a Muslim perspective. The original seems to have had three parts. The first, the "Book of the Beginning," quite literally began with Creation and passed down through the history of the Prophets, biblical and Arabian, to where it was thought Arab history began. This first part, which is known chiefly from Tabari's (d. 923) incorporation of parts of it into his *History*, seems like an attempt to fill out, along biblical lines and surely with the assistance of Jews and/or Christians, the Sacred History that lies behind the Meccan suras of the Quran where the prophets are adduced to illustrate the Quran's moralizing history of revelation.

The second section, the "Book of the Sending Forth," began with an overview of early South Arabian history—another version, like that of the Persian Tabari, might begin with the early history of Iran—material that might easily have come from the royal annals of one or other of those literate societies. Thence it passes into the "Book of Raids," the heart of the Islamic enterprise that begins with Muhammad's "migration" (*hijra*) from Mecca to Medina and is structured around the raids (*maghazi*) on an ever-widening arc of Arabian settlements conducted by Muhammad.

As just remarked, we no longer have Ibn Ishaq's original work. It may in fact have been driven out of circulation—in the medieval Muslim world that would mean it would cease being publicly performed and/or recopied—by an edited version by one Ibn Hisham (d. 813) called—and this is the first occurrence of the title in this context—"The Life (*Sira*) of the Messenger of God." Whether edited down or not, Ibn Ishaq's material and approach seem quickly to have become the standard treatment of the Prophet's life and times, and it is possible to see his work in somewhat less distinct versions in other historians.

The Sira Tradition

When it comes to discerning how the Meccan and other Arabian societies of that day organized their memories for recollection, transmission, and performance, we are on difficult terrain. There is little antecedent literature to guide us, but it would appear that the collective memories of those preliterate Arab societies were preserved in the form of tribal genealogies, which are all about tribal memory and kinship ties; anecdotal tales (*qisas*) whose primary objective seems to have been entertainment and instruction rather than a mere recollection of the past; and finally, a *maghazi*, or "raids," genre commemorating tribal derring-do in its scuffles with its neighbors. This last appears to have been of Bedouin provenance—the settled Arabs like those in Mecca and Medina were normally not much given to raiding—but was likely preserved in more urban settings out of the town dwellers' prideful nostalgia for their own not very remote past.

If this is an accurate appraisal, the literary form of the Arabic *Sira* or "Life" must be a later creation cobbled together in the first instance from those other older and more primary elements of performed memory. It would certainly seem so in the avatar of the genre, Muhammad's own "Life." It was not so much concerned with genealogy because it was notoriously unconcerned with tribalism as such.[13] Both the *qissa* and the *maghazi* are, however, very much in evidence in the *Sira*, the first during the Meccan period of the Prophet's life when there was no raiding activity; the latter, as we might expect, from the first eye-opening plunder foray at Badr Wells in 624 onward to Muhammad's death. The sequencing or order of Muhammad's expeditions out of Medina could probably be easily recalled, but for the Meccan matter as well as isolated nonraiding incidents at Medina, the contrivers of the earliest Muhammad sira used the Quran, whose units of revelation they attempted to locate in events, real or imagined, in the Prophet's life, after which the anecdotal reminiscences were strung along this not terribly substantial thread.

It is argued by one strain of modern non-Muslim scholarship that the *Sira* is the product of a much later milieu than the Prophet's own—Ibn Ishaq's career began in provincial Medina but ended in cosmopolitan Baghdad—and this seems very likely. The Muslim Arabs of late eighth-century Iraq were surrounded by peoples familiar with narrative biography, and indeed the Christians among them, who were surely still close to a majority of the population, based their faith on just such biographical narratives, the Gospels. It is difficult to imagine that the new Muslim intelligentsia, who showed themselves familiar with Greek philosophy and science, were not also influenced by those emblematic Christian texts in shaping their own new venture in biography.

Ibn Hisham's Sira

Ibn Hisham's edition of Ibn Ishaq's epic history reflects historians' reactions to an emerging narrative of Islamic origins that was already overgrown with legend and hearsay. Like most of his fellow historians, Ibn Hisham was trained as a *traditionist*, that is, he specialized in the accurate transmission of traditions or reports about the Prophet. Not only did he reduce the Ibn Ishaq original into a more manageably sized and focused biography of the Prophet; he wielded a severe scalpel on material within the *Life*. Great swathes of poetry were removed as well as what seemed to him like Jewish or Christian interventions that had come from new converts to Islam. In the same vein, he was opposed to storytelling, though it would have been difficult to remove all those elements, particularly from Muhammad's career at Mecca. As a corrective he attempted to tie the events of Muhammad's life as closely as possible to the givens of the Quran. And Ibn Hisham had quite another, and quite unhistorical, agenda: he wanted the *Life* to be edifying and so he also removed whatever he thought was inappropriate to the Messenger of God.[14] This, then, is the basic biographical torso the later historian has to work with, the *Sira* of Ibn Ishaq in the Ibn Hisham version, and whatever else we can glean of the original from the fragments and treatments embedded in later writers.[15]

Beyond Ibn Hisham

Those later writers are principally Waqidi (d. 823), Ibn Sa'd (d. 843), and finally, and preeminently, Tabari (d. 923). The first was the author, with an assist from Ibn Ishaq, of a clear-cut *Raids* which shows us rather exactly what the original core of a Muhammad biography looked like.[16] The second composed a *Life*, again relying on Ibn Ishaq material, to stand at the head of his *Classes,* a kind of biographical dictionary that is not, however, arranged alphabetically but by generation, proceeding from Muhammad's own contemporaries, the "Companions of the Prophet," down to the time of the writing. It was for the use of traditionists and lawyers interested in investigating the "chains" of authorities attached to various traditions concerning the Prophet. Finally, Tabari is the author of the *Annals*, a monumental chronological progress through the history of Islam from its Iranian background—which was Tabari's own—down to the present day. The life of the Prophet is a long and rewarding stop on that parade. Tabari relied heavily on Ibn Ishaq and, what is useful for us, in a version different from the one Ibn Hisham had before him.

Bukhari and the "Prophetic Reports"

With our last authority, Bukhari (d. 870), the author or better, the editor of the celebrated collection of Prophetic traditions called "The Sound" (*al-Sahih*), we have left history-writing as such and entered into the domain of the lawyer. Islamic law is peculiarly a law of precedent; it stands, however, not *ex decisis* but *ex revelatis*. The basis of all Islamic law is the revealed Quran, but where the Quran is silent or nonspecific, the law resorts first and principally to the precedent of "the custom of the Prophet." The latter is preserved in individual case, or better, incident, reports. These are the celebrated, and notorious, "Prophetic traditions" (*hadith*), vignettes that embody the sayings or deeds attributed to Muhammad and are attested to by an attached chain of authorities going back to eyewitnesses to the Prophet's career. These Prophetic traditions began to be assembled and scrutinized in the ninth century, a subject to which we shall return, and one of the most famous and influential of the collections was that of Bukhari, with its guarantee that all the traditions contained therein were "sound" (*sahih*), that is, authentic.

Bukhari's *Sahih* is a book by a lawyer for the use of lawyers. The Prophetic traditions are arranged topically for easy consultation, but it opens in a manner of interest to the historian as well. The first chapter is titled "How the Revelation to the Apostle of God Began." After five traditions on the effect of the revelational experience on Muhammad, there begins what is not marked as a new chapter, but appears to be such, on "The Merits of the Prophet's Companions." These "Companions" are, of course, the eyewitnesses to Muhammad's behavior and their merits are rehearsed to establish their bona fides as witnesses. These are immediately followed by twenty-nine sections covering, in chronological order, episodes in the life of Muhammad. It is not in uninterrupted narrative form—the Prophetic traditions are still discrete entities—but it has obviously been influenced by the historian's concerns with events and chronology rather than the lawyer's need for case precedents.

Western Historicism and Its Discontents

If there is any authenticity in the material in Ibn Ishaq's biography and Waqidi's classical version of "The Raids," it surely rests upon the preserved reminiscences of Muhammad's contemporaries.[17] That there were such can hardly be doubted, but our problem is discerning whether any such is represented in the material at hand. To solve it, we must inquire how and for what reasons the material was transmitted in the three or three-and-a-half generations between Muhammad and Ibn Ishaq. There are two general paths of transmission that can be discerned, that of the Prophetic traditions (*hadith*), where the transmission may have been written or oral and the motives legal or historical, and that of the entertaining narratives (*qisas*) passed down orally in the first generations of Islam.

The first possibility carries us into one of the most crucial and debated areas of Islamic history. The great bulk of the preserved Prophetic traditions have to do with legal issues, for which they could be cited as a clinching argument. Such, for example, are most of those collected in Bukhari's *Sahih*. They are designated "sound" or "healthy" because in the ninth century Muslims were beginning to have doubts about the authenticity of many of these hadith and subjected them to intense scrutiny. The scrutiny focused on the chains of transmitting authorities—whether each *could* have transmitted the tradition in question and was of reliable moral probity—that was put at the head of every tradition.

A new scrutiny of the hadith began on the part of Western scholars in the nineteenth century, and concluded that a great many of the Prophetic reports were forgeries concocted to advance political or sectarian aims or to support what was in fact nothing more than local legal traditions. Initially the investigation had to do with the legal hadith, but in the early part of the twentieth century it was extended to the historical hadith, the stuff of Ibn Ishaq's life, and with equally negative results. A strong current of skepticism continues to run through most Western studies of the hadith, including the historical ones. In the eyes of the skeptics, the Prophetic traditions were orally transmitted for a century and a half after Muhammad's death and during that period underwent substantial transformation. If the *Sira* is composed of hadith material, it is generally held, then it's only doubtfully reliable as history.

Tales of Wahb

If the hadith arouse historical skepticism, so too does another element of the sira, the "story" or "tale" (*qissa/qisas*). What is disturbing to the historian is the not unlikely possibility that all the preserved biographies of Muhammad may owe far more to the art of storytelling than to any actual historical recollection. Here the critical figure is Wahb ibn Munabbih (d. 728 or 732). His family, of Iranian origin, was long domesticated in the Yemen, and Wahb himself, a

Muslim from birth, was considered a specialist on Judeo-Christian matters—his sources on these were two Jewish converts whose lifetimes overlapped that of the Prophet. He wrote and lectured on the history of the prophets and the history of South Arabia, both topics that loom large in Ibn Ishaq's work, and composed a now lost "Book of Campaigns," the antecedent, if not the source, of both Ibn Ishaq's and Waqidi's compositions on that subject.

Later, more self-conscious authorities hastened to disassociate themselves from Wahb since he was not a traditionist, a transmitter of hadith with presumably high standards of verification, but a storyteller (*qass*), an entertainer, who, like others of his guild, enlarged on the Quran by supplying pleasant (and plausible) contexts in the life of Muhammad for this revelation or that. Plausible does not, of course, mean true, as may be seen on the almost infinite variety of traditions on any given moment in Muhammad's life. We have fragments of one of Wahb's versions of early Islamic history but both Ibn Ishaq and Waqidi likely had—and used—other complete versions of tales of the prophets and tales of Muhammad, a likelihood that casts profound doubts on the veracity of what we read in those latter authors.

Toward a Life

The extant *Lives* of Muhammad thus represent a serious methodological problem for anyone attempting to reconstruct the biography of the Prophet of Islam. It is difficult to deny that some of the material found there is grounded in historical fact, and it is not inconceivable that accurate memories may be passed on orally over three or even four generations. But who passed them on, and why, is what gives us pause. Polemicists and storytellers do not make the best of historians, even—or, as it turns out, especially—when their accounts are introduced by long and impressive chains of authorities. We shall return to these problems in the course of our own reconstruction of Muhammad's life, but from the outset, it must be understood that the Quran is our soundest guide.

But not our only one. All the modern biographers of Muhammad have attempted to combine the two sources just described, the Quran and the narrative sources. The biographical tradition, no matter how suspect in its intent, unconvincing in its methodology, and uncertain in its details, has been used to provide a chronological—or at least a *sequential*—framework over and against which to arrange whatever data may be wrested from the Quran. Some of this framework can be authenticated from the parsimonious allusions in the Quran, but these invariably have to do with Muhammad's career at Medina.

For the Meccan period of his life, his call to prophethood, the circumstances of his earliest preaching, the rise of an opposition and his reaction to it, and the private and public travails that eventually led to his flight to Medina, the Quran gives us little or no guidance. It is here then, in the critical formative period of Muhammad's life and calling and the matrix of nascent Islam, that the historian must confront the issue of the historical reliability of the basic biographical sources and what the Muslim tradition adds beyond them, just as he or she does with the New Testament.

Muslim Patristics

Beyond the foundation biographies of Muhammad lies a poorly charted and treacherous sea of data just referred to as "the Muslim tradition," a phrase that recurs often in these pages. What the catchall term refers to is the great body of writing on Muhammad and the Quran that is preserved for us from circa 750 onward. It represents, in effect, the authors who would be called in Christianity the "Fathers of the Church." This Christian construct of "patristics," and the authority attached to its representatives, is thought to have ended with John of Damascus (d. ca. 754) in the East and Gregory the Great (d. 604) in the West, but Muslim patristics is a very different matter. The tradition on Muhammad and the Quran is embodied, like its Christian counterpart, in full-blown literary works like those of the biographer Ibn Hisham (d. 813), the historian al-Tabari (d. 923), the exegete Muqatil Ibn Sulayman (d. 767), and the traditionist al-Bukhari (d. 870), but much of it originated, as we have seen, in those "bytes" of information that are the hadith and that were thought to transmit the authoritative testimony of the "ancestors" (*salaf*), as the Muslims call what we might term the "Apostolic Fathers."[18] Though many of the hadith were incorporated into the works just mentioned, many too continued to circulate, often orally, as individual reports and thereafter surfaced as new and authoritative testimony to the Prophet and his Book as late as in the work of al-Suyuti (d. 1505), the prodigious Egyptian polymath—he told one of his students he had memorized one hundred thousand hadith— who constitutes, in effect, the finis of Muslim patristics.[19]

Afterthoughts: The New Testament and the Quran

There are two different epistemic systems at work in the New Testament and the Quran. With the Quran the secular historian starts with the investigative premise that it is the voice of Muhammad he is hearing through the received text. The Muslims who were responsible for transmitting that received text, and perhaps the very earliest believers who created the Quran as a text, believed no such thing. They heard the all but immediate voice of God. The sounds may have come forth from the lips of Muhammad but he was merely enunciating and not creating them.

In the case of Jesus, the historian, whether Christian or not, recognizes from the outset that he is dealing with texts that had human authors, whose very names stand in fact at the heads of the texts that constitute the New Testament as certainly as no one's does at the head of the Quran. The investigative premise is that the texts, particularly the Gospels, report the teachings (and describe the acts) of another human personage, namely, Jesus of Nazareth. The Christian immediately adds that that same Jesus was *also* the Son of God and so what was proceeding from his lips was the reported speech of God. It was not, however. The words of Yahweh heard and reported by Moses from Sinai or the words of Allah pronounced by Muhammad in Mecca and Medina were God's reported words; what proceeded from Jesus' lips was a revolutionary new discourse, the words of a man-God, a human voice with the gravity of the Divine.

The Critic at Work: Coming of Age

THE ACTIVE CAREERS of Jesus and Muhammad, which in both instances began with the public preaching of a religious message, were undertaken in the early middle age of both men, Jesus when he was "about 30" (Lk 3:23) and Muhammad at likely about the same age, though the Muslim tradition makes him, without good reason, forty. At some point in their careers a number of their contemporaries began to pay heed to what the public Jesus and the public Muhammad were saying and from that point onward we have firm reports for each. But the Christian and Muslim biographical traditions on their foundational figures were understandably unwilling to pass over in silence all that had gone before in the life of each. Their biographies, the Christians' Gospels and the Muslim versions of the *Sira*, undertook to fill in those thirty-odd years in the *Life* of Jesus and Muhammad in a manner that would both edify and instruct the believers. Those preludes, the biographical chapters covering the birth and early nonpublic years of Jesus and Muhammad, are the subject of this chapter and present an opportunity to illustrate something of the critical method that has been employed in the attempt to disentangle the "historical" Jesus or Muhammad from the mass of myth, legend, theological construction, and simple wishful thinking that now surrounds each.

Jesus' Infancy Narratives

The Gospels of Mark and John, as well as the sayings source Q—hence all of our independent narrative sources—begin Jesus' biography with Jesus' association with John the Baptist and, more specifically, with his baptism by John. Matthew and Luke also describe Jesus' baptism but their Gospels do not begin there. Each has a rather prolonged account (Mt 1:1–2:23; Lk 1:5–2:52) of Jesus' (and in Luke even John the Baptist's) conception, birth, and, more briefly, his early years. Each has also included a genealogy of Jesus that purports to provide his family tree. The point being made here is that Jesus is descended from David, and each genealogy passes through that king and messianic prototype, Matthew's (1:1–16) forward from Abraham to Joseph, the husband of Jesus' mother; Luke's (3:23–38) backward from Joseph to Adam.

These chapters, which are present only in Matthew and Luke and differ one from the other, constitute the so-called Infancy Narratives and they immediately raise doubts about their own authenticity and the integrity of the Gospels. We note at the outset that each of the two Jesus genealogies is itself notoriously different from the other in many details, from their near starting points (Mary for Matthew, Joseph for Luke), to their end points (Abraham for Matthew, Adam, or indeed God himself, for Luke), and with many divergences in between. It is of little matter to the Christian, perhaps, since in both instances the purpose was grossly theological rather than historical. But they catch the attention of the historian. We know a good deal about undocumented genealogies, and the most common judgment concerning them is that they are not very reliable beyond three generations, though in this case Matthew and Luke, or their editorial helpers, could not even agree on Jesus' paternal grandfather.

Editorial Fingerprints on the Gospels

Even if we regard them materially, the Gospels are not all of a piece. The ancient manuscript tradition reveals rather clearly that a later hand or hands tacked on an appendix to the Gospels of Mark (16:9–19) and John (21) to flesh out, interestingly enough, testimony to the empty tomb and the resurrected Jesus, elements that had apparently taken on a new importance since the originals were written.

There are other rather obvious examples of later editorial additions to the Gospels, like the parenthetical comment in Mark (7:3–4) explaining for the reader the presumably unfamiliar Pharisaic, and Jewish, custom of washing the hands. Then there is the rather bold editorial conclusion tacked on to Jesus' remarks on inner versus outer purity (Mk 7:19), arguing that Jesus had thereby pronounced *all* foods clean. Consider too the strenuous disclaimer in John (4:2) that Jesus had ever performed baptisms himself, this immediately after the same Gospel asserts quite clearly that Jesus was baptizing. Finally, there are a series of internal signs that point to entire passages having been introduced into the text at some later point.

This latter is almost certainly the case in what have been called the Infancy Narratives, the accounts of Jesus' miraculous conception and miracle-surrounded birth that are found in the early chapters of both Matthew's and Luke's Gospels. The Church never had any problems with these passages—we know this because they are never missing in the ancient manuscripts—and they are quite obviously the foundation of the Christian celebration of Christmas. But modern scholarship, even of the most traditional kind, has its doubts as to whether these two Infancy Narratives in the opening chapters of Matthew's and Luke's Gospels were part of the original Good News of Jesus Christ, a doubt shared here.

Jesus of Bethlehem

The grounds for doubting the authenticity of the stories of Jesus' *Life* before his public ministry are all internal to the two Gospels and are, generally speaking, the tendentiousness of the enterprise and the incoherence of the manner in which it is achieved. "Tendentious" means that a text is being driven by some unacknowledged motive or agenda. Here in both Infancy Narratives the first unacknowledged intent is to make the case that Jesus, who is elsewhere referred to exclusively as "Jesus of Nazareth," was really "Jesus of Bethlehem," that is, he was born in David's native city and hence a true scion of that royal messianic line. Indeed, John's Gospel tells us that Jesus' messianic claim was mocked precisely because he was *not* from Bethlehem (7:41–42; cf. 1:45–46, "Can anything good come from Nazareth?").

To achieve this counterintuitive objective each author has to resort to extraordinary means. Matthew opens his account with Joseph and Mary already living in Bethlehem, where Jesus is born (2:1), and then has to resort to a series of angel-inspired dreams to move the family first to Egypt and then, after a stay there, to Nazareth in Galilee, where Joseph settled because "he heard that Archelaus had succeeded his father Herod as king of Judea (and) he was afraid to go there" (2:22).

Luke seems to concede that Nazareth was indeed the original home of Mary and Joseph and so has the problem of getting them from there to Bethlehem, where Jesus will be born. To do so he entangles himself in some highly implausible *realia*. "In those days," he begins, "a decree was issued by the Emperor Augustus for a census to be taken throughout the Roman world. This was the first registration of its kind; and took place when Quirinius was governor of Syria. Everyone made his way to his own town to be registered" (Lk 2:1–3). "In those days" would presumably be before or about Herod's death in

4 BC. But whether before or after, Roman history, which makes Quirinius the governor of Roman Syria in AD 6 when Judea was annexed to the Roman Empire, knows of no such empirewide census and certainly knows nothing of the unusual registration procedure of making everyone return to his home-town. But despite the absence of all evidence for such, it is difficult to believe that the editor who formulated this piece, and who doubtless lived in the Roman Empire, would simply have so flagrantly invented an empirewide cen-sus that everyone alive could immediately identify as having never occurred. It is more likely that either he or we have misunderstood the intended histor-ical marker.

Again, it should be remarked that, outside these two narratives, nowhere in the New Testament is Jesus identified as coming from Bethlehem, not even by Matthew and Luke, who were supposed to have provided that information to begin with. More generally, from all that we know of the ancient world, absent all archaeological and documentary record keeping, little formal atten-tion seems to have been paid to infants or children; public note was taken only when they had become public figures, as Jesus did when he emerged from the waters of the Jordan after his baptism by John. It is safe to think that the public record of Jesus' *Life* begins there, just as it does in Q and the Gospels of Mark and John. Where accounts of children do occur in ancient literature, they invariably depict the infant or child displaying whatever it is that will later make him famous. Hercules, for example, is described as strangling snakes in his cradle. Here Jesus does the others one better: he is *born* the Messiah.

Recognitions

But there is far more at work here than getting Jesus from what was, on all the other evidence, his native village of Nazareth—he is invariably referred to as "Jesus of Nazareth," never as "Jesus of Bethlehem"—to the Davidic, and hence messianic, town of Bethlehem. Another motive, not quite so obviously per-haps, is at work in the infancy accounts, namely, that Jesus did not *become* the Messiah, which is a conclusion that might be readily drawn from reading the other Gospels, or even from Matthew and Luke once past the Infancy Narra-tives. In all these other accounts Jesus receives his messianic validation imme-diately after his universally attested baptism by John, when a heavenly voice confirms that he is indeed the Son of God. The Infancy Narratives would push that moment back to Jesus' birth, when angels proclaim his divine status and it is recognized in one form or another by Herod, by the Magi from the East and the shepherds in the Bethlehem fields.[1] In fact, it is Jesus' "Coming

Out," his Epiphany, that is celebrated with great pomp by Eastern Christians on January 6 rather than his birth on December 25.[2]

A Virginal Conception

Embedded in both Infancy Narratives there are other powerful motives at work. Each puts forward the claim of Jesus' virginal conception, that is, the assertion that he was not the offspring of a sexual union between a man and a woman.[3] He was certainly born to Mary, all agree, a maiden betrothed to a certain Joseph. In both accounts she is discovered to be pregnant: in Matthew the news is announced to Joseph and in Luke to Mary herself by an angel. It happened "through the Holy Spirit," according to Matthew (1:20). Luke is somewhat more forthcoming. "The Holy Spirit will come upon you," the angel tells Mary, "and the power of the Most High will overshadow you" (1:35).

This is an extraordinary turn of events, extraordinary not merely because of its miraculous nature but also because nowhere else in the Gospels or in Paul is Jesus' virginal conception mentioned or even alluded to. Our primary sources, as well as the later rabbinic writings, do seem to indicate, however, that the paternity of Jesus, who is quite remarkably called "son of Mary" (Mk 6:3), was problematic, or at least unusual. The likely motive behind the explanations in the Infancy Narratives appears in Matthew immediately after we are told of this miraculous conception. "All of this happened in order to fulfill what was said through the prophets" (1:22). The prophet in question is Isaiah (7:7) and the apparently messianic prophecy begins, "A virgin (or a young girl) shall conceive and bear a son . . ." Whether Jesus' early followers read "virgin" or "young girl" in their Greek version of Isaiah is not exactly to the point, since either fits Mary at that point. What is remarkable is that they understood it to mean that she *conceived* virginally, and that she was still a virgin after the conception.

The Gospel's reading of Isaiah raises an interesting point about how contemporary Jews understood their own Bible—the Dead Sea Scrolls are of enormous importance here—but more pertinent to our purpose is the possibility that here, and often throughout the Gospels, particularly Matthew's, that biblical prophecy is driving—read *creating*—events in the *Life* of Jesus. The fulfillment of prophecy is in fact invoked on five different occasions in Matthew's Infancy Narrative to explain an event. The stories that occur in Matthew's Infancy Narrative, from Jesus' miraculous conception through Herod's search for the newborn and his slaughter of all the male infants under two years in Bethlehem—an event that has left no trace in Josephus' highly detailed history of Herod's reign or in any other source; the Magi/astrologers "from the East" who follow a new star to Bethlehem; and finally, Joseph and Mary's flight with their newborn into Egypt, must all have been in early and wide circulation in Christian circles, and here Matthew or his editor has integrated them into a single, somewhat disjointed tale held together by the formulaic "This happened to fulfill what was said through the prophets."

The Infancy Narrative in Luke represents a somewhat different point of view. Whereas Joseph had been the prime mover of the action in Matthew, here it is Mary. Luke's version in fact opens with a long and circumstantial treatment (1:5–80) of the (almost as miraculous) conception of John the Baptist on the part of the elderly priest Zechariah and his equally aged, and barren, wife Elizabeth, who was also of priestly descent and who was, we are told, Mary's cousin. And when the pregnant Mary visits the now pregnant Elizabeth, John the Baptist leaps in his mother's womb in joyful recognition of his Lord. Mary remains with her cousin for three months and then returns home. This part of the Infancy Narrative concludes with an account of the Baptist's circumcision.

The Nativity

The Lukan story of Jesus' own birth and earliest years fills the entire second chapter of that Gospel. Mary (and the reader) was earlier informed of her imminent pregnancy by an angel (1:26–38)—in Matthew, Joseph (and the reader) learns she is already pregnant—and there now occurs the census that forces Joseph and Mary to take the road to Bethlehem. "While they were there the time came for her to have her baby, and she gave birth to a son, her firstborn. She wrapped him in swaddling clothes and laid him in a manger, because there was no room for them at the inn" (2:7). Matthew, who spends a good deal of time explaining Mary's pregnancy, has none of this detail. He says simply, "Jesus was born at Bethlehem in Judea during the reign of Herod" (2:1). This part of Luke's narrative concludes with the story of how angels told local shepherds of the birth and hymned the newborn Messiah from the heavens (2:8–18).

In the Temple

There follows in Luke a brief mention of Jesus' circumcision and naming (2:21) and a somewhat longer account of two other Temple rituals that the author seems to have run together, the prescribed purification of the mother after childbirth (Lv 12:2–4)—the text says "their purification" as if the narrator mistakenly thought both Mary and Joseph had to undergo purification—and the traditional ritual of the buyback of a firstborn Israelite male in the Temple (2:22–24; cf. Ex 13:1–2, 13). There is a further confusion of the prescribed offering for maternal purification and male redemption: Luke transfers the former, two doves or two pigeons, to the latter.

This account of these rituals leads into two further recognition stories, both set in the Temple precincts. One is by a certain Simeon, a charismatic—"the Holy Spirit was upon him"—who had been told from on high that he would live to see the Messiah, whom he now sees in the infant Jesus. "This is," Simeon hymns, "a light that will bring revelation to the Gentiles and glory to your people Israel" (2:32). And, now speaking directly to Mary, "This child is destined to be a sign that will be rejected. And you too will be pierced to the heart" (2:34). Another figure enters the narrative, Anna, an elderly widow—she is rather precisely eighty-four—and a "prophetess" (2:36), who spent her days and nights over long years worshiping in the Temple. She too recognizes the infant as one for whom "all were looking for the liberation of Jerusalem." Joseph and Mary then return with Jesus to Galilee and to "their own town of Nazareth," where "the child grew big and strong and full of wisdom" (2:39–40).

Bar Mitzvah

The final episode in Luke's Infancy Narrative is a disconnected piece about the twelve-year-old Jesus. He is accidentally left behind in Jerusalem when Joseph and Mary are visiting the city to celebrate Passover. They return to find him in the Temple engaged in a discussion with the astonished sages there. "Didn't you know," he asks his worried parents, "that I was bound to be in my Father's house?" (2:49). The narrative ends with Jesus returning to Nazareth, while "his mother treasured all these things in her heart."

The historian would like to know, of course, where these intimate stories of Jesus' infancy and boyhood originated. Herod's murderous pogrom and the Magi are probably folktales based on we know not what actual incidents. But Joseph's dreams and more private memories could of course have been provided by Mary, and the Lukan version, where she is far more prominent than Joseph, rather clearly suggests that it was Jesus' mother, who otherwise does not play an important role in the Gospels, who provided at least some of the memories, since "Mary treasured all these things and pondered on them" (Lk 2:19, 51).

One Man's Family

Jesus has a family in the Infancy Narratives, a mother Miryam or Mary and her husband Joseph, who was not, we are assured, Jesus' father. Joseph was a carpenter of Nazareth,[4] but he effectively disappears from the Gospels after the Infancy Narratives. The Christian tradition explained this absence by stipulating that he had died before Jesus, then about thirty, began his public career. According to the Proto-Gospel of James, Joseph was already an aged widower—and so he is inevitably portrayed in Christian art, elderly and often a little detached—when he was selected by lot to marry the twelve-year-old Temple maiden Mary. Another, somewhat later apocryphal work, *The Story of Joseph the Carpenter*, is as usual much more explicit. Joseph died, age 111, in AD 18 or 19, when Jesus would have been twenty-two or twenty-three. The elderly Joseph is not only a guarantee of Mary's ongoing virginity; he is also, again according to a postevangelical tradition, the father, in an earlier marriage, of those individuals called in the Gospels Jesus' "brothers and sisters" (Mt 13:44), and thus Mary's virginity could be sheltered *ante, inter*, and even *post* the birth of Jesus.

As a carpenter or, more accurately perhaps, a woodworker (*tekton*), and in all likelihood the son of another such, Jesus would have grown up not in the peasant class of subsistence farmers but closer to what we might think of as a pinched middle class of tradesmen and craftsmen, though in a society quite differently stratified from our own. He was certainly Aramaic-speaking, though it is not inconceivable that he knew some Hebrew (learned in the local synagogue), some Greek, and perhaps even a smattering of Latin patois. And the odds are good—the direct evidence is uncertain—that Jesus of Nazareth was literate. Scriptural learning was still largely orally acquired and transmitted in that day but not entirely so in a famously clerical Israel, and Jesus' familiarity and apparent ease with Scripture and its tropes suggests something more profound than listening. He was not, however, a member of the learned elite, the "scribes" (*grammateis*) who appear often in the Gospels, and certainly not of the priesthood, the hereditary caste that still controlled both Temple and Torah in Jesus' day.

The Women in Jesus' Life

Women have now come to the surface of the Gospels. They have always been in the narrative though it is only very recently that their presence has been remarked and reflected upon. Women appear throughout Jesus' Galilean ministry both as part of his support system (Lk 8:1–3) and as the objects of his particular pastoral care (Mk 1:29–31, 5:21–24, etc., and parr.). Certain of them may even have been regarded as disciples (Lk 10:38–42). The entire complex of relationships, close and largely uninhibited by the usual societal restraints, seems somewhat remarkable in that time and that place. Most extraordinary of all is that women are reported to have been the primary witnesses to Jesus' empty tomb (Mk 16:1 and parr.) and in one instance, a woman, Mary Magdalene, was the first to whom the risen Jesus appeared (Jn 20:14–18).

Jesus appears easy in the presence of women, even in the most awkward of circumstances (Mt 15:22–28; Jn 4:7–5:30),[5] although there is no direct evidence for his own formal relationship with them. No wife is ever mentioned, directly or indirectly, though it must be recalled that it is only by the most casual of asides—when Jesus cures his mother-in-law (Mk 1:30–31)—that we learn the Apostle Peter was married. And yet no one comments on the fact that Jesus was *not* married. There the matter seems to stand. The Jesus movement had, however, an increasingly important investment in celibacy and so there has been a constant insistence from within the Christian tradition that Jesus himself was celibate.[6] That is possible in a Second Temple Jewish society where celibacy was not all that uncommon, and it is perhaps even likely, given the absence of all evidence to the contrary.

Afterthoughts: Editorial Opportunities

The Synoptics are rich in editorial opportunity. Matthew's and Luke's unmistakable use of Mark displays for us the evangelical author-editors in action. We have their source before us in Mark and we can take the measure of what each did with it. It was perhaps that happy circumstance that provoked the further step of reconstructing a second source used by Matthew and Luke, namely, the sayings source Q. But in this instance we must imagine the source: Q, as we have seen, is a reconstruction back from Matthew's and Luke's edited versions. Here we are, or should be, sobered by the realization that we could not have conceivably reconstructed Mark solely on the basis of its traces in the two later Gospels. Our hesitation is, however, assuaged somewhat by the conviction that Q was simply a collection of sayings, where the intent of the text lay, as it does in the Quran, in the sayings themselves and not in their contextual framing.[7]

Nor is that the end of it. Luke's announced second volume, the Acts of the Apostles (see 1:1–2), provides us with the rather exact context within which he wrote his Gospel; not the precise when or where—though its ending with Paul's arrival in Rome in the opening 60s is certainly suggestive—but what he believed about Jesus of Nazareth and why. Luke's account of what happened in AD 29–30 was written in the light of the crucial events that occurred between at least 30 and 60. His Gospel may in fact have been written circa 80–90, as many think, but, unlike the matter covered in Acts, we have no idea how much Luke knew of those later events, like the Jewish insurrection, or what he thought of them.

John's Gospel represents a different kind of opportunity. The evidence is convincing that John was working on both a collection of Jesus' sayings not unlike what is found in Mark and Q as well as a collection of Jesus' miracles, or "signs" (*semeia*), as John characteristically calls them (2:11). There is not much hope of recovering or reconstructing the original form of either, not least because John's own authorial hand was a particularly heavy one, as can be seen by his transformation of Jesus' almost certainly aphoristic teachings into lengthy discourses. But the mere existence of a "*Semeia* Source," like that of Q, tells us something about Jesus' earliest followers. The fact of their collection as such shows that Jesus' miracles had an importance of their own, that they were, like the "signs" that fill the Quranic accounts of the prophets (including Jesus!), a form of validation, and quite explicitly of prophetic validation.

The "Infancy Gospel of Islam"

When we turn from the Gospels to the *Sira* tradition on the birth and early years of Muhammad, we find ourselves in a different time and place, late sixth-century Western Arabia, but on a very similar narrative landscape filled with many of the same motifs on display in the Jesus Infancy Narratives. But whereas we can trace many of these latter themes back to their Scriptural prototypes, we stand mute before their *Sira* counterparts. The folkloric background of the *Sira* (and of the Quran!) has disappeared in the wreckage of "The Barbarism," as the Muslims called their own pre-Islamic past; we are left merely with "types," the topoi or commonplaces of hagiography.

The Birth of Muhammad Ibn Abdullah

The biographical tradition on Muhammad opens with a familiar theme, an "annunciation" from on high, this one reported on the authority of its recipient, the Prophet's mother, Amina, though with a modest disclaimer from the author:

> It is alleged in popular stories—and only God knows the truth—that Amina, daughter of Wahb, the mother of God's Apostle, used to say when she was pregnant with God's Apostle that a voice said to her, "You are pregnant with the lord of this people, and when he is born, say: 'I put him in the care of the One from the evil of every envier'; then call him Muhammad." As she was pregnant with him she saw a light come forth from her by which she could see the castles of Bostra in Syria. Shortly afterwards Abdullah, the Apostle's father, died while his mother was still pregnant.[8]

Thus rapidly does Muhammad's father pass from history. Other versions of the story have a light emanating from the Prophet's father, a light that made him sexually attractive to other women but which was quenched as soon as he had impregnated Amina.

> The Apostle was born on Monday, the 12th of First Rabi'a in the Year of the Elephant. . . . It is said that he was born in the house known as Abu Yusuf's, and it is said that the Apostle gave it to Aqil ibn Abi Talib who kept it until he died. His son sold it to Muhammad ibn Yusuf, the brother of al-Hajjaj, and he incorporated it into the house he built. Later Khayzuran separated it therefrom and made it into a mosque. (69–70)

What is driving this particular piece of the narrative is a rather obvious interest in—or dispute over?—a piece of Meccan real estate owned by the famous al-Hajjaj, the Muslim strongman who put down an insurrection in Mecca in 691–692 and who was subsequently governor of the Hijaz. A good deal of the *Sira*, which is filled with lists of "those present at," is given over to determining the service-based rights, privileges, and property of a later generation of Muslims.

"The Men Who Have the Elephant"

"The Year of the Elephant" was not an uncommon way of dating an event. Tying it to another exceptional or remarkable happening fixed it in the common memory. This happening particularly recommended itself since it was referred to in one of the Quran's very few historical allusions: "Don't you (Muhammad) see how your Lord dealt with the men who had the elephant? How He completely confounded their plans? He sent ranks of birds against them, pelting them with pellets of baked clay. He reduced them to rubble" (105). The reference, the Muslim historians tell us, was to an attack on Mecca by a Yemeni army that had a war elephant among its weapons. It was led by one Abraha, the Ethiopian viceroy in the Yemen, a verifiably historical personage and in this scenario a Christian who had vile designs on pagan Mecca.

Ibn Ishaq sets the scene. We are now clearly in the presence of an entertaining storyteller, a *qass*:

> In the morning Abraha prepared to enter the town and he made his elephant ready for battle and drew up his troops. His intention was to destroy the shrine and then return to the Yemen. When they made the elephant—its name was Mahmud—face Mecca, Nufayl ibn Habib came up to its flank and taking hold of its ear said: "Kneel, Mahmud, or go straight back whence you came, for you are in God's holy land!" He let go of its ear and the elephant knelt, and Nufayl made off at top speed for the top of the mountain. The troops beat the elephant to make it get up but it would not; they beat its head with iron bars; they stuck hooks into its underbelly and scarified it; but it would not get up. Then they made it face the Yemen and immediately it got up and started off. When they faced it towards the north and the east it did likewise, but as soon as they directed it toward Mecca, it knelt down. (25–27)

Ibn Ishaq then ties, with amplification, what happened afterward to the unspecified event described in sura 105:

> Then God sent upon them birds from the sea like swallows and starlings; each bird carried three stones, like peas and lentils, one in its beak and two between its claws. Everyone who was hit died, but not all were hit. They withdrew in flight the way they came, crying out for Nufayl ibn Habib to guide them on the way to the Yemen. . . . As they withdrew they were continually falling by the wayside, dying miserably by every waterhole. Abraha was smitten in his body, and as they took him away his fingers fell off one by one. Where the fingers had been there arose an evil sore exuding pus and blood, so that when they

brought him to San'a he was like a young fledgling. They allege that as
he died, his heart burst from his body.

And then in a final note, Ibn Ishaq offers, almost as an aside, what may
have actually befallen the expedition:

Ya'qub ibn Utba told me that he was informed that that year was the
first time that measles and smallpox had been seen in Arabia. (27)

Muhammad's birth was thus remembered to have occurred in the same
year that God, to protect His holy Meccan house, the Ka'ba, miraculously
defeated Abraha's army, whether with smallpox or a lethal avian flyover. But
which year? The Muslims were not entirely certain, but many placed it forty
years before Muhammad's call to prophecy in 610, which would date the
Prophet's birth in 570. There is, however, a South Arabian inscription that
describes an Abraha-led military engagement east of Mecca that seems to
belong to the same campaign. It bears the date in the local era that yields AD
552, which places both Abraha and his military foray far too early to be connected to the birth of Muhammad.

An Uncertain Chronology

Ibn Ishaq's confident chronology that places Muhammad's birth on the
twelfth day of the spring month of First Rabi'a in the "Year of the Elephant"
is belied not only by the physical evidence but by most of the other information we possess about the *Life* of the Prophet. To begin with, not all the
authorities date his birth in the so-called Year of the Elephant. Muhammad
himself, like most others of his contemporaries, and people in similar circumstances for many centuries after, had little or no idea when he was born and
thus of his exact age at death, and the historians give wildly different figures.
Most authorities make him anywhere between sixty and sixty-five years old
when he died, a quite advanced age in that culture and quite at odds with the
impression given by the sources of his vitality and of the unexpectedness of
his death when it did occur.

As it turns out, the reported age of Muhammad was a function not of the
memory of his followers, who had no way of knowing it, but of a calculation
based on quite another set of considerations. Note this quite typical explanation from a later historian:

The Quraysh reckoned (time), before the (beginning of the) era of the Prophet, from the time of the Elephant. Between the Elephant and the Sinful Wars, they reckoned 40 years. Between the Sinful Wars and the death of Hisham ibn al-Mughira they reckoned six years. Between the death of Hisham and the (re)building of the Ka'ba they reckoned nine years. Between the (re)building of the Ka'ba and the departure of the Prophet for Medina, they reckoned 15 years; he stayed five years (of these fifteen) without receiving the revelation. Then the reckoning (of the usual chronology) was as follows. (Ibn Asakir, *Ta'rikh* 1:28)

One nonhistorical element in the calculation was the notion that the Prophet should have been at the ideal age of forty when he received his first revelation, and another, less frequently invoked, is that he should not have yet reached the age of responsibility when he took part in a somewhat reprehensible Meccan enterprise, the so-called Sinful Wars. The consequent calculations have led to numerous anomalies, like obliging his wife Khadija to bear Muhammad eight children after she had passed the age of forty, in a land, as has been remarked, "where there were twenty-two-year-old grandmothers!"

Later Muslim authorities seem to give tacit recognition to the uncertainty of any of the chronological indications passed on about the Prophet's *Life* at Mecca. They, like us, must have felt that the historical ground grew firm only at Muhammad's migration to Medina; it was that date and not, as we might expect, the first "sending down" of the Quran, that they chose to begin the Muslim calendrical era, and from that point to Muhammad's death, all agreed, was a span of ten years.

Presentiments and Prodigies

If we return to Ibn Ishaq's canonical account of the early years of Muhammad, what has been called the "Infancy Gospel of Islam," we find it filled, as it appears, with the same miracles and presentiments of the future as are found in the Infancy Narratives of Matthew and Luke:

Salih ibn Ibrahim . . . said that his tribesmen said that Hassan ibn Thabit said, "I was a well-grown boy of seven or eight, understanding all that I heard, when I heard a Jew calling out at the top of his voice from the top of a fort in Yathrib [that is, Medina]: 'O company of Jews' until they all came together and they called out to him, 'Confound you, what is the matter?' He answered: 'Tonight has risen a star under which Ahmad is to be born.'" (69–70)

"Ahmad" is an after-the-fact reference to the Quran (61:6), where Jesus is made to say to the Jews: "I am sent to you by God, confirming the Torah that was sent before me and bringing good news of a messenger to follow me whose name will be Ahmad." Ahmad, "the Praised One," is, in meaning at least, identical to the name Muhammad and the *Sira* is here making certain, with an unmistakable reflection of the evangelical star over Bethlehem, that the proper identification of Ahmad-Muhammad is made.

Ibn Ishaq returns to the same point again just before the beginning of Muhammad's public mission:

> The following is, among other things, what reached me about what Jesus the Son of Mary stated in the Gospel [Injil] which he received from God for the followers of the Gospel, in applying a term to describe the Apostle of God. It is extracted from what John the Apostle set down for them when he wrote the Gospel for them from the Testament of Jesus, the Son of Mary [Jn 15:23]: "He that hateth me hath hated the Lord. . . . [v. 26] But when the Comforter has come whom God will send to you from the Lord's presence, and the spirit of truth which will have gone forth from the Lord's presence, (he shall) bear witness of me, and ye also, because ye have been with me from the beginning. I have spoken to you about this that ye should not be in doubt." The *Munahhemana* (God bless and preserve him!) in Syriac is Muhammad; in Greek he is the Paraclete (*baraqlitis*). (103–4)[9]

The Opening of the Breast, the Cleansing of the Heart

A foster mother was found for the newborn, a certain Halima from among the Bedouin tribe of the Banu Saʻd ibn Bakr, and this suckling interval in his *Life* was the setting for some of the more extraordinary stories that grew up around Muhammad, in which he lays claim to the Quranic prophecy regarding the future "Ahmad":

> Thawr ibn Yazid, from a learned person who I think was Khalid ibn Maʻdan al-Kalaʻi, told me that some of the Apostle's companions asked him to tell them about himself. He [Muhammad] said: "I am what Abraham my father prayed for and the good news of my brother Jesus.

When my mother was carrying me she saw a light proceeding from her which showed her the castles of Syria. I was suckled among the Banu Saʻd ibn Bakr, and while I was with a brother of mine behind our tents shepherding our lambs, two men in white raiment came up to me with a gold basin full of snow. Then they seized me and opened up my belly, extracted my heart and split it; then they extracted a black drop from it and threw it away; then they washed my heart and my belly with that snow until they had thoroughly cleaned them. Then one said to the other, "Weigh him against ten of his people." They did so and I outweighed them. Then they weighed me against a hundred and then a thousand and I outweighed them. He said, "Leave him alone, for by God, if you weighed him against all his people, he would outweigh them." (72)

We think we know where this latter story began. The classic biography of the Prophet seems to have been constructed in part at least out of the Quran. Various incidents in Muhammad's *Life* have been developed to explain or enlarge verses in that Sacred Book, which was in existence and being recited before any of the *Lives* were composed. In this instance it is undoubtedly Quran 94:1–3 that is being unpacked, where God is made to say, "Did We not open [or expand] your breast and remove from you the burden that galled your back and raised the esteem of you?"

The Quran provides no context for the remark but Muhammad's biographers did. The agents of the act were God's angels and the cleansing was spiritual, though it is here described in physical terms. Where in the Prophet's *Life* the event was located depended on the theological point being made. Placed here, early on, it functions as Muhammad's Immaculate Conception; it frees him from any taint of Meccan paganism prior to his call. Placed later, as it is in other versions of the story, just before Muhammad's Night Journey and Ascension into heaven, it signals the purgation of soul that precedes his initiation into full prophethood.

An Arab Prophet

The account in Ibn Ishaq continues, and we discover perhaps the point of the infant Muhammad's sojourn among the Bedouin:

The Apostle of God used to say to his companions, "I am the most Arab of you all. I am of the Quraysh and I was suckled among the Banu Saʻd ibn Bakr." (72)

Thirty years after Muhammad's death it was already becoming common for the Arab Muslim elite to send their sons to be raised among the Bedouin, the *echt* Arabs in the eyes of the new Muslim townsmen, and the most authentic speakers of Arabic. Muhammad's stay among the Banu Sa'd was patently a validation of both the Arab and the Arabic authenticity of the Prophet.

There follows an incident remarkably like Luke's Infancy Narrative account (2:41–51) of Jesus' being left behind in Jerusalem. Ibn Ishaq begins with a not untypical disclaimer:

> It is alleged by some, but God knows the truth, that when his foster-mother brought him to Mecca, he escaped her among the crowd while she was taking him to his people. She sought him and could not find him, so she went to Abd al-Muttalib [the Prophet's paternal grand-father] and said: "I brought Muhammad tonight and when I was in the upper part of Mecca he escaped me and I don't know where he is." So Abd al-Muttalib went to the Ka'ba praying to God to restore him. They assert that Waraqa ibn Nawfal and another man of Quraysh found him and brought him to Abd al-Muttalib saying, "We have found this boy of yours in the upper part of Mecca." Abd al-Muttalib took him and put him on his shoulder as he went round the Ka'ba confiding him to God's protection and praying for him; then he sent him to his mother Amina. (72–73)

The story concludes with a recognition scene:

> A learned person told me that what urged his foster-mother to return him to his mother, apart from what she told his mother, was that a number of Abyssinian Christians saw him when she brought him back after he had been weaned. They looked at him, asked questions about him, and studied him carefully, then they said to her, "Let us take this boy and bring him to our king and our country; for he will have a great future. We know all about him." The person who told me this alleged that she could hardly get him away from them. (73)

Coming of Age in Mecca

If the stereotypical "recognition" stories in Muhammad's infancy narratives inspire little historical confidence, there appears to be some factual kernel embedded in anecdotes like the following as well as the already remarked concern to establish or confirm existing privileges and prerogatives:[10]

> The Apostle lived with his mother Amina, daughter of Wahb, and his grandfather Abd al-Muttalib in God's care and keeping like a fine plant, God wishing to honor him. When he was six years old his mother Amina died.... Thus the Apostle was left for his grandfather.... When the Apostle was eight years of age, eight years after the Year of the Elephant, his grandfather died.... When Abd al-Muttalib died his son al-Abbas took charge of Zamzam and the watering of the pilgrims, though he was the youngest of his father's sons. When Islam came it was still in his hands and the Apostle confirmed his right to it and so it remains in the family of al-Abbas to this day.... The Apostle lived with his uncle Abu Talib, for (so they allege) the former had confided him to his care because he and Abdullah, the Apostle's father, were brothers of the same mother.... It was Abu Talib who used to look after the Apostle after the death of his grandfather and he became one of his family. (73, 78–79)

Bahira

We have already seen how Muhammad was recognized and acknowledged by both the Jews, at the moment of his birth, and later by certain Abyssinian Christians, as God's own Apostle. A similar recognition takes place in a meeting at Mecca with an itinerant fortune-telling pagan seer, and indeed there are extended passages in the *Life* devoted to this theme.[11] But by all accounts the most famous and detailed of all these recognition incidents is the one that reportedly occurred during Muhammad's adolescence in the course of a commercial journey to Bostra or Busra in Syria.

> Abu Talib had planned to go on a merchant caravan to Syria, and when all preparations had been made for the journey, the Messenger of God, so they allege, attached himself closely to him so that he took pity on him and said that he would take him with him.... When the caravan reached Busra [Bostra] in Syria there was a monk there in his cell by the name of Bahira, who was well versed in the knowledge of the Christians.... They had often passed by him in the past and he never spoke to them or took any notice of them until this year, and when they stopped near his cell he made a great feast for them ... and sent

word to them, "I have prepared food for you, O men of Quraysh, and I should like you all to come, great and small, bond and free . . ."

So they gathered together with him, leaving the Messenger of God behind with the baggage under the tree, on account of his extreme youth. When Bahira looked at the people he did not see the mark which he knew and found in his books, so he said, "Do not let one of you remain behind and not come to my feast." . . . One of the men of Quraysh said, "By al-Lat and al-Uzza, we are to blame for leaving behind the son of Abdullah ibn Abd al-Muttalib." Then he got up and embraced him and made him sit with the people.

When Bahira saw him he stared at him closely, looking at his body and finding traces of his description (in the Christian books). When people had finished eating and had gone away, Bahira got up and began to question him [Muhammad] about what happened in his waking and in his sleep, and his habits and affairs generally, and what the Messenger of God told him coincided with what Bahira knew of his description. Then he looked at his back and saw the seal of prophethood between his shoulders in the very place described in his book.

When he had finished he went to his uncle Abu Talib . . . and said "Take your nephew back to his country and guard him carefully against the Jews, for, by God! if they see him and knew about him what I know, they will do him evil; a great future lies before this nephew of yours, so take him home quickly." (79–81)

The Sinful Wars

One of the few events in the history of pre-Islamic Mecca in which the youthful Muhammad was reportedly involved was the so-called Sinful Wars, which fall somewhat uncertainly in the period of his *Life* before his marriage, reportedly at age twenty-five, to Khadija. Ibn Ishaq passes quickly over the events of these "wars" in his biography of the Prophet, but there seems little doubt that some such conflict did occur, whatever the role the future Prophet of Islam was assigned by the sources to play in it.[12] The issue was a violation, or rather, a series of violations of the "truce of God" during the holy months, whence the name "Sinful Wars." Though Muhammad was generally thought to have taken part in one or more of the engagements, the sources were uncertain what he did and, more importantly from the point of dogma, how old he was at the time. The entire business of the Sinful Wars was obviously a violation of customary religious law at the time, and Muhammad's participation in it raised serious questions, particularly in what later developed as the doctrine of the Prophet's "impeccability," his freedom from sin even before his prophetic call.

Marriage to Khadija

This is as much as we know about the adolescence of Muhammad. The next event in his *Life* is his marriage to the widow Khadija, which is reported quite attentively by Ibn Ishaq:

> Khadija was a merchant woman of dignity and wealth. She used to hire men to carry merchandise outside the country on a profit-sharing basis, for the Quraysh were a people given to commerce. Now when she heard about the Prophet's truthfulness, trustworthiness and honorable character, she sent for him and proposed that he should take her goods to Syria and trade with them, while she would pay him more than she paid others. He was to take a lad of hers called Maysara. The Apostle of God accepted the proposal and the two of them set forth till they came to Syria. (82)

There then occurs in Ibn Ishaq's narrative another recognition scene, or likely a doubling of the Bahira story, since here too the agent is a Christian Syrian monk, though anonymous in this version. Ibn Ishaq's account then continues to describe a transaction which appears to be barter, the exchange of goods for goods, and may represent what actually occurred in Meccan commercial transactions of that era:

> Then the Prophet sold the goods he had brought and bought what he wanted to buy and began the return journey to Mecca. The story goes that at the height of noon, when the heat was intense as he rode his beast, Maysara saw two angels shading the Apostle from the sun's rays. When he [that is, Muhammad] brought Khadija the property she sold it and it amounted to double or thereabouts. Maysara for his part told her about the two angels who shaded him and of the monk's words. Now Khadija was a determined, noble and intelligent woman possessing the properties with which God willed to honor her. So when Maysara told her these things she sent to the Apostle of God and—so the story goes—said: "O son of my uncle I like you because of our relationship and your high reputation among your people, your trustworthiness

and good character and truthfulness." Then she proposed marriage.
Now Khadija was at that time the best born woman in the Quraysh, of
the greatest dignity and the richest as well. All her people were eager to
get possession of her wealth if it were possible. (82–83)

Both families are in agreement and the marriage is contracted, without
ceremony or fanfare.

She was the mother of all the Apostle's children except Ibrahim,
namely, al-Qasim—whereby he [that is, Muhammad] was known as
Abu'l-Qasim—al-Tahir, al-Tayyib.

As the Muslim commentators themselves point out, these latter two des-
ignations are not names but rather epithets—"the Pure," "the Good"—that
applied to the single son, al-Qasim, that Khadija bore to Muhammad. He did
not survive.

. . . (and the girls) Zaynab, Ruqayya, Umm Kulthum and Fatima. Al-
Qasim, "the Pure and the Good," died in paganism. All his daughters
lived into Islam, embraced it, and migrated with him to Medina.
(82–83)

The results of this marriage to one of Mecca's more successful entrepre-
neurs were extremely fortunate for Muhammad, as the Quran itself seems to
recognize. God is addressing Muhammad, here in the third person:

By the morning brightness, and the night when it is still, your Lord has
not forsaken you, nor does He hate you. And truly, the last is better for
you than the first. And truly the Lord will give to you, so that you will
be content. Did He not find you an orphan, and He gave you refuge?
He found you wandering (*dallan*) and guided you? He found you poor
and made you rich? (Q. 93:1–8)

This reading of the opening of sura 93 did not find much favor among the
commentators. As we have seen, its open acknowledgment that Muhammad
was once orphaned and poor as well as a pagan ("wandering") were not popular themes among later Muslims. Ibn Ishaq's *Life* makes no mention of the
Prophet's poverty during the guardianship of Abd al-Muttalib and Abu
Talib, and though it reports the marriage to Khadija, there is no reflection on

the riches or even prosperity that followed from it. There was no room in the "legend of Muhammad" for suffering or poverty, and so none for the precise point of Quran 93:8: God had indeed found Muhammad poor and made him rich, not by the performance of some divine miracle, but by his providential marriage to the wealthy and successful Khadija.

Muhammad the Trader

In the later Arab retelling of the history of pre-Islamic Arabia, a central figure in its commercial *Life* is Hashim, Muhammad's great-grandfather, who reportedly initiated Mecca's career as a trading center. As the story was told, Hashim was granted a trading concession by a Byzantine authority—the sources somewhat implausibly suggest it was by the emperor himself—and thereafter concluded a series of alliances with the Bedouin along the route to Syria. These arrangements enabled Hashim to send annual trading caravans into Byzantine territory and so make the fortune of Mecca.

From this story depends a great deal of what both medieval and modern historians make of the history of Muhammad's Mecca and the origins of Islam. The problem is, it happens not to be true, neither the story nor the conclusions drawn from it. In the eyes of its medieval chroniclers, Mecca was, in the wake of Hashim's commercial innovations, a rich merchant republic, Arabia's premier trading center whence caravans went forth winter and summer, carrying the luxury products of the east, onloaded in the Yemen, to the markets of Byzantine Syria and the Mediterranean. But the Hashim story is, itself, in all its variations, simply an exegetical gloss on the early sura 106 of the Quran, which reads in its entirety:

> In the name of God, the Beneficent, the Merciful.
> For the covenants of security of the Quraysh,
> The covenants (covering) the journey [or caravan] of winter
>   and summer.
> Let them worship the Lord of this House,
> Who provides them with food against hunger and security
>   against fear.

This is the by now standard translation/interpretation of the sura, but the few lines are filled with grammatical as well as exegetical difficulties. The first are best solved by connecting this sura with the preceding sura, 105, which tells of God's miraculous defeat of an invading force from the Yemen; the resultant unity yields a quite different meaning for the verses of sura 106. The "covenants" disappear, replaced by the "easements" of the Quraysh, something effected by the defeat of the abortive invasion, and guarantee the security of Mecca, so the prosperity that came to the Quraysh not from *trading caravans* "of winter and summer" but, in this new understanding, from the two seasonal *pilgrimages* that centered on Mecca and its environs.

Once the notion of "covenants" or commercial treaties is no longer squeezed out of this sura, the annual Quraysh caravans to Syria and the Yemen disappear, and with them, the entire fable of Hashim the trader and Mecca as a kind of sixth-century Venice-in-the-Hijaz. There was no support for either proposition to begin with. Pre-Islamic Mecca gives no sign of having the ready cash to conduct such a trade or of enjoying, in the form of investment in public or private buildings—the kind of evidence on such visible display at the other Arab caravan cities of Petra, Palmyra, and Hatra—the alleged profits of this commerce. The kind of luxury trade envisioned by the Muslim sources and many of their modern interpreters, though it had enriched other Arabs in the second and third centuries, no longer existed in the Near East in the sixth and seventh. The Iranians controlled most of the East Asian ports of origin for such goods, and the once thriving incense economy of the Yemen lay in ruins. If there was any trading going on in or around Mecca in the sixth century, as there assuredly was, it was probably in raisins and leather, and it inevitably had some connection with the shrine there. And it was in that trade that Muhammad had, thanks to Khadija, a modest share.

Afterthoughts: Where Do We Stand?

How much of these two accounts is reliable information about the historical Jesus and the historical Muhammad? The Infancy Narratives in the Gospels of Matthew and Luke are openly tendentious. They assert, through two contradictory and not very convincing genealogies, that Jesus was a descendant of King David. This might or might not be true—we have no way of knowing—but it is a constitutive element in the Christians' ongoing case for Jesus' messiahship and so the information must be regarded at least with suspicion.

Jesus' birth in Bethlehem, on the other hand, which has the same argumentative objective, is flatly contradicted by all the other evidence we have on the subject: this latter demonstrates that Jesus was regarded by all (including Matthew and Luke!) as being from Nazareth. More, the birthplace assertions, like much else in the Infancy Narratives (and elsewhere in the Gospels), are adduced to demonstrate that Jesus literally fulfilled the messianic prophecies that his followers found in the Bible. Finally, the stories of Jesus' conception elude the categories of history and by such a wide margin that even conservative and traditional critics prefer to address the issue not as a matter of fact but as a *theologoumenon*, a species of theological truth that "prescinds from facticity" but is rather "a notion which supports, enhances or is related to a matter of faith."[13]

Some of the same forces are at work in the opening chapters of Muhammad's biography. There are no biblical prophecies to fulfill—Muhammad's own proof of his prophethood is in effect the Quran: "bring *suras* like these," he challenges the doubters (11:13)—but there are attempts to enlarge and enhance the Quran's meager givens, that the Prophet was an orphan and perhaps suffered poverty till God granted him abundance (93:6–8). The recollected kernels of wheat and the legendary folkloric chaff mingle uneasily in the *Sira*.

We throw up our hands at the chronology. We may be assured that Muhammad died in AD 632 at Medina, where he had arrived ten years earlier after a forcibly ended career at Mecca. We might add that he was typically a young man when he had earlier married there and that he was equally typically in his maturity when called to prophethood. We can be assured that he was not born in the "Year of the Elephant," an event whose date we can fix in 552. Even the traditional fixing at 570, which is arrived at simply by counting back the stereotypical forty years from his call to prophecy, is almost certainly much too early for Muhammad's actual year of birth.

Yet there is no reason to doubt that Muhammad was early on orphaned, first of his father, Abdullah ("Devotee of Allah"!), and then of his mother, Amina, and that he was subsequently raised by his paternal grandfather and then his uncle, Abu Talib. We can affirm too that he entered into an arranged marriage with the relatively well-off Khadija, who bore him all his surviving children, all daughters, and through whom he gained a share in Mecca's modest commercial life. What may be doubted, however, as firmly as they are in Jesus' case, are all the recognition scenes in Muhammad's early life. Both may have been good young men; it is unlikely that either had a light over his head.

4

The Living Voice

THE AVAILABLE SOURCES present Jesus to us in four narrative portraits that are named "The Good News" and that include Jesus' sermons, lessons, and even his conversations. For Muhammad we have, among other things, what professes to be a transcription of his pronouncements that calls itself, quite simply, "The Recitation."[1] In both instances, then, we are led to believe that we are hearing the living voice of the principal: in one instance, as recalled by others; in the other, as simply transcribed. In a world where reported speech was notoriously invented, is this truly the case?

Jesus Speaks

Our early sources do not merely describe Jesus; they show him to us in a dramatic context.[2] We see him acting; we hear him speaking. In our Gospels Jesus' speech is embedded in a narrative frame that is loose and rudimentary in places, and in others, in the Passion Narratives, for example, highly detailed. These were, we are given to understand by the authors, the sayings of Jesus. Our modern sensibilities about reported speech—we take to be accurate whatever is enclosed in quotation marks—has been inclined to turn these sayings, Jesus' logoi, into his exact words.

Jesus' Words

We should pause here. We live surrounded by devices for recording and transmitting speech, but even the most primitive of those devices, stenography or speed writing, was quite rare in the ancient world and nonexistent out in the fields or inside the synagogues where Jesus spoke. And from their own testimony it is clear that ancient historians like Thucydides and Livy composed speeches for the personae in their works, and that such speeches can be thought of, in our more trusting moments, as perhaps representing the *sense* of what might actually have been said on a given occasion. But Jesus' words recorded in the Synoptic Gospels are generally not speeches—John's Gospel of course has Jesus delivering long discourses that are, as all agree, John's work and not Jesus'; rather, Jesus' own teaching was generally dispensed as aphorisms and parables, forms that were quite memorable and readily memorizable in that still very oral society. Someone might very well have memorized, and they or others have eventually written down, the sayings of Jesus of Nazareth.

Modern historical criticism has accepted that possibility and has devoted a great deal of ingenious labor to attempts at determining which of the reported sayings are likely to be authentically the dearly sought *ipsissima verba* of Jesus of Nazareth. We shall eventually return to that aspect of Jesus' sayings, but here we note that somebody had already done exactly that, and long before the modern quest began.

The Discovery of Q

In the nineteenth century, it should be recalled, once the Gospels began to be printed synoptically, that is, side by side, it quickly became apparent in the matchup process that there were more than two hundred verses that were identical, or almost so, in Matthew and Luke but not found in Mark's Gospel. It had already been ascertained that Mark was earlier than either Matthew or Luke and that they, in the verses they shared with Mark, had likely used that earlier Gospel as a source. Thus, it was reasoned, these other two hundred-plus shared non-Markan verses must represent a quite distinct second source for Matthew and Luke. This is the so-called Two Source Hypothesis, and by the end of the nineteenth century this equally hypothetical second source had already begun to take on a kind of life of its own and was being called "Q."

Once that much has become clear, it is possible to go even further and add to our reconstituted Q those passages that occur in Mark but are found in *an identically different version* in Matthew and Luke, like John the Baptist's preaching (Mk 1:2–6, 78 = Q 3:2, 7–9, 16–17) or Jesus' temptation in the wilderness (Mk 1:1–13 = Q 4:1–13). These might have come from a third source, a hyperhypothetical 2Q, but it is more Ockham-like to think that here too Matthew and Luke were simply following Q.

The Making of Q

On inspection, the Q verses, or, to recognize this source's increasingly realistic existence, the verses of Q, turned out to be somewhat remarkable. First, almost all the Q verses that occur in Matthew and Luke are constituted of reported speech or sayings (*logoi*); narrative stories of Jesus were minimal. As best we can understand, some of Jesus' earliest followers heard his pronouncements in their original Aramaic, but since a number of them possessed bilingual skills, something not all that uncommon in Jewish Palestine, they had remembered and collected them in Greek.[3] Bilingual speakers have no need of formal "translation"; what they heard in Aramaic they could immediately voice in Greek, though possibly in a manner that still trailed some of the original Aramaic flavor. Very soon these remembered pronouncements were committed to writing in that very clerical society. All of this must have been at about the same time as Mark's Gospel was being composed, or perhaps even earlier; certainly before Matthew and Luke came to be written, which, as we have seen, is generally, but not always convincingly, put at AD 80–90.

Q and Mark

More recently the emergence of the sayings source Q has introduced another dating criterion at the margins of the Synoptics. Internal evidence leaves little doubt that Mark and the hypothetically constructed Q were both used by Matthew and Luke in writing their Gospels. Mark shows no signs of knowing Q as we have reconstructed it, nor Q of knowing Mark. Hence, Mark and Q must represent two independent sources for the life of Jesus; indeed, they are our oldest such. But which is the earlier? Formally, it would appear that Q came first since Mark's narrative gospel has apparently taken a collection of Jesus' sayings something like Q and embedded them in his "Jesus in Galilee" section. There they are contained within a primitive narrative framework held together by the simplest possible connectives: "Next," "And then," "Immediately." In the first half of Mark's Gospel Jesus moves randomly from place to place; time passes in indeterminate and indistinct segments. Mark's true literary creation is the Passion Narrative, what is here called "Jesus in Jerusalem."

Q seems not only formally more primitive than Mark; it also appears earlier in what has been called its "theologically undeveloped" content: it knows nothing of Jesus' death and his resurrection. For us it is inconceivable that its compilers knew of such things, particularly the resurrection, and neglected or chose not to mention them. Two other possibilities present themselves, however. It is possible that these things never actually happened, or that they had not yet happened at the time of the collection. But whatever the reason for their omission, the absence of a passion and a resurrection narrative has been taken as an indication of the early date of Q by those most closely engaged in Q research and by many more broadly ranging Jesus questers as well.

The Q Text

When once it was necessary to imagine Q, now it is possible, thanks to modern sensibilities, to read it in a resurrected, or perhaps more accurately, reconstructed state and it is often printed as a freestanding document, which we are invited to appreciate as such. The verses extracted from Matthew and Luke are printed in the order (and with the numbering) found in Luke's Gospel since it is judged that that Gospel best preserves the original sequence of the collection, a decision that has not prevented its modern editors from juggling the order to fit their vision of the original. The current numbering practice is followed here: the citations of Q are noted according to the chapters and verses as they occur in Luke's Gospel.

Jesus and John

The Q passages begin at Luke 3:7 (= Mt 3:7), not with Jesus but with John the Baptist's full-throated judgment (3:7–9) against the unrepentant "spawn of Satan." John then turns to the subject of the Messiah who is to come (3:16–17). John is not the Messiah; it is, rather, an unnamed other who is far more worthy than he but who will be an equally severe judge. Jesus enters the scene rather quietly, and his baptism by John is uncertainly represented in Q (perhaps 3:21–22). The first time the Q text expands fully on Jesus, he is said to be "filled with the Holy Spirit," which guides him into the wilderness where he undergoes the familiar temptations (4:1–13). There follows Jesus' preaching from a mountainside, first the Beatitudes and Woes (6:20–26), in the Lukan version, then advice to love one's enemies and other moral teachings that are continuous down to the end of Luke's chapter 6. We return with Q to the concrete in the story of the cure of the Roman centurion's servant (7:1–10), which has far more to do with the centurion's faith than with the miraculous cure, which rates barely a line (7:10).

John's disciples reappear at 7:18–20, inquiring on John's behalf whether Jesus is the Expected One. They are told to report back to John what they have witnessed, which is a resume of Jesus' cures and exorcisms (7:22–23). It is a summary, but it is sweeping enough to indicate that behind this spare sayings collection there is an awareness that this preacher was also a wonder-worker. At their departure Jesus delivers an encomium of the Baptist (7:24–28), followed perhaps—the passage may have become displaced—by what is an important programmatic statement in which a firm line is drawn between Jesus and John: "Up to John you have the Law and the Prophets; since then the Kingdom of God has been proclaimed as the Good News and everyone is struggling to gain entry" (16:16).

"A Wicked Generation"

The thread of Q resumes in Luke's text (7:31–35) with Jesus' criticism of "this generation" who said of the Baptist that he was possessed and of Jesus himself that he was "a glutton and a drunk, a friend of tax-collectors and sinners." Next (9:57–62) there is Jesus' severe advice to would-be followers, followed by an extended (10:2–12) commission and some rather detailed advice to those Jesus is sending forth with the message: "The Kingdom of God draws near."

At Q 10:13–16 occurs Jesus' fierce damnation of the two Galilean towns of Chorazin and Bethsaida for being unresponsive to the miracles he performed in them, an unusual singling out that points perhaps to the immediate environment that produced the collection. Jesus' meditation on the fatherhood of God and his own sonship comes next (10:21–22). After noting the privilege of his followers in witnessing him (10:23–24), Jesus instructs them in the Lord's Prayer (11:2–4) and the Father's generosity toward those who ask (11:9–13). There is a long passage on exorcism (11:14–26), including a response to those who claim Jesus drives out spirits by the power of Beelzebul.

Jesus then turns to this "wicked generation" that asks for a sign (11:16, 29–32) and offers himself as that sign, just as Jonah was to Nineveh and the "queen of the south" to Solomon. "Note," he says, "here is someone greater than Jonah." Next it is the turn of the Pharisees, who are condemned fiercely and at length for their hypocrisy (11:39–52). Embedded in this chastisement is Jesus' reflection on the murderous deaths visited on God's prophets and with an unmistakable reference to Jesus' own, all of which will be paid for by "this generation," and this same harsh judgment is leveled specifically at Jerusalem (13:34–35).

Teachings

Luke 12 is mostly Q text and includes amid its moral teachings—"There's more to living than food and clothing" (12:23)—Jesus' references to himself with the messianic title of the "Son of Man" (12:8, 10) and a prediction that his followers will be persecuted "in the synagogues" and "before the rulers and authorities" (12:11–12).[4] The instruction continues in this vein through most of chapters 13–17 and 19:12–26, now with the liberal use of similes ("The Kingdom of God is like . . .") and parables ("A man was giving a big dinner party and sent out many invitations . . ."). Notable is an aphoristic correction of the Mosaic Law on divorce (16:18), which Matthew will later repeat but attempt to soften (Mt 5:32), plus a long apocalyptic passage (17:22–37) where Jesus once again refers to himself as the "Son of Man." Q also included Jesus' formal appointment of those—the Twelve?—designated to share at his royal banquet and "be seated on thrones and sit in judgment over the Twelve Tribes of Israel" (22:28–29). In Luke the passage is situated within Jesus' instructions at his last supper on the evening before his death, but Matthew (19:28) has Jesus saying it even earlier on his way to Jerusalem and as a response to Peter.

Looking under the Hood

With Matthew and Luke we are in the enviable position of being able to observe what each did with his Markan source and to surmise why. We note the editorial cutting and expanding, the explanations and even at times corrections elided into the text of the older Gospel. We can trace the redactional process because we too have Mark before us. But in the case of our hypothetical Q, we have only two redacted versions, namely, what Matthew and Luke have chosen to give us. We know what they left out of Mark; what did they leave out of Q? Matthew and Luke obviously redistributed Q, and so perhaps we can assume that Q, which many critics think was a literary composition with its own intentions, was merely a collection (like our other Q, the Quran!). Thus its sequence was unimportant and the two evangelists felt free to distribute its members wherever they most suited the narrative framework they had taken over—and also modified!—from Mark.

Jesus in Context

Mark's story line, like the similar and perhaps borrowed one in both Matthew and Luke and the somewhat different version in John, provides a context for what was remembered as Jesus' speech. In the Galilean sections of those Gospels—the situation is quite different in the Passion Narratives—there is the frequent impression that a context has been created, a generic "the next morning at the lakeside" in which to frame Jesus' sayings.[5] All those sayings, if authentic, must in fact have had a quite specific life-context, the *Sitz im Leben* of New Testament scholarship, but the collectors of Q had no interest in preserving them. What are reproduced there are the bald "sayings," remarks whose principal importance we must assume resides in the words themselves, quite apart from the context. That assumption is confirmed when we inspect Matthew's and Luke's recontextualization of the same sayings in their Gospels. That enterprise seems perfunctory at best. Matthew in particular has assembled Jesus' "discourses" into five large units (5–7, 10, 11, 18, 24–25), with only the slightest indication of a specific *Sitz im Leben* for each. Mark, who had received his logoi in some form other than Q, worked in much the same way.

What Is Q?

There is little doubt that Q presents, and perhaps even represents, an early view of Jesus and one that is strikingly different from the portrait of Jesus presented in the Gospels, even in the earliest of them, the Gospel of Mark. What then is this Q thing we have contrived for ourselves? And, if it really existed, as seems almost certain, who composed or collected the sayings in it, and to what end? If they were authentic early followers of the authentic Jesus, why did they make no mention of his crucifixion and resurrection? As just remarked, Q is for some modern critics not simply a collection; it was, they argue, a genuine (written) literary work, a composition, and, what is more, it was, like its sibling, the "Gospel of Thomas," a true gospel—in fact, the original form of the "Good News." On this view, Q represents the authentic Good News of the authentic Jesus.

Was Q a Gospel?

Q may indeed have been a "Gospel" in the original sense of that word. Jesus seems to have used the term "Good News" as a specific denomination of his message, which is summed up in our Gospels as "Repent. The Kingdom of God draws near" but which obviously also encompasses Jesus' teachings recorded in those Gospels. The Christians changed the meaning of the word, however. As the Acts of the Apostles describes and as our Gospels illustrate, the "Good News" his followers preached from the outset was in part *from* Jesus, but more substantially it was *about* Jesus. And in its most profound sense, as in Paul, for example, Jesus *was* the Good News. Neither of those two latter senses is visible in the reconstituted Q, and indeed, the two events that make Jesus more than merely a teacher, his death and resurrection, are not even mentioned in that collection of Jesus' sayings.

Q and Jesus

We have now moved far beyond mere chronology to fundamental judgments about the person and mission of Jesus. If, as some think, Q, particularly if it is bolstered and complemented by that other sayings source called the Gospel of Thomas, really does represent the authentic Good News about the authentic Jesus, then the authentic, original Jesus was apparently little other than a Galilean preacher-teacher, perhaps on the Cynic sage model, as some would have it, or a radical peasant upstart, as has also been suggested. On this latter view, Jesus was radical and troublesome enough to bring on his own death: this Jesus, like John the Baptist, died not for the sins of humankind but for his own intemperate remarks.

Q and the Death of Jesus

What are we to think, then, of Q's seeming unawareness of, or lack of concern for, Jesus' death? One solution to this odd disconnect between Q and what we find in the canonical Gospels may lie in the Q verses (= Lk 11:47–51) that record Jesus' wrathful remarks on the death of the prophets and what appears to be his presentiment of his own death at the hands of "this generation." Jesus' death may, then, have been known to this earliest group of his followers who collected and treasured his teachings. But if so, it surely did not represent the redemptive and even triumphal death so solemnly signaled by Paul, a death that was in turn illuminated by the resurrection that followed. It is not so much the missing death of Jesus that troubles us about Q so much as this missing resurrection, the linchpin of the post-Jesus movement, which of course raises other equally profound questions about this sayings collection.

Q as a Literary Work

There are other issues raised by assuming that this hypothetical collection of Jesus' sayings was a finished literary work, questions that arise from both the composition as such and the Jesus it presents to us. To begin with, Q has left no literary trace whatsoever apart from its phantom residue in Matthew and Luke. There is no independent evidence that such a sayings source, much less a Sayings Gospel, was ever in circulation among the early Christians. That argument from silence is not fatal, perhaps, but the troubling Jesus query remains unanswered. Why does Q sound so different from Paul, who is after all our earliest preserved source on Jesus?[26] Why the exclusive interest in Jesus' words rather than what he did and said and what happened to him? Why would the author(s) of such a work have omitted both the death and the resurrection reported in all our other accounts of Jesus, and particularly Mark's? Was it because they never occurred? Some, perhaps many, modern critics might be willing to embrace that conclusion regarding the resurrection of Jesus, but the evidence for his death by Roman execution seems incontrovertible. What is more often proposed is that the compositors of Q knew of Jesus' crucifixion but chose not to mention it, presumably because it had no significance for them; or more, because it was a reversal, an embarrassment that was best forgotten.

One current explanation of the genesis of Q is that its collectors were engaged in the preparation of either a catechism for the instruction of Jesus' early followers or, more likely, a proselytizing document. Q, it is argued, was what we might call a "teaser" or "recruitment brochure," that is, a collection of Jesus' sayings designed to introduce the prospective convert, possibly an interested Gentile, to the easily digestible Jesus *the teacher* without the more "difficult" message of (1) Jesus' messiahship, (2) the theology of a redemptive death, or, we might add, (3) the promise of immortality guaranteed by Jesus' own resurrection from the grave.

Not all of this can be true. There is no single motive that explains the composition of Q. The Q sayings put a great deal of emphasis on the local Jewish phenomenon of John the Baptist, who would mean nothing to a Gentile, but they say nothing about messiahs. In Q Jesus is made to speak often of himself as the "Son of Man," an apocalyptic title from Daniel, and in an eschatological setting. Some critics have solved these anomalies by claiming that Q is itself a composite document, that the original core of sayings—now dubbed Q^1—underwent perhaps two subsequent redactions in which the portrait of Jesus was altered.

Redaction criticism of Mark's Gospel, the study of the editorial revisions of a text, began in the nineteenth century. That on Q is a much more recent affair, but it is based on the same principle applied to Mark. In brief, it looks for the presence of internal signs that point to authorial or editorial intent. Such is the arrangement of the material, providing we can determine the original order of Q before Matthew and Luke redistributed its parts to serve their own purposes; or whether the compositional units into which the material has been arranged betray an argument that is being proposed or a case that is being made by what has been somewhat delicately called "the purposeful juxtaposition of originally independent sayings."

The Themes of Q, and of Jesus

On the basis of those criteria, it is argued, the Jesus of Q, who is closely linked to John the Baptist, is being presented by the author(s) of Q as emphasizing, in and around his calls for repentance and moral reform, three major themes. The first is unmistakably that of the coming Judgment, the same leitmotif that dominates the Synoptic Gospels. Part of that judgment is the divine vengeance visited upon Sodom for its treatment of Lot. This leads to the conclusion that the same will inevitably fall upon Chorazin and Bethsaida and even Jerusalem for their treatment of the prophetic Jesus. Finally, there is the powerful and traditional theme that runs through both Q and the books of the Bible from Deuteronomy through Kings, that of "a cycle of sinfulness, prophetic calls to repentance which are ignored, punishment by God followed by renewed calls to repentance with threats of judgment."

When, Where, Who?

These, then, are the Jesus themes that seem to have most interested whoever it was who composed Q and that, in their eyes, constituted the "Good News of Jesus," good news which, it must be conceded, sounds like very bad news indeed: sin, judgment, divine vengeance. And the collection and editorial arrangement of these Jesus logoi was done, we guess, on the basis of its geographical references and local knowledge, in Jesus' home territory of Lower Galilee, the towns around and west of the Sea of Galilee, and likely centered on Capernaum. And early on. On the face of it, Q was composed before the full impact of the atonement and redemption theology that is so prominent in Paul—who came from a quite different Jewish world—was felt among Jesus' followers. On the basis of what is in it and what is not, Q may in fact have been put together by Jesus' Galilean followers in the 30s, immediately in the wake of his death.

The People of Q

There have been attempts to peer more closely into the text of Q and to find there the lineaments of the original Jesus movement as it existed in that Galilean milieu in Jesus' lifetime and immediately after. "Itinerants," "charismatics," "radicals," and "pacifists" have all been found in and between the lines of Q, all with a distinct impulse toward proselytizing among their fellow Jews. "Itinerants" has since morphed into the more resonantly modern "homeless" and "vagrants" in some quarters, and Jesus, with a somewhat unlikely literary nod toward Hellas, into a Cynic-type preacher with a cortege of deliberately disreputable followers.

At some point, perhaps with the appearance of Mark's Gospel, Jesus' followers must have stopped using Q and turned to the full Gospels as we know them. The text of Q survived long enough for Matthew and Luke to use it for their own very different theological purposes. Other groups, like the sectarians who cherished their own Q called the "Gospel of Thomas," may have circulated it for a spell. But Q did not survive as a separate and freestanding testimony to Jesus, which it apparently once was. Was it simply outdated by the appearance of the narrative Gospels or was it superseded by the fact that Jesus turned out to be something more than a rather ill-tempered Galilean preacher and End Time crier?

Muhammad Speaks, or Sings

The Muslims' Q is fortuitously named "Quran." The Arabic word means "recitation" and it is a name that the work applies to itself (10:15, etc.; an "Arabic Quran," 39:28, 41:3, etc.). And it is appropriate. The collected Quran began as an individual oral recitation on the part of Muhammad and it continues to live today not only as a printed book (and before that as an oft-copied manuscript) but also as an ongoing recitation. Quran recitation is one of the most esteemed works of Muslim piety.

Q and Quran

Both works, the Christians' Q and the Muslims' Quran, are collections of the pronouncements of the charismatic and sanctified individuals who stand at the head of worldwide communities of believers that affirm that these were in fact the words of God. The pronouncements recorded in each began as oral performances delivered to audiences who could scarcely have imagined the consequences of what they were hearing. The sayings of Jesus collected in Q were scattered here and there in the narrative Gospels of Matthew and Luke, and Q quickly passed out of existence as an independent work, if it was such. The Quran's "recitations," in contrast, seem to have achieved the status of Scripture from the outset. It was the reciter-collector himself who persuaded his listeners that the words they were hearing were not his but God's very own.

The first voice heard in Q is that of John the Baptist (= Lk 3:7). And it is reported speech; we are hearing it through someone else's ears: "So John used to say to the crowds who came out to hear him . . . 'You spawn of Satan!'" Jesus enters only in the wake of John, abruptly and without introduction (= Lk 4:1). If we attempt to open the Quran at its beginning, we cannot find it. As already remarked, whoever assembled the logoi in the Quran combined many of them and then arranged the new units, the suras, in an order that is difficult to fathom, though it appears to be from longest to shortest. The Jewish and Christian Scriptures present themselves in the overarching form of history and thus have a beginning and an end. The Quran, without a genuine beginning or end, is a kind of Möbius recitative looping through eternity.

Muhammad, Prophet and Poet

Nowhere does the Quran introduce Muhammad, and neither it nor our biographical texts provides any form of preliminary discourse whereby the Prophet explains to the Meccans the extraordinary experience of revelation that he had undergone and what it was that he was about to recite to them. Perhaps Muhammad had no need to explain what he was doing. Perhaps the very manner of his doing it told his listeners. On the evidence of what are judged to be the earliest Meccan suras, Muhammad spoke from the outset like a prophet, if we understand that term in its broadest sense of someone pronouncing on behalf of God. How did his audience know that, since there is nothing in the Quran, nor even in the biographical tradition, that describes the beginning of Muhammad's public ministry?

No matter which sura modern Western or traditional Muslim scholarship designates as the earliest in the Quran (e.g. 96, 74), it is clearly not the first in an absolute sense: everything in even the earliest suras points to the fact that something had gone before. Hence we can only speculate about how Muhammad's mission began, how he presented himself, or how he was understood by the first Meccans who heard this familiar man, now in his full maturity, raise his voice in this new fashion. And since there is no sign that at the very outset he attempted to explain his calling and its consequences, we can only conclude that he was identified as something already familiar to the Meccans' experience, something that required no explanation.

Our suspicion is borne out by the Quran. Scattered through the early suras, and echoed and amplified in the biographical tradition, are allegations that Muhammad was someone unusual but familiar, a poet or a seer. Our scanty evidence suggests that the two were not always identical in ancient Arabia, but there is nothing in the Quran to suggest that the Meccans cut the distinction very fine when it came to Muhammad. There was something about the style of his utterances—the frequent oaths, the insistent rhyme or assonance, the emotive verse, the highly wrought language, the often enigmatic expressions. And perhaps there was something about his personal demeanor as well—"O you wrapped in a cloak!," sura 69 begins—that reminded them of a well-known type, a public crier who was inspired, possessed by a higher force. Muhammad spent some considerable time thereafter attempting to correct this impression (52:29–30, etc.), which he eventually did, but it was his reputation as a charismatic bard that first seized the attention of the Meccans and got him his first hearing.

Both the characterization as bard and the style of those early suras draws our attention to what Muhammad was about. We now read what he said, but in the original setting he was not writing but speaking; or, if we take seriously the evidence of the text and the judgment of his contemporaries, Muhammad was, in the manner of the *vates*, singing or chanting. Suddenly, the ground grows firmer beneath our feet. We need not overdetermine the case, but thanks to the analysis of the Homeric epic and its parallels, even of pre-Islamic poetry, we know a good deal about such bardic singers. Such poet-performers composed as they declaimed, and once again we must make the distinction between oral composition and oral transmission. The Meccan Quran shows signs of both, but they are separate problems and we are here concerned with only the first, oral composition.

Revelation as Oral Composition

We are now on the track of the composition of the Quran, not of *our* Quran, which the Muslims call a *mushaf* or "copy,"[7] and which is the product of a redaction, but of the original pronouncements that are collected in our Quran. The Quran as such has no structure; or rather, whatever structure is manifest in the arrangement of the suras, and there is very little certitude about that, or, even more obscurely, in the composition of the current suras out of smaller "recitation" units, is not the result of the author's intention but that of the Quran's anonymous editors. So from our perspective, Muhammad's intent resides solely in the words or in whatever original "recitations" we can rescue from their packaging in the mushaf.

On inspection, the early Meccan suras, which are closer to being original units of composition than the longer suras that follow, betray all the indices of oral composition: a notable, even insistent, rhyme scheme; intense rhythmic patterns; short *stichoi*; enjambment; and recurrent formulaic themes. More, the putative *Sitz im Leben* of those suras corresponds to the circumstances of oral composition: first, a society of mixed orality-literacy where, though writing may have been known, oral composition was still the standard form of expression. The circumstances of preaching point in the same direction: the Meccan suras constituted a message for the society as a whole delivered to a public audience. And it should be recalled once again that audience remarked the notable resemblance of what they were hearing to the compositions of oral bards and seers in that society.

There are other clues that point to a live preaching setting for the Meccan suras. It has been pointed out that there are passages in the Quran, like the Judgment scenes in sura 37 (50–61) and sura 50 (20–26), that are difficult to follow unless we imagine them as performances, where gesture and verbal intonation alone make clear, as our written text does not, who is speaking and to whom. One conclusion from this is that we are here in the presence of an oral recitation, which no one doubts, but the logic may lead to a more profound, and radical, conclusion, that Muhammad belonged to a tradition of oral poetry and so was composing as well as declaiming: singing, performing, and composing are closely connected acts in an oral tradition. They are moreover often accomplished through "inspiration," assistance from a higher power.

It is possible to go even further. As with the other oral bards who have been studied, it is difficult to imagine that Muhammad's "songs" were not declaimed more than once, and, in the manner of oral performances, somewhat differently on each new occasion. Thus, as we shall see, many of our preserved Meccan suras, all other editing concerns aside, might have caught one "performance" of the revelation. That is not, however, the impression we are given in our version of the Quran. There we are clearly dealing with a fixed text, and that fixing must have taken place early on. We are thus confronted with an essential difference between Muhammad and the oral bard. Whatever the similarities in style and matter, some at least of Muhammad's audience went away with the conviction that they had heard the words not of a poet but of God.

The Objective

On the witness of their own contents, the objective of the suras delivered at Mecca to an audience of pagans was a change in worship from polytheism to strict monotheism, and the method chosen for its achievement was preaching. The Meccan suras constituted a message for the society as a whole (with both a carrot and a stick prominently displayed in it) and delivered to a public audience. But this particular preaching was neither spoken nor read; it was "recited" or declaimed, that is, cantillated in a manner and form that was precisely God's own (75:18) and that immediately identified the performer to his audience as either a *kahin*, a "seer," or a "poet." The Quranic recitations had, at any rate, an identifiable style sensibly removed from ordinary speech and ordinary language and ordinary behavior. And there must also have been gestures: as already noted, many of the dramatic presentations of the Judgment—the just on one side and the unjust on the other (50:20–26 and 37:50–56, e.g.)—would be unintelligible without identifying gestures or perhaps changes in vocal register.

The Poet and the Performer

All we know about poets and poetry in an oral society like Mecca's in the Prophet's day—and Islamic culture for long afterward—indicates that the "recitation"/performance was rarely completely improvised, that the poet, who was a skilled professional, devoted time and pains to crafting his work in private before performing it in public. We may even have been given an oblique glance of Muhammad at work (with God!) in sura 73 (1–8, with a later insertion at 3–4). But what the poet finally did perform in public was not entirely what he had composed in private: oral poetry of all types gives indications of responding to audience reaction as it unfolds so that the recited work was, in the end, the product of both preparation and a "live" reaction-improvisation, even, we must believe, when the content embodied the words of God.

The Quran shows an ongoing awareness of audience reaction. There are, as we have seen, on-the-spot explanations—introduced by "What will make you understand . . . ?"—that are obviously cued by audience reaction (101:9–11), or in these instances, perhaps a lack of it. There are direct answers to both questions and criticisms (2:135, etc.). And there was, finally, the charge that the "revelations" were somewhat too improvised, that Muhammad was in effect making it up as he went along, with one eye steadily fixed on the main chance (21:5, 52:33). No, he recited only what—and when—he had received from God (10:15–16). Not all of these responses had necessarily to occur in the original performance, however, since these performances were certainly and, in the case of the Quran, necessarily, repeated, and there was an opportunity for the poet, or the prophet, to make adjustments.

The Revelations Memorized

Some in that Meccan audience were convinced and had become "Submitters" (*muslimun*) and so began the next part of the Quran-process. The Quran itself does not tell us much about the Muslims' repetitions of "The Recitation." Its instructions on the recitation of the Quran are directed at the Prophet himself—"Repeat it slowly and clearly," he is told from on high (75:16)—and not to the Meccan Muslims, even though these latter understandably applied the directives to themselves. But what does seem certain is that the Quran was memorized from very early on and likely in some sort of liturgical setting, though obviously not in the same one in which Muhammad originally recited it: the Muslims were repeating, not originating the Recitation. This was not a nascent society of *kahins*: the Muslims were not speaking in tongues like the early Christians who had received "the gifts of the Holy Spirit"; they were repeating what was now a *text*. Nor were they Arab *rawis*, the highly trained "carriers" or transmitters of the poetry of others. They were, it appears, worshipers who used as a form of worship those recitations that had been prophetic utterance in the mouth of Muhammad but were now sacramentalized: Muhammad's recitations had become the Muslims' prayer.

If this supposition is correct, we must also imagine Muhammad guiding the memorization process. It was he who had to choose out of his multiple performances of a given sura the version that would now become liturgical, that would constitute the Muslims' prayer. If Muhammad in fact shaped or composed his revelations into his recitations, as has already been suggested, the range of the variations in them would be narrower than if he had simply improvised, that is, delivered them even as they were being revealed to him. But there would still be choices to be made, and in this very fundamental sense, Muhammad was the first editor of the Quran. It was he who selected, and perhaps modified, or even recomposed the verses for memorization, and it was he who guided the memorization itself. The Arabic of the Recitation was, after all, unfamiliar diction, a species of art-speech that was the poets' stock in trade rather than the vernacular of the Meccan streets.

"The Recitation" was thus taken up not by professional rawis, the trained transmitters of poetical texts, but by the "Submitters" themselves, the simple believers who possessed neither the license nor the professional skill to reperform this particular text. We can only imagine them repeating the recitations with Muhammad, or better, after Muhammad, and with his guidance. The Recitation became for them a public declaration of their trust in God and in His message, and at the same time a prayer, an act of worship.

The memorization itself must not have been difficult in the still-oral society of Mecca. The same techniques that aided the poet in his composition—the insistent rhyme and rhythm and the formulaic diction—were equally helpful to the believers in their memorization of the Recitation. And nothing, apparently, was edited out. All the original dialogue directed by God to Muhammad was faithfully repeated as originally chanted. They were not imitating the Prophet; they were repeating the Words of God. Thus the matter too of the Recitation lent itself not merely to memorization but to stability.

A Singer of Tales

Was then Muhammad a poet or a seer, as some in his audience seemed to think? Did he compose and perform in the same ways as those familiar figures in the Meccan Haram did? Medieval and modern distinctions between the style of the poet and the seer, and between them and the Quran, are somewhat beside the point. Muhammad's audience knew far more about such things than we, and they certainly thought he filled the bill; and they had moreover their own theories of how he worked. It took no great sophistication to recognize him as a poet; what was proceeding from his lips was poetry by any standard: the characteristic oaths that either begin or occur in the early suras, short-lined rhymed verses, chanted not spoken, and with high emotive content. And his performance behavior too, about which we are not very well instructed, may likewise have identified him as a poet. And his listeners drew the appropriate conclusion, that these were "old stories" and that he must have gotten his poetry from someone else, and even that what he was "reciting" had been "recited" or "passed on"—this is not the same word as that referring to the Quran—to him (25:4–5).

There is a larger issue at stake here. If Muhammad was composing within a fixed idiom, was he also composing within a fixed tradition, that is to say, was he, like the other known oral poets, working new variations on traditional, and hence familiar, themes? By his own lights, Muhammad was absolutely original: his message was God's, not of his own, devising, and as a matter of fact, we know of no one else in that place or that era— poet, seer, or other— who was doing what he did. To some at least of Muhammad's listeners, who knew what they were hearing, he was simply repeating old themes, "tales of the ancients" (25:5); but for us, who know more about the making of oral poetry, he was, to use Homeric terminology, a "singer of tales." If the characterization is true, then the Muhammad of Mecca fits comfortably into the tradition of the oral bard, a skilled artist redoing familiar themes in a familiar, though difficult, style.

Muhammad denied the charge, and we must agree: the themes of his "recitation" are nothing like the stereotyped ones that appear in contemporary poets. One of the chief thematic settings of the Quran is in fact a biblical one of prophets and prophecy: Adam and Abraham, Noah and Moses, David and Solomon, among many others, march back and forth across the suras, carrying with them their values and their vocabulary. And judging from the audience response as reflected in the Quran itself, the biblical themes were comprehensible if not always entirely familiar to the Meccans who were hearing about those matters, and apparently not for the first time.

Story and Storytelling

The establishment of at least some of the literary forms in the Quran is not difficult; but once differentiated, we must attempt to integrate them into the Prophet's intent. The first objective is rather obvious, to gain the attention of his audience. The striking oath clusters that introduce many of the early suras are clearly directed toward this end, and the repeated eschatological mis-en-scène beginning "And when . . ." had much the same purpose. The Judgment passages have another function however: they also begin to shape the listeners' behavior and consciences to the new morality, particularly when the descriptions of the rewards and punishments of the Afterlife were accompanied by vivid depictions of what led the denizens of Paradise and Gehenna to their respective fates (38:55–64, 70:15–44).

As the revelations unfold, so too does the scope of the instruction. Examples taken from Sacred History, God's History, gradually replace the eschatological threats and promises. Biblical and Arabian examples of divine retribution, not so much against immorality as against disbelief, are put before the listeners, at first merely allusively and then in far more detail as salvation stories,[8] either because the allusions were not working or perhaps because of obvious audience interest in this new historical storytelling approach to Muhammad's message.

Muhammad's Religious Repertoire

Where did this information come from, save from God? The question will be addressed more broadly later,[9] but here the issue is Muhammad himself. The Muslim insists that the Quran is not from Muhammad but from God. Let us, then, pose the question somewhat differently. Where did the Prophet's apparently pagan audience receive an understanding that matched his own? The pre-Islamic poets may have had, as some maintain, some notion of biblical *ideas*, but they certainly know nothing of the biblical *stories* with which Muhammad and his audience were seemingly familiar. Even a cursory look at the Bible and Gospel material mentioned in the Quran reveals that its author had not been exposed directly or indirectly to the Scriptural texts themselves but rather in some fashion or another—we simply do not have enough information to say precisely how—to what the Jews called *midrash*, the retelling of the contents of Scripture, often embellished with extraneous details for the enlightenment, edification, or entertainment of the audience.[10]

We have no preserved examples of Jewish literary *midrashim* from Arabia in that era, but there were Jews in both South Arabia and in the oases that stretch out in a chain northward from Medina, and it seems more than likely that their acquaintance with Scripture, and so Muhammad's own grasp, was oral-midrashic rather than literary-textual. What we have in extensive segments of the Quran are nothing less than the scattered members of a seventh-century midrash on the Bible.

The same is true of the Gospel material in the Muslim Scripture. The Quran's stories of Jesus and Mary, again allusively told or referred to (e.g., 19:16–23, 3:35–44), find their immediate parallels in the apocryphal Gospels and not in the canonical texts. We know less about the apocrypha, and of the Eastern Christian popular literature on Jesus generally, than we do about the Jewish midrashim, but the accounts of Jesus in the Quran have some distinctly marginal as well as legendary elements vis-à-vis the Great Church's beliefs. In the Quran Jesus is said not to have died on the cross, but "there was a similarity to him" (4:156–59), a substitute victim according to most Quranic commentators. The way Muslims read the Quran, Jesus, the human prophet, is now on high with God (3:55) and will return to suffer his mortal death at the End Time, perhaps as the *Mahdi* or "Guide" who plays a Messiah-like role in Islamic eschatology.

The Mantic Seer

Muhammad baffled his contemporaries. Though their familiar Muhammad was playing, or better, performing, the poet, *they* knew that he had never been trained as such, that he was not a member of the guild. In Arabia poets were both born and, at the same time, made. But the Meccans had a theory. Muhammad, they thought, must be a jinn-possessed or jinn-inspired poet

(21:5, etc.), or perhaps a mantic kahin or seer (52:29, 69:42). They had the testimony of their eyes and ears, and for us the impression is reinforced by what seem to be some early Muslim traditions about the Prophet. They relate that Muhammad told his wife Khadija à propos of his revelations, "I see light and hear a voice. I fear I am becoming a kahin!" The accounts make Muhammad out so fearful of a demonic experience that he contemplated suicide! We must grant the story some credence since it too would be a rather unlikely invention by a pious Muslim tradition.

The seer and the poet both provided access to what the Arabs called *al-ghayb* (6:59, 3: 44), the "unseen world" of the supernatural. Each was a familiar of the jinn, the *daimones* or *genii* of the Arabian spirit world,[11] and both poet and seer were, on occasion, jinn-struck (*majnun*) or, as we might say, inspired or possessed, though the flavor of the Arabic is closer to the latter. To the poet the jinn gave the skill to tell the tribal tales of bravery in war or sorrow in love; the poet was the memory and panegyrist of the tribe, the "archive of the Arabs," as he has been called. The kahin had somewhat more practical skills. His special knowledge made him a tribal counselor and arbitrator in matters great and small. Both were known from their speech, the rhymed prose (*saj'*) of the seer and the more poetically elaborate ode of the poet.

The prosody of Quran bears little resemblance to the highly formalized metrics of the ancient Arabic ode, but does it show the characteristics of the kahin's saj'? The subsequent Muslim literary tradition says "No," as indeed it must since to grant that the Quran is a form of saj' is to concede in effect that Muhammad was a kahin as charged. More, those same critics were careful to so define *saj'* that the Quran's diction could not possibly qualify as such. Yet, if the definition is left broadly open as rhymed cola with a loose metrical structure and a penchant for opacity or enigma, the Quran fits comfortably into the paradigm. But only for a time. At Medina the reluctant kahin began to disappear behind the Prophet's new role as preacher.

But not before Muhammad's identification as a kahin changed his life and the course of human history. In 622 CE, after twelve years of publicly "reciting" his message in the crowded Haram of Mecca, and when the Meccan authorities were making efforts to assassinate him, Muhammad migrated—his famous *hijra*, or Hegira—to the oasis of Medina at the invitation of the people there. The Medinese were in the grip of a civil war and they thought that this Meccan, whom we would regard at this stage as simply a troublesome and troublemaking God-crier, was the one to solve their political and social problems. The invitation to Medina is odd, however, only if we are persuaded, as the Muslim tradition would persuade us, that there is no conceivable way that Muhammad could be confused with a kahin. The phrase "Envoy of God" may have had one sound in the Prophet's ears, but it assuredly had quite another for the Medinese. They spelled "prophet" with a "k" and they were more than willing to take their chances with this particular one.

The Miraculous Quran

We are as baffled by Muhammad and the Quran as the seventh-century Meccans who first heard it from Muhammad's lips. We do not know where this minor merchant of Mecca learned to make poetry. For the Muslim tradition there was necessarily no issue here and so it offered no explanation; both the content and the diction of the Quran—its language, style, and very tropes—were from God. Hence, the Muslims quite correctly concluded, the Quran itself is a miracle and so is literally and literarily inimitable. Muhammad (or God speaking through him) claimed as much in response to his critics: let them try to produce suras like these (2:23, etc.)! And, if a miracle is an event with no natural causes, then the Quran is indeed a miracle. Whether it was the "fine magic of the language" that brought it to pass, as one early nineteenth-century critic thought, or simply an act of God, there was no sensible way by which an untrained Meccan—the question of Muhammad's illiteracy is irrelevant; most oral poets, and certainly the best, have been illiterate—could have produced such sophisticated verse as we find in the Quran. Like Caedmon's in Bede's tale,[12] Muhammad's singing seemed to come from some other place.

Afterthoughts: Q and the Hadith

By one of the curious but meaningless quirks with which life abounds, the collection of Jesus "sayings" (*logoi*) that nineteenth-century scholarship extracted from the Gospels of Matthew and Luke was called "Q." The curiosity consists in the fact that the other famous "Q book," the Muslim Scripture called the Quran, is nothing more or less than a similar collection of the logoi of Muhammad.[13] Or rather, the logoi that proceeded *from* Muhammad since, on the Muslim view, the Prophet simply repeated what he had heard from God.

Neither collection has any strong claim to completeness. There are many *agrapha logia* of Jesus that are not in Q, nor even in Luke or John, but are attested to in the Christian tradition, whether (1) they are embedded in an apocryphal gospel, (2) they occur in other logoi collections like the so-called

Gospel of Thomas, or (3) they are cited in passing in a wide variety of works, including some by Muslim authors, for whom Jesus was an important pre-Islamic prophet. The majority of Muhammad's reported sayings occur in fact outside the Quran. They are incorporated in his biographies, just as Jesus' are in the Gospels, and a great number of them are preserved in the form of hadith, the reports of Muhammad's sayings (or acts) transmitted on the testimony of eye- and ear-witnesses among his contemporaries.

The hadith are in a sense deutero-canonical Scripture for Muslims in that they do not directly represent God's thoughts as do the Quranic logoi but rather Muhammad's own. Muhammad was nevertheless the ideal Muslim and the best interpreter of God's will and so his utterances are in the form of the preserved hadith and they are invoked *pari passu* with the Quran in determining what a Muslim should believe and how he or she should act. Both the Quran and the hadith purport to reproduce what came from Muhammad's mouth, and yet there is no confusing the two. There is a profound difference between the "high" diction of the Quran and the everyday prose of the hadith. Even the Medina suras of the Quran, which were composed in a markedly lower poetical register than the Meccan suras that preceded them, stand a world apart in tone and diction from the flat didactics and pedestrian storytelling of the hadith.

5

The Message: Jesus in Galilee

WITH MARK WE LEAVE the narrow confines of the sayings source Q and venture onto the broader and better-lit landscape of the narrative Gospels. If the original attempts at capturing the essence of Jesus of Nazareth in fact took the form of a collection of sayings, his followers soon turned to a more spacious form of recollection. This is what their Greek-speaking contemporaries might have recognized as a *bios* or "Life" but which the members of the Jesus movement preferred to call, in their own jargon, the "Good News." The makers of Q had mostly contented themselves with Jesus' bare sayings, joined by the briefest of connectives and with little or no narrative framing. The new Gospel form put the sayings found in Q and elsewhere inside a more robust frame. The settings of Jesus' remarks were expanded: we are taken inside synagogues and the homes of some of his followers, along the shore of the Sea of Galilee, into crowded town centers and onto the plains and mountainsides.

There is a general chronological vagueness surrounding the Galilean Jesus, the itinerant teacher and preacher who moved some of his followers to collect and memorize his words. Apart from his cures and exorcisms, few facts or events were retained as Jesus moved about a landscape of villages and countryside and sea, which, if authentic, is also generalized, and his passage from one such setting to another is most often marked by a simple ". . . and then . . ." or "Early on the next day . . ." Eventually Jesus goes up to Jerusalem and the narrative tone immediately changes to one of precise times and places. Historical personages appear: the Roman procurator Pilate, the tetrarch Herod Antipas, the high priest Caiaphas, all of whom stand in sharp contrast to "a centurion," "a man born blind," and the "scribes and Pharisees" of the Galilean account.

The Galilean authors/editors of Q had allowed their choice of themes and their arrangement of the sayings to communicate what they thought was the intent of their teacher. The authors of the Gospels, whose location we cannot pinpoint exactly but who very probably composed their Gospels outside Galilee and possibly outside Palestine, are now discernible *inside* their Gospels, where they speak through glosses, explanations, and a range of editorial comments, not the least common of which is the argumentative ". . . as was said by the Prophets . . ."

Neither Q nor Paul's letters tell us much about the events of Jesus' life. Q, as we have seen, is a collection of sayings and Paul was more interested in the significance of Jesus than what he said or did beyond his death and resurrection, events he does not, however, describe. So for a more complete view of Jesus' life we must turn to the narrative Gospels, Mark in the first instance and whatever Matthew, Luke, and John can add to the portrait from their own resources. As we have seen, both Matthew and Luke used, and modified, Mark and Q in writing their Gospels, but they had additional material as well, though we cannot make out its nature or form. And John, who may or may not have been reading the Synoptics (or something similar), certainly had access to other information, some of it convincingly authentic, about Jesus.

The Shape of the Gospels

Structurally the narrative Gospels, and the three Synoptics in particular, seem to fall into two parts or perhaps, if we are inclined to see Jesus' life as a drama, into two acts, what are being called here "Jesus in Galilee" and "Jesus in Jerusalem." They are preceded by other matter, notably, the already described Infancy Narratives in Matthew and Luke, and in John by a theological prologue (1:1–18) on Jesus as the eternal Word of God. There is also in each a relatively brief epilogue covering the discovery of Jesus' empty tomb and his reported appearances after his resurrection from the dead.

These two sections, "Jesus in Galilee" and "Jesus in Jerusalem," are developed quite differently. After the Baptist connection is explained and the Twelve chosen, the rest of Act One of the Gospels consists of Jesus' teaching or preaching, most of which is provided with some kind of simple setting of time and place. These are combined into larger discourse units that seem to move forward in chronological order, though differences among the Gospels suggest that the imposed order is somewhat arbitrary. Interspersed are accounts of the wonders performed by Jesus, mostly cures and exorcisms, as well as his arguments and disagreements with various competing Jewish groups. It all plays out in a Galilean landscape over the course of what seems barely a year, though in John's version, Jesus' active ministry appears to have been spread over two or perhaps three years.

John the Baptist and Jesus

The first piece of evidence about Jesus that confronts the investigator is his unmistakable connection with the man called John the Baptizer or Baptist, a figure also noticed by the historian Josephus.[1] John's career and his prominent place at the head of all the Gospels sharpen our focus on the mission and intent of Jesus. We note at the outset that, except for Jesus' own baptism by John, we are shown no actual baptisms being performed in the Gospels. The evidence is, however, suggestive (Jn 4:1–2) that from the outset of the new movement, Jesus' followers continued the Baptist's practice of using a public washing to signal a spiritual rebirth in an outward and formal way. What is more certain is that, as time passed and its institutionalization proceeded, a baptism ritual was used to seal and signal membership in the Jesus movement (Mt 28:19; Acts 2:41; 1 Cor 1:14–17). Jesus' own participation in the rite is more problematic. John's Gospel seems almost offhandedly to mention that Jesus was baptizing (3:22, 26), and then later, in what is obviously an editorial comment, and equally obviously a defensive one—there was a rumor that Jesus was by then winning more followers and baptizing more people than the Baptist himself—the Fourth Gospel loudly announces (4:2) that "Jesus was not in fact baptizing; it was his disciples who were doing the baptizing!"

The latter comment seems like another evangelist attempt to put distance between Jesus and the Baptist. But for all the awkwardness that the connection with the Baptist posed to his later followers (and presumably to John's own), there is no reason that Jesus should not have been doing what John was doing before him and his own followers were doing after him, eventually in his name. We are not the first to think so. Herod Antipas, the ruler of Galilee and son of the Herod who had reportedly pursued the infant Jesus, heard and believed the report that Jesus was the Baptist come back from the dead (Mk 6:14 and parr.). And when Jesus inquired of his own followers what people were saying about him, he was told that some people thought he might John the Baptist (Mk 8:27–28 and parr.).

If, in the popular mind, Jesus was closely associated with the Baptist, there was good reason. The two men had the same vision of an approaching End Time understood as the arrival of the "Kingdom of God." They preached righteous living rather than fastidious observance as the best preparation for the coming Judgment, and they both used submission to the familiar ritual act of "washing" as a signal that one accepted this new charge. And in the end both were put to death by the state authorities, John by the Jewish puppet prince Antipas and Jesus by the Roman procurator Pontius Pilate. But Jesus was no clone of the Baptist. Jesus was an itinerant; John seems to have remained in place. John was an ascetic attached to the wilderness, Jesus was not: he seems social, gregarious. Jesus was a wonder-worker and exorcist; John apparently confined his activities to preaching.

The Twelve

One point of similarity between Jesus and the Baptist is that John had disciples—*mathetai*, literally "students," though hardly here in an academic sense—and so too did Jesus after he left the fellowship of John. We do not know much about John's followers—Paul found some of John's followers at Ephesus in the 50s (Acts 18:25, 19:3), but in Jesus' case the function and actions of his disciples are described in some detail. What is here being called a "movement" was at the outset two or three concentric circles of individuals surrounding Jesus himself. The first circle is unmistakable; it is that of "The Twelve," the individuals chosen and personally called by Jesus—"Have I not chosen you Twelve?" Jesus says (Jn 6:70). The movement remembered the Twelve clearly as a group but less certainly as individuals since their names differ in the various New Testament lists (Mk 3:16–19; Mt 10:2–4; Lk 6:14–16; Acts 1:13), a fact that points toward a collective rather than an individual identity and function.[2] That function is already defined in Q as an eschatological one, to rule over the restored Twelve Tribes of Israel (Mt 19:27; Lk 22:30). Three, however, escape the general anonymity—Peter, James, and John—who are singled out for special attention, most notably as witnesses to Jesus' "Transfiguration," his divine epiphany atop a hill in Galilee (Mk 9:2–13 and parr.), and they attended his final personal agony in the Gethsemane garden (Mk 14:32–35).

Though they later became the directors of the movement, during Jesus' own lifetime the Apostles, or "The Sent" as they were also called, appear generally to have had no administrative responsibilities, with two apparent exceptions. The first is the occasion in Matthew 16, where, after Peter confesses that Jesus is indeed the Messiah and "the son of the living God" (v. 16), Jesus says (v. 18): "You are Peter, and upon this Rock"—a pun on Peter's (Jesus conferred?) Aramaic nickname, Kepha (Greek *Cephas*)—"I will build my assembly (*ekklesia*)." There is no question that Peter enjoyed a prominence among the Twelve not only in all the Gospels, but in Acts as well and even in Paul, who was not much of an admirer; but that Jesus appointed him to head a "church," or any other kind of institution he was founding, is contradicted by all the other evidence of Jesus' intentions and the earliest history of his followers. Somebody, perhaps beginning with our "Mark," was making a later case for Peter's *institutional* importance.

The other "appointment" is less direct but more likely. John (12:6) remarks of Judas, one of the Twelve, and the one who betrayed Jesus for money (Mk 14:10–11), that "he was a thief, and he held the purse and carried the things that were put into it," suggesting that Judas was a kind of treasurer who managed the offerings to the group and paid out their expenses. This rather strongly implies that, as far as Jesus and the Twelve were concerned, goods were held in common. But the arrangement may have been broader than that. Jesus' own teaching, while not specific about common property, advocated a trust in God's providence about even the basic requirements of life (Mt 6:25–32), and it would not be surprising if Jesus and his most dedicated followers lived in exactly that fashion.

Spreading the Good News

Except in the case of the Twelve, whose "call" was immediate and charismatic— indeed, as it is described in Mark (1:16–20), Peter, Andrew, James, and John, the first called, do not even appear to have known Jesus or who or what he was—Jesus seems to have exposed his message broadly and publicly. It was a general ethic for the generality of Jews, not an appeal to a sectarian fellowship, an openness to all that incurred the displeasure of the Pharisees in particular, who were attempting, by both prescript and example, to inculcate a higher degree of ritual purity among their fellow Jews. Jesus generally taught by examples rather than by prescriptions. There is one instance, however, where there was a prescription, and it was a severe one. As the Synoptics tell it (Mk 10:17–30 and parr.), Jesus was approached by "a man of great wealth" who asked him how he might have a share in the Afterlife.[3] Jesus replied in traditional fashion: observe the Torah. The man insisted that he was observant. "Go, then," Jesus replied, "sell everything you have, give it to the poor— you will have treasure in heaven—and come follow me" (Mk 10:21).

The man declined the invitation, and his refusal triggered Jesus' more general reflections on property and wealth, many of them collected in Q where they are the basis of the modern judgment that Jesus was at base a social reformer. In the narrative Gospels they have a more diffuse impact, however. Here they are delivered to Jesus' own followers: "How difficult it will be for the wealthy to enter the Kingdom of God!" (Mk 10:23). The disciples were amazed. Jesus spells it out again: "It is easier for a camel to enter the eye of a needle than for a rich man to enter the Kingdom of God" (10:25). The amazement of the disciples grows, though it is not clear why: the statement is a more concrete echo of the "Beatitude" beginning "Happy are the poor . . ." But the sequel is interesting. "What about us," Peter asks, "who have left everything to follow you?" The "everything" in this instance is home, family, and livelihood, for all of which they will be "repaid many times over," they are assured, in the eternal life to come (10:29–31 and parr.).

An Itinerant Preacher

As was already clear in the Q collection, a plain reading of the Gospels shows Jesus, after his separation from John, as an itinerant preacher-teacher who went about with his followers spreading his message, or better, messages, in a variety of public and semiprivate venues across Galilee. This was the largely rural and agricultural domain of Herod Antipas, the puppet ruler who administered his allotment under the regarding eyes of the Romans next door in Judea. It seems no longer possible, however, to give a "plain reading" to these heavily freighted texts, and certainly not in the opening decade of the twenty-first century. Galilee is no longer just a painted rural landscape against which the career of Jesus unfolded. It is now regarded, variously and concomitantly, as the seat of a "colonial, cosmopolitan, peasant, purity and patriarchal ('androcentric') society."[4] Nor, as already remarked, do the evidentiary texts themselves constitute a homogenous account. By resting on one rather than another text, the interpreter/reader can produce dramatically different portraits of Jesus, all of them in current, and popular, circulation: Jesus as healer or magician; prophet or sage; visionary or revolutionary.

We proceed, then, carefully. Jesus had once had an occupation—carpenter— as did his circle of the Twelve. But whatever their previous work, as the Gospels unfold, Jesus and his followers no longer seem to be employed. The evidence is indirect, but indications are that they were supported by some of his more prosperous followers in whose homes they stayed as they traveled through Galilee, including a number of women (Lk 8:2–3), a circumstance that appears, to our limited knowledge, unusual for that time and place, though no one takes particular note of it. Jesus and his circle seem to have moved from place to place as the occasion, or perhaps just chance, dictated.

Some patterning is discernible, however. After a hostile reception, Jesus himself explicitly and deliberately chose never to return to Nazareth (Mt 13:54), which both Matthew and Luke here call his "hometown" (Mt 13:54; Lk 4:23), since his neighbors there had no faith in him. Nor did he present himself in Galilee's only two cities, Sepphoris and Tiberias. The reason, some have speculated, was because of the Gentile/pagan quality of those two places but, as archaeological exploration has now revealed, the population of both cities was predominately Jewish. Scripture may be inspired, but the historians' guesses often are not.

What Was the Good News?

The Gospels generally characterize Jesus' activity as preaching, teaching, and working what the ancient world generally knew as "wonders" (*thaumata*) but what the Gospels prefer to call "deeds of power" (*dynameis*) or, and this is particular to John, "signs" (*semeia*). The distinction between the first two activities, preaching and teaching, is maintained throughout. "Teaching" (*didaskein;* noun, *didaskalia*) is used for the imparting of instruction, in most cases, moral or ethical instruction. "Preaching" (*keryssein;* noun, *kerygma*) is more accurately rendered as "proclamation" or "announcement," in this instance, of the "Good News" (Greek *euangelion;* Hebrew and Aramaic *besora*).[5]

The characterization of his proclamation as the "Good News" may be Jesus' own—the Gospels' and Q's insistence on the term suggests it was—and the content of that pronouncement, and so the substance of the "Good News," is unmistakable in the summaries provided by the Gospels. Right at the outset of his Gospel (1:14), Mark sums up Jesus' Galilean career: "After the arrest of John, he came to Galilee proclaiming (*kerysson*) the Good News of God (and saying) that the Kingdom of God was approaching. Repent and trust in the Good News.[6] Matthew's Gospel similarly says of Jesus, with somewhat more emphasis on his instructional mission, that "he went about in all of Galilee, teaching (*didaskon*) in the synagogues and proclaiming (*kerysson*) the Good News of the Kingdom and healing every disease and illness among the people" (4:21). Even more pointed than these editorial summaries is what Q reports from Jesus' own mouth. Approached by some of John's own followers with the imprisoned Baptist's question whether he was the Expected One, Jesus answers, "Go and tell John what you have heard and seen: the blind see, the halt walk, lepers are cleansed and the deaf hear, the dead are raised and the lowly are told the Good News" (= Lk 7:22).

The content of the Good News is presented to us, then, if not by Jesus, then by his reporters, in a remarkably straightforward fashion. Or so it seems, at least at a first reading and with the kind of editorial underlining just quoted from Mark, the earliest of the Gospels: "The opportune moment has arrived," Mark has Jesus say. "Repent and trust in the Good News." Both the notions embedded in the summary, that of "changing your mind, changing your attitude," which is a more exact translation than the traditional "repent," and the appeal to an eschatological "Kingdom," come directly from the Baptist's own version of the message. Jesus may, however, have reshaped John's eschatology somewhat by describing the End Time as the "Kingdom of God."

The Kingdom

End of Days messages were no novelty among the Jews of that time and that place. A variety of "Apocalypses" or "Unveilings" that offered a detailed and highly imaginative scenario of the events of those terrible, and eventually glorious, days were the favorite reading of many Palestinian Jews in the years after the Exile. But in what is a rare consensus on matters pertaining to Jesus, New Testament scholars are now agreed that the expression "Kingdom of God" to describe God's final rule is authentically Jesus' own. It does not appear exactly as such in the Hebrew Bible and only very rarely in the body of noncanonical Jewish writings of the Second Temple period. In the Gospels it is almost always Jesus, not others, who uses the phrase, while it does not much occur in the rest of the New Testament. There can be no doubt that the "the Kingdom of God," or "of Heaven"[7] was a central concept in Jesus' message during his Galilean ministry, even though the notion, or at least the term, appears to have rather quickly faded from view in the sequel; it is not a critical element in the End Time preaching of the Apostles or Paul in the decades after Jesus' death. There is agreement too that what is usually rendered "Kingdom" in that phrase is better understood as active sovereignty or rule rather than the statelike construct suggested by the English "Kingdom."

The noun, "kingdom," when joined to its predicate "approaches," raises additional issues. The word "kingdom" is elastic but not ambiguous. The Greek *basileia* can mean both kingship or sovereignty and the state that follows from such—a kingdom—and modern translations swing between the two: "Kingdom of God" or "God's imperial rule," for example. The Roman overlords of Judea were familiar with both senses, *rex* and *regnum*, and were still close enough to their republican roots to be wary of both. *Rex*, king, was a title they condescendingly granted to their clients like Herod and then denied to his sons who had to settle for diminished claims to sovereignty. And *rex*, it should be recalled, was a repeated element of Pilate's charge against Jesus (Mk 15:2, 9, 12, 18), and *Rex Iudaeorum* was precisely the indictment attached to his cross (Jn 19:19–20).

However the Romans might have heard the term, there is no certain sign that Jesus ever intended "kingdom" in a political sense. But its anticipated future presence—"May Your kingdom come, may Your will be done" (Mt 6:10–11) was Jesus' own invocation of it—implies a change, and likely a massive change since the present human condition does not represent "God's imperial rule." The Kingdom preached by Jesus would represent, then, a new order, and certainly a new moral order, but there are a few clues about its shape or form. One is that "The Twelve" were commissioned rather precisely to sit as "judges over the Twelve Tribes of Israel" (Mk 10:37; Mt 19:28), a notion that somewhat bafflingly underlines both the real and the ideal side of the Kingdom. The restoration of the long-since scattered ten tribes was an idea, an almost cosmic notion, but the appointment of twelve very concrete individuals gave it an unmistakable reality.

When Does the Kingdom Come?

All Jews believe that God has in some degree guided His creation since its creation, but with very imperfect results. The complete fulfillment of the divine will, God's rule, will occur only at the End Time. The weight of the evidence of Jesus' sayings on the subject strongly suggests that he understood, and probably preached, that God's rule, His Kingdom, still lay in the future. But some passages seem rather clearly to express Jesus' expectations of the Kingdom in the very near future; indeed, while some of his listeners were still alive (Mk 9:1; Mt 16:28; Lk 9:27). With the passage of time that latter instruction, as clear and as direct as it seemed, grew increasingly unlikely. Jesus' followers had to imagine other possibilities for themselves, and in the end they, or rather, the "assemblies" or "congregations" (*ekklesiai*), the institutionalizing forms of the Jesus movement, settled on a straddling answer: God's sovereignty was established in the first instance, or better, re-established, either by Jesus' incarnation, the en-fleshing of the God-man, or by his redemptive death. It would be followed, at some unknown future time, by the cosmic arrival of the Kingdom in the old-fashioned Jewish apocalyptic sense.

Whatever later Christians came to believe about Jesus' postponed return, there can be no mistaking the immediacy of the expectations of Paul and the congregations in his care, which are on full display in 1 Thessalonians 4 and 1 Corinthians 15. It is difficult to think that these first believers were so quickly mistaken or deluded about Jesus' teaching on the Kingdom that they missed his point that the Kingdom was actually *now* and preferred to think that it was *soon*. The catastrophic events of AD 70 might have later turned the minds of Jesus' followers from a "spiritual" to a vividly eschatological Kingdom, but in the 50s Paul was writing to Diaspora communities of Jews who had as yet no sense of an impending military or political disaster.

To return to Jesus, the embryonic community that had gathered around him was not quite a spontaneous formation around a charismatic leader; the Gospels underline the fact that Jesus had quite deliberately "called" the men who formed its nucleus and then had not only assigned them an eschatological role—the Twelve as rulers of the restored Twelve Tribes of Israel—but had also given them a mission, to go forth as *apostoloi*, or "sent ones," to carry his Good News to others.

Did, then, this array of Jesus and his followers represent the community of the Kingdom? If so, it could represent little more than an interim arrangement since Jesus also quite obviously expected a transforming apocalyptic event out of which the "Kingdom of God" would emerge in its fullness. It was that latter that he described in his "apocalyptic" discourse (Mk 13 and parr.) and that his followers were awaiting in Jerusalem after his disappearance from their midst. Perhaps this is so, but there are, disconcertingly to modern scholarship, a few other sayings that broach another possibility. In Matthew Jesus says, a propos of his casting out demons, that if he accomplished it by the Spirit of God, then "the Kingdom of God has come upon you" (12:28 = Lk 11:20), and in a Q passage (Lk 17:20–22), Jesus says, "The Kingdom is not coming with signs to be observed. The Kingdom is among you," though the latter is immediately followed (vv. 23–37) by a prediction of a *future* coming.

A Dual Kingdom?

Without ruling out the strong possibility of later editorial tampering and adjustments to the still-evolving text, the most sensible course is perhaps to think that Jesus did in fact mean both a future and in some sense a present Kingdom. The main thrust of the preserved pronouncements is that the Kingdom, over which he would preside, lay in the very immediate future. Its coming, moreover, would be by a miraculous act of cosmic proportions wrought by God and not one brought about by human diligence or striving. And if "kingdom" was the primary figure of the new condition, it was also symbolized as a messianic banquet (Mk 14:25 and parr.) to which all the just would be summoned, even from among the Gentiles (Mt 8:11–12; Lk 13:28–29), and where the poor, the humiliated, and the downtrodden would find their quittance (Mt 5:3–12; Lk 6:20–23).

But there is also no denying that in Jesus' mind the Kingdom could, to some extent, be inaugurated, or perhaps, in the later language of the rabbis, be "hurried" by human moral effort. That effort is embodied in the ethic described and urged on his audiences throughout Jesus' Galilean ministry. It is even conceivable that it might be achieved by more extraordinary means; witness the thinking behind Jesus' dispatch of his disciples (Mt 10:23) and, even more persuasively, as will be seen, by Jesus' own acts in the Temple in Jerusalem.

Messiahs and The Messiah

If the "Kingdom" represents, now or in the future, the fulfillment of God's plan, what was to be Jesus' role in it? If, as seems likely, his own immediate followers confessed him to be the Messiah (Mk 8:29 and parr.), then it would be natural for them to think of him as the ruler of the future Kingdom, God's vicar or caliph, so to speak. There is no clear evidence that Jesus claimed such—Was the protestation "My kingdom is not of this world!" (Jn 18:36) his or his followers?—but it would be nonetheless natural that Messiah Jesus should be the ruling power in God's Kingdom.

Christian apologetics often give the impression that in the first century AD there was a universal locked door recognized by all Jews and named "The Anointed" (Hebrew *mashiah*; Greek *christos*). Into its lock only one key would fit: the tumblers would turn, the door open, and the Messiah emerge. Then, in the midst of a tumultuous End Time, he would bring salvation to Israel and the Nations. Many keys might be offered and tried, but the only one that fit perfectly was, on the Christian view, Jesus of Nazareth. His life and work and, as it turned out, even his death matched every identified and recognized prophetic messianic passage in the Jewish Scriptures. Jesus was undoubtedly the Anointed One, the Christians argued, the promised Messiah of Israel.

Soon the testing of that lock faded away. *Mashiah* meant little or nothing to the non-Jews who began to constitute the main following of Jesus, and the more familiar *Christos* quickly morphed from a title into a name for the God-man. Jesus Christ was still the Messiah, but he was also, and more importantly, Lord and Savior, the Redeemer of humankind. The need for Jewish validation diminished and with it interest in the historical issue of Jewish messiahs. Jewish scholarship has never lost its interest in messiahs, however, particularly since, according to many, the expectation of such is *now* an essential feature of Judaism. Essential or not, messianism remains a lively issue among Jews, and that interest has led to new and thorough research on messianism in Second Temple times.

The Messianic Evidence

The results of a close inspection of Jewish messianic thinking in Jesus' day are quite different from those long advanced by Christian apologists. Where the term "the anointed" (*ha-mashiah*) appears in the Bible, it is not used as a title but simply as a descriptive word that is regularly and normally applied to a priest or, more generally, a king, and never to a figure from the onrushing End Time. There is no eschatological messiah in the voluminous writings of either Josephus or Philo. While it is certain that there was no general Jewish expectation, or even understanding, of someone called "The Messiah," messianic-type figures, eschatological saviors, do appear in Second Temple–era writings. There is, in short, present in the writings of that time abundant evidence of messianism, if not of a unique "Messiah."

The actual messianic background against which Jesus appeared is illustrated in the extrabiblical books called 1 Enoch (the so-called Similitudes), 2 Baruch, and 4 Ezra, in addition to a number of messianic reflections in the Dead Sea Scrolls. The figures identified as such are called by a variety of names like "Chosen One" or "Son of Man" and display diverse characteristics ranging from a celestial figure to a warrior to a teacher. No matter how many Jews awaited a savior ex machina—some others simply took up arms in a hopeless effort to save themselves—there was clearly no messianic consensus in Jewish expectations before or after AD 70, no agreement on either the who or the what of a messiah, or the exact context in which such might appear.

Reading the Scriptures

There is by now an extensive scholarly literature on how exactly we are to understand the messianic titles like "Son of Man" that appear in Second Temple writings from Daniel to the Book of Enoch. The exercise is interesting, if somewhat pointless. The early followers of Jesus, like Jesus himself and like most of their fellow Jews, read religious texts in an "open" fashion. They were not limited by the same "constraints of history" as ourselves about what we consider a historically accurate—that is, a contextual— understanding of a given text, whether Isaiah or Daniel or Enoch. There were no "authentic" readings, just hopefully persuasive ones, and the New Testament is a florilegium of such, drawn from a variety of sources and without a great regard for either provenance or philology. The product was not terribly different from our other body of sectarian exegesis in the Dead Sea Scrolls or the way the Bible was understood by the author of the Book of Jubilees, for example.

The Jesus Key

The problematic nature of the notion of Messiah is revealed in the strenuous efforts that the evangelists made to fit the Jesus key into that baffling messianic lock. We do not know how the other claimants to the title validated themselves, but the proof offered throughout the Gospels is that Jesus, by his words and his deeds, fulfilled the biblical passages thought to refer to a future Messiah. The assumption that the Bible was looking forward in that fashion was certainly not the invention of either Jesus (Lk 4:15–17) or his followers. It seems to have been accepted as legitimate by contemporary Jews, some of whom, like the Essenes of Qumran, were doing much the same thing as Jesus and his followers for similar or different purposes.

If they accepted the method, contemporary Jews did not necessarily believe that the "messianic" reading of any given passage was the correct one. It should also be recalled that the texts in question were being "read" then and later in their translated Septuagint or Greek version. This seems to have aroused no qualms at the time, but the Christians' continuing use of this rather freewheeling version of the Bible eventually provoked the Jews to retranslate the Septuagint no less than three times.

In the end the issue became moot. Jesus as the Messiah was a claim that was never vacated by Christians, embedded as it is in the fabric of the Gospels. But, as just noted, messianism makes sense principally, and perhaps exclusively, to Jews, and with the rapid Gentilization of the Christian assemblies, "Messiah" became, in its Greek translation, *Christos*, first a name—as it is already in Paul, "Jesus Christ"—and then a generic title of honor that was elided with the far more Gentile-resonant, and intelligible, title of "Savior" (*soter*). The Gentile Christians could far more easily grasp "Son of God" than the venerable but obsolescent (and Jewish!) "Messiah."

A Reluctant Messiah

On the evidence of the Gospels, and particularly Mark, Jesus seems particularly elusive and reluctant on his own messianic claims, a posture that has been somewhat portentously dubbed "the Messianic Secret" in William Wrede's famous 1901 book. Jesus appears often in Mark's Gospel to pull back from an open identification of himself as the Messiah, and he warns those who had experienced his extraordinary curative powers "not to tell anyone," not to reveal that he was the Messiah (8:30) or the "Son of Man" (3:12). In addition to Wrede's own hypothesis, two general explanations have been put forward for this rather odd reluctance. The first, the standard Christian one, was to prevent misunderstandings of his messianic purpose, as there certainly were in his day. The more secular explanation is that Jesus was himself uncertain of his role in the unfolding movement that he (or the Baptist) had set in train.

Signs and Wonders

There are a few "events" in Jesus' Galilean ministry. He preached in parables, fashioned with realistic but idealized scenes where the characters—kings, landowners, farmers, tenants, laborers—are recognizable but anonymous. The actual places and persons among whom this itinerant preacher moved appear in fact in much the same fashion: a town, a synagogue, or someone's house, a hillside, a lakeshore, all realistic in detail but never quite real. A few of the Twelve, like Peter, James, and John, take life briefly from time to time but then quickly recede back into the faceless crowds of the curious and the convinced, those who came to follow or merely to watch or listen.

It must have been the watching and the word of mouth that followed that drew most of his audience, the reports of wondrously instantaneous cures: limbs straightened, the veil of blindness lifted, ritual impurities, even chronic conditions like leprosy or dysmenorrhea, cleansed on the instant, and, what has almost disappeared from our own repertoire of miracles, the exorcism of evil spirits. Generally the cures were effected by a word or touch, though there are traces of the healing *process*, the utterance of certain words that the Christian tradition remembered in their original Aramaic, perhaps because of their intrinsic power (Mk 5:41, 7:34), the placing of fingers into deaf ears and of spittle on a dumb tongue (Mk 7:33), and even the rubbing onto blind eyes of a mudlike concoction of dust and spittle (Jn 9:6). Remarkable too is the *progressive* cure of a blind man (Mk 8:22–25) who *begins* to see, albeit imperfectly— "men walking—they look like trees"—after Jesus touches his eyes and applies spittle and then only later regains his full sight. It is these "process" miracles, which are seemingly effected *ex opere operato*, that have seemed to some to place Jesus' miracle practice well within the widely diffused ancient magic tradition.

The Gospels present a portrait of a Jesus who is not only the particular object of God's signal favor and providential activity, in his virginal conception, for example, or his transfiguration and resurrection, but who himself possesses both a supernatural knowledge and the ability to work wonders. In the four canonical Gospels alone—the number would rise dramatically if *all* the Jesus gospels were tallied—there are by one count thirty-three distinct miracles performed by Jesus himself, in addition to other summary statements simply attesting to similar activities on his part.

" . . . and more than a prophet"

As we have seen, behind the Gospel of John there appears to lie a collection of Jesus' miracles, a "Book of Signs," as it has been called. Even earlier, the Q source, which was not particularly interested in miracles, reports a Jesus tradition (= Lk 7:18–23) on the subject. When the Baptist's disciples are dispatched to ask him whether he is the Expected One, Jesus instructs them to tell John what they have witnessed, namely, his miracles (7:22). Jesus was citing them as a validation of his eschatological role, and this may be the motive behind John's semeia source collection. But the miracles seem to have been read by many, just as the Quran was, as the more familiar signature of a prophet. There can be no doubt that some at least of Jesus' contemporaries thought he was a prophet (Mk 8:28 and parr.; Jn 4:19), as Jesus himself recognized: "What did you come out to see? A prophet?" (Mt 11:9). "Yes," he continues, "and more than a prophet." More indeed. In one of the most extraordinary episodes recorded in the Gospels (Mk 9:2–8 and parr.), atop a mountain in Galilee Jesus appears to Peter, James, and John, the favored three among the Twelve, dazzlingly "transformed" or "transfigured" and conversing with Moses and Elijah, two of the most famous—and long-dead—of the "sign" prophets.

Skepticism, Ancient and Modern

The modern reader of the Gospel accounts may be torn between assent to a supernatural miracle and a deep-seated skepticism for which the "wonder" at its worst scents of charlatanism and at its best illustrates either mass popular hallucination or the misinterpretation of natural processes. The young girl that Jesus raised from the dead perhaps really was, as Jesus himself remarked, merely "sleeping" (Mk 5:39). But such skepticism is all modern; no trace of it arises out the Gospel narratives themselves, nor from Josephus, who calls Jesus simply "a doer of wonders." Jesus' onlookers show no reluctance to accept the actuality of what they had witnessed; their question was rather, "By whose power was this accomplished, God's or Beelzebub's?" (Mk 3:22–30).

The ready acceptance of the wondrous on the part of Jesus' contemporaries is but one more sign that we live in a world quite different from Jesus' own. But the fact of Jesus' miracles is not the most important thing about them. What was likely more striking than their occurrence—the ancient world had a plentiful supply of wonder-workers, including Jewish ones—was Jesus' own connection of what he had wrought with the subject's prior act of "trust" and the concomitant remission of sin since disease and moral transgression were linked in the medical and ethical calculus of that day. "Who has sinned," the bystanders asked in an attempt to understand the condition of a blind man, "this man or his parents?" (Jn 9:2).

Since the inception of the critical study of the life of Jesus, the miracles have been viewed with suspicion and skepticism by historians, chiefly, one supposes, because they are reluctant to admit the a priori possibility of acts contravening the laws of nature. But on purely evidentiary grounds, some at least of the miracles are among the best attested of Jesus' deeds, and the strength of that evidence has constrained a majority of scholars to the pinched concession that Jesus was indeed known as one who healed the sick and cast out demons. Jesus' exorcisms (Mk 3:11–12) and the closely linked charge that they were done through the power of Satan are multiply attested to in our available sources and, more convincingly, show up independently in both Mark (3:33) and Q (= Lk 11:15). Nor is the charge of diabolical assistance likely to be the kind of thing invented by the early Church! Finally, non-Christian sources from Josephus and the second-century pagan polemicist Celsus down to the Talmuds all regard Jesus as a wonder-worker. That Jesus was in fact a wonder-worker in the eyes of his contemporaries seems beyond serious doubt.

Jesus, then, was generally regarded, however we might judge such activity, as a charismatic worker of wondrous deeds, in the tradition of such biblical figures as Moses, Elijah, and Elisha, and perhaps, as has been suggested, like a known type of Galilean Jewish *hasid* or holy man with wonder-working powers whose examples date from roughly the same era. And Jesus' miracles, it appears, were performed not to verify his other claims, messianic or otherwise, but rather to confirm and reward the faith of those on whose behalf they were performed: "Thy faith has made thee whole" is a frequent and apparently authentic Gospel refrain.

The Twelve, as we have seen, were all quite specifically "called"—"Come, follow me," Jesus says (Mk 1:17)—but we cannot tell whether Jesus' immediate following, which seems to have waxed and waned during his brief career, was attracted by his teaching or his wonder-working. It is perhaps of little importance since at his death that following appears to have vanished at an instant and the Jesus movement had to be reconstituted almost anew by the Apostles, which, as the Acts of the Apostles describes, they accomplished by their preaching and their own miracles (3:1–10) and, above all, by their testimony that they had experienced the risen Jesus.

A Jewish Teacher

By all the evidence, Jesus himself was an observant Jew as that designation was understood in the first century in Palestine. Circumcised on the eighth day according to Jewish law (Lk 2:21), Jesus worshiped the One True God of Israel, and, on the evidence of "the Lord's Prayer" (Mt 6:9–13) composed for his followers, Jesus too prayed to his "Father in heaven" (Mk 14:35–36). Though we are never shown him actually participating in Temple rituals, there is no reason to think that he did not do so, and not merely at Passover, but at Sukkoth (Jn 7:2–14) and Hanukkah (Jn 10:22) as well. Like most contemporary Jews, Jesus observed the Sabbath and the dietary laws, though he disagreed with the Pharisees on some of the finer points of both observances, and principally and particularly with the wall of separation that the latter were attempting to erect between the Gentiles and their own "unclean," that is, unobservant, Jews on one hand and, on the other, the purified "nation of priests" they were attempting to foster.[8]

Much of Jesus' traditional Jewishness is unstated, as is that of a Pharisee of his own day and that of the rabbis of a somewhat later era. Most of these latter would quickly embrace the Gospel's "Great Commandment": "Love God and love your neighbor" (Mk 12:29–31 and parr.). For Jesus no less than for them, this was the heart of the Torah. And however sensitive the subject of the Sabbath, more than one Pharisee would have agreed with Jesus that "The Sabbath was made for the sake of men and not men for the Sabbath" (Mk 2:27). What are chiefly and explicitly preserved are his talking points, emphases, and new directions. To the Torah-derived Great Commandment Jesus adds his new, very personal prescription, "and love your neighbor as well," underlined by a series of very concrete illustrations (Mt 5:38–48; Lk 6:27–32).

Jesus and the Torah

There are the occasional moments when local politics, which were urgent for many Jews, intrude on Jesus' pacific world. The political and sectarian issues that dominate Josephus' account of contemporary Palestine do arise—Jesus is confronted, for example, with questions regarding taxation (Mk 12:13–17 and parr.)—but they seem remarkably marginal when viewed through the prism of the Gospels. The main thrust of Jesus' program lies elsewhere, in redrawing the template of contemporary spiritual life, particularly in its social aspects, and in the light of an impending eschatological showdown. And though much of contemporary Q- and Thomas-riveted Jesus scholarship thinks otherwise, it is End Time imminence that gives urgency to Jesus' message and not the political circumstances of life in Palestine.

Jesus' criticisms of his Jewish contemporaries are chiefly directed at the Pharisees, and not so much at their views as at their actual practice, which is, in his eyes, often hypocritical and generally concerned with the letter of the Torah rather than with its spirit. The Torah itself is another matter. Jesus seems to meet actual or anticipated objections to the Torah-orientation of his teaching by the retort direct. According to Matthew (5:17–18)—the passage is not in Mark—Jesus flatly declares, "Do not think that I have come to abolish the Law or the Prophets; I have not come to abolish them but to fulfill them. I tell you the truth, until heaven and earth disappear, not the smallest letter, not the least stroke of a pen, will by any means disappear from the Law until everything is accomplished."

So he said, but as a matter of fact, Jesus' specific teachings do on occasion appear to confront and correct the Torah, and that in two main areas. The first is his rather direct, indeed, almost confrontational modification of the Mosaic Law, in the matter of divorce, for example (Mk 10:2–12 and parr.), and adultery (Mt 5:27–32).[9] Secondly, there are passages, notably Mark 2:18–20, that strongly suggest a "suspension" of the Torah by reason of the onset of the anticipated messianic era, a condition, incidentally, that none of Jesus' immediate followers— none at least save Paul—appears to have recognized after his death.

These and other Torah-modifying texts are not cited by Paul, who seems to have thought that his own authority as an interpreter of Jesus was sufficient warrant for his own pronouncements. Paul had a far more radical view of the effect of Jesus on the Torah, not by his teachings, assuredly, but by his redemptive death. That particular notion appears nowhere in the Gospels, however, where Jesus' death, though the Gospels have him predicting it to his inner circle (Mk 8:31, 9:31–32, 10:32–33, and parr.), was effectively a bolt from the blue that caught those same followers by surprise.

A Teacher with a Difference

But if Jesus was familiarly Jewish, he was also different from many of his con-temporaries, in degree if not in kind. Jesus was advocating a more individual, more internal, conscience-driven morality. His concern was for the lust in the heart (Mt 5:28), the inside of the cup (Mt 23:26), the defilement within (Mk 7:15). Jesus was grounded in the Torah, but he took spiritual wing above it. The figure is a gentle one, but to "rise above" can with remarkable ease become to "fly away from," to transcend. It is difficult to say if Jesus understood his—and others'—relationship to God as transcending the Torah, but in less than a generation, some of his followers, most notoriously Paul, when attempting to transfer Jesus' teachings to non-Jews (for whom the teachings came associated with, but different from, the Torah), were forced to concede that it did. And beyond Paul the gap between Jesus' teachings, now interpreted and expanded by non-Jewish followers, grew progressively more distant from the Torah roots, a discordant separation whose grating echoes already sound in the Gospels.

But these are the convictions of the later more fanatic age when opinion had hardened on both sides and, more, when both Jesus' followers and their opponents could take measure of the profound consequences of the new faith. In that later day there was among the believers an acceptance not only of the messiahship of Jesus but also of his divinity and the worship of "the Lord Jesus" that followed; a growing acceptance of Gentiles into the Covenant; and the progressive erosion of the Torah by the Christians' extravagant application of allegorical interpretation to the dietary and liturgical prescriptions of the Law.

In Jesus' own day these developments could scarcely be imagined, even though some of them have leached backward up into the Gospels and somewhat contaminated the portrait of the historical Jesus. But even if most, if not all, of what Jesus said and did is recognizably Jewish, as that term was understood early in the last century before the Common Era, the fact remains that he was arrested and executed with the cooperation, or at least the connivance, of both the Jewish and Roman authorities of that time and that place.

Afterthoughts: The Man and the Message

It seems clear that the two great sections of the Gospels, what has been called here "Jesus in Galilee" as well as the "Jesus in Jerusalem" that will follow, have two different purposes that are manifested in the Synoptics at least—the distinction is blurred somewhat in John—by two narrative styles. The first, which has concerned us here, was to record Jesus' teachings. We are presented with a portrait of a teacher with the emphasis not on his life but on his teaching. Jesus is a teacher of Jewish values to a Jewish audience. This Jesus is not an unfamiliar figure. Though most of the parallel examples emerge later when the rabbis' own logoi are collected in the Mishna of circa AD 200, there were similar types in Galilee in Jesus' day.

Jesus was somewhat different from those other early examples, however. First, like his predecessor and perhaps model, John the Baptist, Jesus had profound eschatological concerns, while the later rabbis had been largely purged of these by the cataclysm of AD 70, when the entire Jewish enterprise in Palestine collapsed in flames. But more startlingly, and this was noted by his audience, Jesus spoke and acted "with authority" (Mk 1:27; cf. Lk 4:36) and not like the rabbinic teachers who are invariably "traditionists" in that they taught on the authority of their masters or, more simply, on the "tradition of the fathers."

There was then a claim that lay behind Jesus' teaching, an unstated (or obliquely stated) claim to authority by reason of what he was. Who he was was clear enough to his contemporaries: "Jesus, the son of the carpenter and of Mary" (Mk 6:3; Mt 13:55). But neither carpenters nor their sons pronounced in this fashion. They might point out signs of the End Time and call for "radical spiritual change," which was the burden of John's and Jesus' *metanoia*, but they assuredly did not set down ethical markers or revise the Mosaic Law, as Jesus did.

As baldly expressed in his message slogan, Jesus seems to have claimed no role in the coming kingdom; at first sight he was, like John before him, a mere "crier," a *vox clamantis*. But as Jesus' Galilean message unfolds and then, with even greater urgency, in the events at the end of his life, there appears the true problematic of Jesus' career: was Jesus in fact a key figure in the End Time, the Anointed One (Hebrew and Aramaic *mashiah*) who appears as an agent of God's will in many of the apocalyptic scenarios? And if so, where was the political and cosmic upheaval that was generally thought to accompany his arrival? If the figure of a Messiah is somewhat ambiguous in the imaginative literature of postexilic Judaism, there was no mistaking the other shattering events of the End Time. Jesus' audiences surely must have had problems with this as well, and those who did accept him as the Messiah must have thought that this particular messiah had arrived *prior* to the End Time and that that terrible event was close upon them.

6

The Message: Muhammad at Mecca

WE HAVE SEEN HOW Matthew and Luke in their Gospels are thought to have taken the sayings source now called Q, provided its individual Jesus sayings, or groups of Jesus' logoi, with a context, and embedded each in the larger narrative framework of a Gospel. Mark and John must have done something similar, though we cannot isolate their sayings sources the way we have Q, and John for his part not only contextualized Jesus' sayings but enlarged them into Jesus discourses. We can nonetheless still discern, through a glass, obscurely, some of Jesus' sayings glimmering behind John's speeches by comparing them with the logoi materials in Mark and Q.

A Preliminary Exercise

A similar process took place between the Quran and the *Sira*. From one perspective, the Quran is a sayings source: it is a collection of the inspired pronouncements that had issued from Muhammad at Mecca and Medina over the course of twenty-two years of his life. They were arranged, like the material in Q, in a manner to suit the purposes of the editor(s) of our Quran. Later—the final version emerged about a century after the Prophet's death—Muhammad ibn Ishaq had embedded small, now contextualized portions of those pronouncements in his narrative life of the Prophet. But these are mere bits and pieces of the Quran. We would be hard-pressed to reconstruct any intelligible version of our Quran from Ibn Ishaq's *Sira*; nor, indeed, any sense of Muhammad's highly eventful life from our Quran.

We proceed, then, to "Muhammad at Mecca" with both texts before us, *Sira* and Quran. But not the present Muslim Quran, or rather, the Quran in its present condition. As already noted, if the Quran is to serve as a biographical resource, it is necessary to determine the chronological order of its suras or chapters, to sort the revelational units back into the order of their pronouncement, and, if possible, to discern the original units of revelation within the present suras. The task is not a simple one. To begin with, we are not certain what exactly were the units of revelation since many of the present sura chapters are composites and there is no very large agreement on where the seams are.[1] Then again, there is an entire stage of the composition of the Quran that is concealed from our sight, what may be called its liturgical memorization stage. The earliest Muslims memorized the Quran by praying it: they were, in the fashion of many religious communities, repeating God's words back to the deity. And it was surely Muhammad who guided that process of memorization and prayer, by shaping and repeating the text for the benefit of the believers and likely by fashioning repetition units for them as well.

We cannot totally understand that process much less undo it, but Muslim and Western scholarship has each attempted reordering the units of the present text, by arranging the suras at least in what is thought to be a chronological series and then taking guesses at the occasions of some of the smaller units—sometimes just a verse or two—within the suras. The results are not assured but they are accepted, and here too we shall follow the classic division into forty-eight "Early Meccan" suras, twenty-one from the "Middle Meccan" period, and twenty-one as well in the "Late Meccan" category.[2]

The Man Muhammad

There are, as already noted, few hard facts on the early life of the Prophet, but on all the evidence, the young man Muhammad ibn Abdullah—not the forty-year-old of the traditional chronology—had made little or no mark on his native Mecca before his emergence into the political limelight. He was married; his earliest followers remembered his wife Khadija, and fondly.[3] It was thanks to this providential marriage that Muhammad was engaged, like many other Meccans, in the local regional commerce in skins and raisins, though not, it would appear, in what must have been the far more lucrative business of the care and feeding of pilgrims.

How far afield that commerce took him, we cannot say since the Quran's awareness of, or interest in, events in the contemporary world is severely limited. Basing itself on a somewhat forced interpretation of such passages as Quran 7:157 and 158, the later Muslim tradition insisted that Muhammad could neither read nor write. The insistence appears apologetic—an illiterate Prophet could not "steal" the writings of the Jews and Christians—but the point may well be moot. If Muhammad was engaged in commerce, it is possible that he possessed some literate skills, however modest; it is even more certain, however, that he had never literally "read," nor was likely capable of reading, the Sacred Books of the Jews and Christians.

Muhammad had heard, of course, the current Meccan stories about Abraham and Ishmael and Mecca's central shrine, the Ka'ba. The Quran alludes almost offhandedly to them (2:125–27) and the audience seems to comprehend. And just as Jesus is understood to have followed the traditional Jewish practices of his day, so Muhammad may be assumed to have participated in the civil religion of Mecca before his call to Islam. Those Meccan rituals included, however, sacrifices to the various shrine gods, among them, though only one of many, the high god Allah. Later Muslims, who had come to think of the Prophet as "the perfect man," were uneasy with the notion of a "pre-Islamic Muhammad"— Muhammad's impeccability had become an unmistakable matter of dogma in an undogmatic religious tradition—and denied the assumption and all its corollaries. Though he protested that he was just a man (17:93, 41:6), Muhammad was declared by Muslims to be as free from sin as Mary was for Christians. Mary just got there a little sooner: she had an "Immaculate Conception"; he had perhaps to await the "Opening of the Prophet's Breast."[4]

But that same tradition insists that Muhammad was not merely shielded from sin; he was also pointed in the right direction. Though the evidence is divergent and even at times contradictory, there runs through the Muslim historical tradition the insistence first, that there was a kind of nascent monotheism abroad in pre-Islamic Mecca. Its aficionados were called *hanifs*, a somewhat mysterious term that is applied in the Quran to Abraham (3:67) and seems to mean a "natural" monotheist, that is, a believer in the One God without benefit of revelation.[5] And second, though Muhammad is, somewhat oddly, never included among those pre-Islamic Arabian *hanifs*, he was reportedly caught up, like some few others there, in a more private and personal and exclusive devotion to the Lord of Ka'ba, the high god called in Arabic *Allah* or "The God."

The Call to Prophecy

It was during one of those devotions in a lonely place near Mecca that Muhammad had the experience that changed his life and all human history after him. The Quran is silent on this extraordinary event, but it is described more than once in the biographical tradition. In Ibn Ishaq's account, which is purportedly from the Prophet himself, it was in the month of Ramadan and Muhammad was in his usual retreat in a mountain cave near Mecca. He was sleeping when the Angel Gabriel appeared, covered him with a blanket, "on which was some writing," and said, "Recite!" The command was twice repeated, each time with the angel pressing on Muhammad's breast, and each time Muhammad answering, "What shall I recite?"[6] Finally Gabriel said:

> Recite in the name of thy Lord who created,
> Who created man of blood coagulated.
> Recite! Thy Lord is most beneficent,
> Who taught by the pen,
> Taught that which they knew not to men.

These latter lines are, as a matter of fact, the opening verses of what was later reckoned as the ninety-sixth sura of "The Recitation," and here in the *Sira* it is being plausibly put forward as the earliest of Muhammad's revelations.

Ibn Ishaq continues his narrative with what is still professedly Muhammad's own account. The Prophet awakens and sees Gabriel, "in the form of a man," astride the horizon. The angel says, "Muhammad, you are the Apostle of God and I am Gabriel." Muhammad continues staring. Everywhere he looks, there is Gabriel in the sky.[7]

Though the account in the *Life* attaches no Quranic passage to this reported vision of Gabriel, we can be sure that what Ibn Ishaq was hearing were the only verses in the entire Quran that describe Muhammad's personal experience of the supernatural. He had been accused by the Meccans of imposture or worse, possession by a malign spirit. This was his retort:

> By the star when it goes down, your companion is neither astray nor misled, nor does he say anything of his own desire. It was nothing less than inspiration that inspired him. He was taught by one mighty in power, one possessed of wisdom, and he appeared while in the highest part of the horizon. Then he approached and came closer, and he was at a distance of two bow lengths or closer. And He inspired his servant with what he inspired him. He [that is, Muhammad] did not falsify what he saw. Will you then dispute with him over what he saw? (Q. 53:1–12)

The same sura immediately continues:

> Indeed he saw him descending a second time, near the Lote Tree that marks the boundary. Near it is the Garden of the Abode, and behold, the Lote Tree was shrouded in the deepest shrouding. His sight never swerved, nor did it go wrong. Indeed, he saw the signs of his Lord, the Greatest. (53:13–18)

Quite typically, none of the pronouns is identified in these verses, though there is little doubt that the recipient of the vision was Muhammad. Who it was who was seen is less clear. If Muhammad's being referred to as "his servant" in verse 10 suggests that it was God Himself who appeared, the Muslim tradition preferred to understand that it was Gabriel in all the other instances, chiefly because later in his own career Muhammad had unmistakably come to the same conclusion (2:97). But it was, after all, merely a vision, an apparition, silent and a little remote, and there is nothing in sura 53 to suggest that it was on either of these occasions that Muhammad received the words of the Quran.

An Experience of the Unseen World

Sura 53 refers quite unmistakably to Muhammad's two personal experiences of *al-ghayb,* "the hidden" or "the unseen world," as the Arabs thought of the supernatural. On the face of it, no words were exchanged on either of those occasions, no revelations granted. The Quran does, however, make very passing reference to two other occasions the Muslims regarded as highly consequential to Muhammad's prophetic calling. The first we have already seen, how the Muslims understood the terse remark in 94:1, "Did We not open [expand] your breast," as an angelic purification of the Prophet, an event that occurred—the biographers were not sure—either in his childhood or just prior to his prophetic call.

The other incident is far more elaborate. Sura 17 opens abruptly with the verse:

> Glory be to Him who carried His servant by night from the sacred shrine to the distant shrine, whose surroundings We have blessed, that We might show him some of Our signs.

That the subject here is God and that the object of God's nocturnal activity, "His servant," is Muhammad is fairly certain since the expressions conform to standard Quranic usage, as does the reference to Mecca as "the sacred shrine" (*al-masjid al-haram*). In sura 53 an earthbound Muhammad was merely a passive beholder of both God and the supernatural signs; here, however, he is carried off on a journey to another place, "the distant shrine" (*al-masjid al-aqsa*), and there "shown what God wished."

A Heavenly Journey

The reading of this opening verse of sura 17 depends principally on how the phrase "the distant shrine" is understood, whether as heaven or as a specific place. In the end the Muslim tradition had it both ways. It produced a harmo-nizing and much enlarged version of that single Quranic verse that described how Muhammad, who was reportedly sleeping in a sacred spot close to the Ka'ba, was first carried on a mythical beast called Buraq to "the distant shrine," the Temple Mount in Jerusalem, and thence ascended into the seventh heaven where he was brought into the presence of God. It was on this occasion, it was later thought, that the entirety of the Quran had been revealed to him, even though it was later "sent down" to him piecemeal, as circumstances dictated (17:106).[8]

There remained, however, a great deal of uncertainty about this verse in Muslim circles. As reported in the *Life*, the story in fact includes its own defense. It describes how Muhammad himself was questioned and then how one Abu Bakr, who had been to Jerusalem and was later a famous Muslim, confirmed the accuracy of Muhammad's description.[9] But doubts must have lingered since a century after the Prophet's death his biographer was still expressing both historical and theological reservations about the pastiche he had composed out of the varying information that had come to him. "The matter of the place [or: time] of the journey and what is said about it is a searching test," the *Sira* avers. "Only God knows how revelation came and he saw what he saw. But whether he was asleep or awake, it was all true and actu-ally happened."[10]

Identification, Validation

The narrative thread in Ibn Ishaq's *Life* continues. After his experience with the angel, Muhammad returns, distraught, to his wife Khadija. He describes the experience and she seems to grasp its significance before he does: "I have hope that you will be the prophet of this people." But she wishes to reassure Muhammad and so seeks out her cousin Waraqa, "who had become a Chris-tian and read the Scriptures and learned from those that follow the Torah and the Gospel." Waraqa listens and confirms Khadija's expectation: "Holy! Holy! Holy! . . . What has come to him is the greatest *Namus*, who came to Moses aforetime. He is, I tell you, and lo, the prophet of this people. Bid him be of good heart."[11]

We are here obviously in the presence of another recognition scene, first by Khadija and then by her relative Waraqa. But something else glimmers forth from the *Sira* account: Muhammad was uncertain what had occurred to him and the identification of the experience comes from an expert and a Christian, which makes it all the more credible. Had not the boy Muhammad already been recognized and acknowledged as a prophet, by the monk Bahira among others?[12] Waraqa tells Muhammad that what has occurred to him was what had once happened to Moses with the sending down of the Torah on Sinai, where *namus* is clearly an Arabic transcription of the Greek *nomos*, the "Law" or Torah. Moses is in fact the prototypical prophet for the Quran, just as he was for the Jews of Jesus' day and indeed for Jesus himself.

Muhammad's Public Preaching

The new prophet's public preaching may not have begun immediately after he received his revelation; rather, it appears to have been confined to his immediate family circle for three years. So at least the Muslim tradition believed, and the belief is reflected in Ibn Ishaq's *Life*. There it is said that Muhammad told of what he had heard only to a restricted few.[13] But converts were made and the word spread until, after three years, God instructed him to "Proclaim what you have been ordered and turn away from the polytheists" (15:94).

The Quran is not a static document. As the suras unfold, the Prophet's confidence grows and his message is enlarged. There are new theological and eschatological concerns. It is trust the Quran now enjoins, trust that God is One—the God Muhammad refers to as his "Lord"—trust in the unlimited power of the One God and now in the fact that that power will be manifested in God's reckoning of humankind on the Last Day. Change your thinking and your life, the Quran warns, since a sure hell awaits the sinner and a bounteous reward the just. "They do not fear the Hereafter," the Quran solemnly intones. "This is, be assured, a warning, and let who will remember it" (74:55).

God

Whatever might have been his beliefs and practices before his visionary experience, the Muhammad who began publicly to preach the "warning" and the "good news" of Islam in Mecca had a new understanding of God. It unfolds in some of the early suras of the Quran. This is not the Allah of the pagan Quraysh, nor yet the Allah of the assertive Prophet of Medina. What is chiefly remarkable, perhaps, is that in the early Meccan suras Muhammad almost invariably refers to the deity not as "Allah" but rather as "Lord" (*Rabb*) or, since God is often the speaker, by the self-referential "your Lord." It is patently not the name of some new divinity, some god whose presence at Mecca was previously unknown; rather, it is an appellative, a reference to a familiar. Who was Muhammad's "Lord"? It is not at all clear, not at any rate at this point, though later it is unmistakably the *Allah* of the Quraysh, and, of course, the Almighty God of the Jews and Christians.[14]

Islam

What God required of the Meccans, the Quran instructed them, was "submission"(Arabic *islam*; one who has submitted is a *muslim*) to God, *the* God, who is none other than the high god Allah worshiped at Mecca; the "Lord of this house," the Quran calls him (106:3), referring to, and probably pointing toward, the Ka'ba, an odd stone shelter, empty within, that was the central shrine of Mecca. Muhammad had no need to introduce the Meccans to Allah; they already worshiped him, and in moments of crisis, he pointed out, they even conceded that he was in fact the only genuine God (29:61, 63; 39:38; 43:87). The trouble was, they worshiped other gods as well, and one of the central aims of the Meccan preaching was to make the Quraysh and other Meccans surrender their attachment to other deities, the idols and empty names they associated with the one true God.

This was the theological or cultic point of the early preaching, but from the beginning Islam was far more than an acceptance of monotheism. The Quran called on the Meccans to change their moral ways. "Repent!" A look at the very earliest suras shows that the reformation was overwhelmingly social, and perhaps economic, in its emphases. The Quran would eventually go on to speak of many things, but the original form of the message was narrowly targeted: it is good to share God's bounty and feed the poor and take care of the needy; it is evil to accumulate wealth solely for one's own selfish good (107, 92, 90, etc.).

The Muslims Pray

The Quran is as much about practice as it is about beliefs: the Meccans must stop *worshiping* their false gods. The Arabs both sacrificed and prayed to their gods before Islam, and if this latter "calling upon the god" was sometimes impromptu and sometimes took place at fixed moments like dawn and sunset, it was generally done in the vicinity of the deity, next to its idol or in a shrine (*masjid*) whose very name, a "place of prostration," indicates that the supplication was accompanied by appropriate postures. We do not always know the contexts in which the Quraysh venerated their gods, which prayers went with which sacrifices, or how the pre-Islamic "retreat" with its prayer and fasting favored by Muhammad was combined with the pilgrimage ritual (*hajj*). But pray and worship the Arabs of Mecca and its environs certainly did, and so when the Quran derisively dismisses it as "nothing but whistling and hand-clapping" at the Holy House (8:35), the judgment is being made from a particularly Islamic perspective.

Prayer, a certain kind of prayer, is, in fact, one of the earliest and most persistently urged elements of Muhammad's message, and prayer precisely as understood by the contemporary Jews and Christians, liturgical prayer, a public worship of God in the form of audibly uttered words. "Do not be loud in your prayer," Muhammad advises the Muslims, "nor speak it softly (as if in secret), but find a way between" (Q. 17:110). When circumstances permitted, this specifically Muslim form of prayer (salat) would be accompanied by the traditional gestures or postures and eventually performed at certain prescribed times.[15]

What Muhammad did himself and what he required of others at Mecca is open to doubt. The few Muslims there lived alone and isolated in a hostile pagan milieu, and it would have been difficult to practice any type of public prayer, which would have visibly set them off from their relatives, friends, and neighbors. It may well have been that the prayers of the earliest "Submitters" were identical in form and setting with the Quraysh's own or else were done privately and spontaneously. There are a number of prayer injunctions in the Meccan suras, but they were more likely addressed by God to Muhammad himself as guidance than intended as prescriptions for general practice.

The early traditionist Waqidi is somewhat more explicit about the Quraysh reaction to Muhammad's prayer in Mecca. He says that the Quraysh had no problems with the Prophet's morning prayer at the Ka'ba, but to perform the prayer at sunset, Muhammad and his companions had to scatter to nearby ravines. Why the Quraysh objected to one and not the other is not entirely clear. But the tradition gives us a rare glimpse of Muhammad apparently praying at the Ka'ba in the same manner and at the same time of the Quraysh.

The Prophet had received at Mecca some rather distinct instructions of when this was to be done: "Stand at [or establish] the prayer from the sinking of the sun until the darkness of the night and the morning recitation (qur'an), for the morning recitation is witnessed to" (17:80). In this last verse prayer is identified as "recitation," apparently of God's own words as indited in "The Recitation" par excellence, al-Qur'an. The Quran's frequent references to itself as "The Book" speaks to the Jewish and Christian tradition of revelation as formal written Scripture (biblion, graphe), while the Arabic qur'an points directly to the oral recitation of God's same words in a liturgical context. Contemporary Jewish and Christian liturgical traditions both enshrined the Book and used its recitation as a form of prayer to God. But even without the evidence of its name, the same conclusion would impose itself from the style and substance of the Quran. The early Meccan suras bear all the stylistic and rhetorical earmarks of what was intended to serve, from the beginning, as prayers.

Growing Pressures

If Muhammad moved cautiously at first, the divinely originated message that was now being publicly pronounced for the crowds assembled in the Meccan Haram began to take some modest hold among those for whom it was intended in the first place, the pagans of Mecca, particularly the wealthy, powerful, and well-connected Quraysh who ruled the shrine-settlement. Muhammad's young cousin, Abu Talib's son Ali, was converted, and a number of others, Abu Bakr and Uthman, and then somewhat later Umar ibn al-Khattab, men whose fidelity never wavered and each of whom would one day rule the community, were numbered among the Muslims,[16] the "Submitters," as the Quran itself called them. But those converts were second-tier Meccans, lesser clansmen or middle sons. The dynasts of the town, the ruling Quraysh, who had begun as skeptics, were turning darker in their resistance: Muhammad ibn Abdullah of the Banu Hashim was not just foolish—the resurrection of the dead? A likely story! (27:67–68)—he was also dangerous.

The Satanic Verses

Allah had competition at Mecca, a great deal of competition in that commercially religious town. Indeed, it was the very proliferation of deities and their attraction to the neighboring Arabs that was the fortune of the town. Prominent in that pantheon were the three goddesses al-Lat and al-Uzza and Manat who were worshiped at Mecca as the "daughters of Allah" and were ubiquitous in the Arab world of the sixth century. The same three goddesses appear—and then disappear—in an extremely curious and much-discussed passage in sura 53 of the Quran. The exact context of this Meccan sura is uncertain, but the collectors of the "occasions of revelation" thought they knew and the traditional explanation is plausible. We are told that Muhammad was anxious and depressed at the mounting Quraysh resistance to his message and, according to Tabari's version of Ibn Ishaq, in his despair he wished that some conciliatory revelation might be sent down by God that would enable him to convince the Meccan doubters.[17] It was at that point that God sent down what is now numbered as sura 53. But when Muhammad came to the words "Have you thought of al-Lat and al-Uzza and Manat, the third, the other?" (vv. 19–20), then, "because of his inner debates and what he desired to bring to his people," Satan cast onto his tongue the words: "These are the high-flying cranes; verily their intercession is to be hoped for."

Satan in the Quran? It is a somewhat startling notion but it has a firm Quranic foundation. Sura 22:52 has God state quite explicitly to Muhammad that "We have never sent a messenger or a prophet before you into whose formulation Satan did not cast something, but God (later) abolished it." The point, the next verse explains, was "to make what Satan proposed a tempta- tion for those whose hearts are diseased." The reason for this latter revelation, the commentators explain, was to reassure Muhammad about what had ear- lier issued from his mouth in sura 53. God would take care of it. But it is equally likely that the story was told precisely to explain, or to put narrative flesh on the bones of the extraordinary and undoubtedly authentic confession in sura 22:52.

The traditional story—it has a number of slightly different versions— continues. When the Meccan pagans heard these, the famous "Satanic verses" of sura 53, they were delighted at the apparent accommodation and began to pay heed to Muhammad's message, while the Muslims, who had complete trust in their Prophet, could not imagine an error, illusion, or mistake on his part. And at the end, all worshiped together, the "Submitters" and the pagans. We are not told how long this blissful accommodation lasted. We know it ended with the "sending down" of the words that now actually stand in the Quran as verse 23 of sura 53.

> These are only names which you and your fathers have invented. No authority was sent down by God for them. They only follow conjec- ture and wish-fulfillment, even though guidance had come to them already from the Lord.

This story, or something like it, has a claim to authenticity. The criterion of embarrassment rises unbidden from its lines: it is impossible to imagine a Muslim inventing such an inauspicious tale. But even without the accompanying story, the implications of a Quranic verse being uttered and then withdrawn are profound for Islamic scriptural theology and jurisprudence. And what is important here is what they reveal of the contemporary regard for the three goddesses. What was first granted and then rescinded was permission to use the three goddesses as intercessors with Allah. It was, as has been suggested, a critical moment in Muhammad's understanding of the distinction between Allah as simply a "high god," the head of the Meccan or Arabian pantheon where the lesser gods and goddesses might be invoked as go-betweens, and the notion that eventually prevailed: Allah is uniquely God, without associates, companions, or "daughters." The goddesses were, as the revision put it, "nothing but names," invented by the pagan Meccans and their ancestors.

Threats of the Judgment

Whether temporarily placated or not, the Quraysh were relentless in their hostility to Muhammad. Like all polytheists, the Meccan oligarchs were not religious fanatics; what they feared was that the monotheism Muhammad preached would lessen the appeal of Mecca as a pilgrimage center, which was surely one of the greatest miscalculations in the history of commerce! Nor did they relish the brand of social and economic reform that underlay the message that the new prophet was publicly propagating in the shadow of the Ka'ba. The early suras of the Quran reflect the mostly anonymous criticism being directed at the Messenger, and the heat of Muhammad's preaching begins to rise in reaction. There are now fierce denunciations of the scoffers and unbelievers: for them is reserved a fiery hell (38:55–58, 70:15–18, 74:27–30, 104:5–9) just as the believers would have as their reward a true paradise of peace and pleasurable repose (43:68–73, 56:10–26, etc.). At this point both the language and imagery suddenly become familiar to the Jew or the Christian. The promised paradise is called the "Garden of Eden" and the threatened hell, "Gehenna."

The Quran early on unveils, in bits and pieces, a vision of the Last Days, not to stress their absolute imminence, as in the New Testament, but to warn the unbeliever that the price of doubt is high and the rewards of submission are great. Though it has its own particular details, the Quran's version of the End is obviously different from anything we encounter among the pre-Islamic Arabs, whose view of the Afterlife was dim rather than apocalyptic, but it is noticeably similar to that current among the Jews and Christians.

The Seal of the Prophets

The threat of the Judgment is one psychological prop that undergirds Muhammad's message. Another equally important one is his own divinely appointed mission. As the Quran unfolds we discover its own elaborate history of prophecy. Muhammad, the Meccans are told, is not the first prophet sent to humankind, though surely he is the last,[18] and his townspeople ignore him at their own eternal peril.

As earlier remarked, the Quran's view of the past is a narrowly focused Sacred History: the listeners are instructed how the divine dispensation, which began at Creation, has unfolded from Adam down to the present (6:84, 19:58). The story of the prophets is rehearsed at length in the Quran, never quite consecutively in the manner of a history, but rather to make the same point that Jesus insists on in the Q source, to wit, when humankind has refused to heed the bearers of God's message, the consequences have been terrible (22:42–43). The lesson here is even clearer than Jesus' own: those who reject this prophet will pay a fearsome price at God's hands.

Thus Muhammad established his own pedigree in the essentially biblical line of the prophets, and as a successor in particular to Moses and Jesus. And this virtual "Scripture" that he was piecemeal pronouncing as it was revealed to him by God, this "convincing Arabic Quran," as it called itself (36:69), was to take its rightful place as an equal beside the sacred Books of the Jews and Christians. Later, when Islam exploded into the populous habitats of these other communities, that claim to parity would take on meaning, but from Muhammad's original audience at Mecca, the references to other prophets were chiefly intended as a warning to reform and not as a prediction that a third great branch of monotheism had arisen out of the other two.

Identifying the Prophet

His poetry and his storytelling made Muhammad culturally identifiable to his contemporaries. What made him particular and what made him a prophet was a great moral earnestness and conviction. Muhammad's spiritual sensibilities and aspirations, which are on display in the Quran, flowed from a Western Arabian religious environment that we only very imperfectly understand and which may be tentatively described as biblical monotheism. We know its likely foundation was the Bible and (perhaps to a somewhat lesser extent) the New Testament, two texts to which Muhammad clearly did *not* have access, however. We know it too from its textual manifestations in seventh-century rabbinic Judaism and that same century's versions of Eastern Christianity. But neither of those is quite adequate to our purpose. What we require, if we are to understand the religious *Sitz im Leben*, the oyster from which the Quranic pearl emerged, is some testimony to seventh-century Arabian Judaism and seventh-century Arabian Christianity or, even more precisely, to the version of each, alone or in hybrid combination, that was available to an earnest man of modest attendance in Mecca in the second decade of that century.

What Was Muhammad Thinking?

We have few resources for approaching Muhammad from the direction of his sources: we can only argue back to him from what we have before us in the Quran. And what the Quran shows is most curious: a rather dense biblical background that is midrashic rather than textual and more familiar with biblical exempla than with Bible history. This seems to point toward Jewish sources or Jewish informants, though we can probably rule out the latter since here it is not only a question of Muhammad's knowledge but that of his audience as well: the Quran as declamation indicates a shared biblical legacy. But we must not proceed too quickly. Muhammad's views on prophecy and prophets give an equal and important role among them to "Jesus the Messiah" (5:75, etc.). It does not appear to be Muhammad himself who put Jesus in that company: to all appearances Jesus had already been integrated into the history of biblical prophecy before that history had begun to be rehearsed in the Quran.

The position of Jesus in Muhammad's thinking appears to rule out a straightforward Jewish source for the thinking on display in the Quran. Nor would an orthodox Christian one regard Jesus, as Muhammad does, as a prophet rather than the Son of God. But there were Christians, or Jews, who adhered to some degree of Torah observance and yet venerated Jesus of Nazareth. This curious hybrid, or what appears as such to modern scholarship, which calls it, with a notable lack of conviction, Jewish Christianity, quite obviously describes the original form of the Jesus movement. By the fourth century it had, however, been swept to the heretical edges of Christianity under a variety of names like Ebionites, Elkasaites, and Nazarenes or Nasoreans.

A Jewish Christian Template for Muhammad?

Nothing is very sure about these Jewish Christian groups, which are chiefly catalog items in heresiographies rather than identifiable communities, except that there certainly existed in Late Antiquity communities of believers whose fellowship was rejected by the main body of Christians because they followed Jewish practices and had a degraded view of Jesus that differed from the high Christology of the official or imperial Church. Indeed, there are indications that such broadly defined Jewish Christian groups survived in the Middle East into Islamic times.

If we place Muhammad's Quranically reflected beliefs and practices against the template of what passes as "Jewish Christianity," there is a remarkable coincidence. Muhammad revered Jesus as profoundly as he did Moses; not assuredly as the Son of God but rather, like Moses, as a mortal prophet and wonder-worker. But he was also, in Muhammad's eyes, the Messiah (*al-masih*)— though the meaning and significance of the term seems long forgotten—as well as both the "Word" and the "Spirit" of God (Q. 4:171). Muhammad prayed thrice daily and facing Jerusalem, practiced ritual purity, abstained from pork and wine, and yet knew about a miraculous Eucharistic banquet (5:112–115). The Judeo-Christian hybrids are generally characterized by an opposition and even a hostility toward Paul. Paul is never mentioned in the Quran, but neither are the Pauline themes of atonement and redemption, nor is there any trace there of Paul's devalorization of the Torah.

Given the schematic nature of our information about the Christian heresies of Late Antiquity and the sparseness of our information about Christianity in sixth-century Arabia, it seems pointless to attempt an exact identification of the version of Jewish Christianity that seems to lie behind Muhammad's religious formation. The sects and sectaries who fill the pigeonholes of Christian heresy-catalogers like Epiphanius of Salamis (d. 402) are almost infinite in their variety and with a bewildering range of beliefs and practices. But the large picture is unmistakable: Muhammad had been exposed to, and accepted as authentic and valid, a monotheistic perspective that embraced both the Torah and the Gospel, both Moses and Jesus. Both the beliefs and the practices of Muhammad conform, in the general terms imposed on us by the nature of our sources, to some variant of Jewish Christianity. More, those beliefs and practices were sufficiently familiar to the Meccans that Muhammad could discuss and incorporate them into his public preaching without elaborate explanation.

There is, however, no evidence that such a sect ever existed at Mecca or that Muhammad was a member of any such group or community. There is no John the Baptist in the Muhammad story and neither clergy nor congregation in the foreground of the Quran. The Jews and Christians, the Quran's *Banu Isra'il* and *Nasara*, are paradigms on the horizon and Muhammad encounters actual members of the first in the *Yahud* of Medina and Christians perhaps only at the end of his life to accept their political submission.[19] We do not know how or whence these putative Jewish Christian convictions came to Mecca. They left no institutional trace but their presence was deep and powerful enough that they made an enduring impression on Muhammad and his fellow Meccans.

Two Prophetic Reformers

Like Jesus, Muhammad was a reformer rather than a revolutionary. Though Muslims later preferred to think of it otherwise, the message of Islam was not intended to destroy or obliterate the religious system in which Muhammad had grown up. His objective was, like Jesus' own, to reform the religious culture of his contemporaries. Where the two men differed was in Muhammad's reform being profoundly conservative, while Jesus' was forward-looking and progressive. Islam preached in the Quran was a self-described return to an original monotheism exemplified in Abraham—Islam was nothing other than the *din Ibrahim*, the "religion of Abraham" (2:135), which was still, despite the travails of a long bout of pagan polytheism, from which Muhammad absolutely disassociated himself (109:6), deeply embedded in the fabric of Mecca. Witness the worship of the One True God at the Ka'ba, the Holy House built by Abraham (2:127), who also prescribed the rituals there (22:26); witness too the pilgrimage, or hajj, another Abrahamic institution (22:27). Muhammad was returning Mecca and the Meccans to a pristine past.

Jesus too saw corruption in the religious culture of his day, nothing as profound as the paganism that had disfigured Mecca, and while he strongly disapproved of what we might call extreme Pharisaism, he never disavowed the Pharisees, or any other Jews, as such. In a sense the Pharisees were irrelevant. Jesus was looking forward not merely to a retributory judgment—that was not what the End Time was about for Jews—but to the future Kingdom in which he and the Twelve would rule over a new order. His followers deepened that vision.

The Plot against Muhammad

As Islam slowly spread in Mecca, the Quraysh, the political and economic elite of the town, appear to have made some initial effort, if not to come to terms with Muhammad, then at least to attempt to negotiate with him. According to Ibn Ishaq, they offered him all the blandishments of Mammon, from money even to kingship. Or, perhaps he was just possessed. In that event they would get him professional help.[20]

These broad promises were likely neither sincere nor altogether practical, but they do attest to the magnitude of the threat Muhammad was thought to pose to the social and commercial equilibrium of Mecca, a city that had combined trade and pilgrimage to its shrine into a profitable enterprise. But Muhammad was not to be swayed. There is no compromise in sura 109:

> Say: O you unbelievers,
> I do not worship what you worship,
> Nor do you worship what I worship;
> Nor will I worship what you worship,
> Nor will you worship what I worship.
> To you your religion; to me my religion.

The negotiations broke off and the Quraysh increased the pressure on their increasingly troublesome fellow countryman. Boycotts and bans were eventually followed by threats against Muhammad's life. The Prophet's reaction was a somewhat unexpected one: he sent some of his followers—eighty-three men and their families—across the Red Sea to asylum in Christian Abyssinia. The Quraysh quickly sent their own delegation to convince the Abyssinian Negus to return the Muslims to Mecca, but he would not be persuaded.[21]

Muhammad's Meccan enemies were persistent, however, and the Prophet's position was eroded by personal setbacks. In 619 he lost to death two of his staunchest supporters, his wife Khadija, the "mother of believers," and Abu Talib, the uncle who had been first his guardian and then his strong political prop against the Quraysh. Muhammad grew desperate. He offered himself to the tribes of Arabs who came to the Meccan fairs, not simply begging asylum but boldly summoning them to Islam and telling them that he was a prophet who had been sent. He asked for their belief and protection only until God vindicated him. No one responded.[22]

The petitioning finally paid off, however. Among those who heard the Prophet's pleas were visitors from the oasis of Yathrib, some 275 miles to the north of Mecca. Yathrib, later named "The City (*medina*) of the Prophet," or simply Medina, was a date-palm oasis, an agricultural settlement of mixed Arab and Jewish population. Ibn Ishaq, with a great deal of hindsight, regarded both the encounter and the presence of Jews at Yathrib as providential:

> Now God had prepared the way for Islam in that they (the Medinese Arabs) lived side by side with the Jews (of Medina), who were people of the Scriptures and knowledge, while they themselves were polytheists and idolaters. They had often raided them in their district and

whenever bad feelings arose the Jews used to say to them, "A Prophet will be sent soon. His day is at hand. We shall follow him and kill you by his aid . . ." So when they heard the Messenger's message they said to one another, "This is the very prophet of whom the Jews warned us. Don't let them get to him before us!" Thereupon they accepted his teaching and became Muslims. (198–204)

The bargaining proceeded. What Muhammad required above all was security for himself and his followers, but though he did not forget he was the Messenger of God, the terms of his removal to Medina did not require that all there should become Muslims. The new Medinese converts carried the terms back to their fellow oasis dwellers for approval, but meanwhile another event commemorated in the Quran occurred, one with enormous political consequences for the nascent Islamic community: the Prophet's formal rejection of passive resistance to persecution and a warrant to turn to the use of force.

A Resort to Violence

The Messenger had not been given permission for the Submitters to fight or to allow them to shed blood before the conclusion of the agreement with Medina. He had simply been ordered to call men to God and to endure insult and forgive the innocent. The Quraysh had persecuted his followers, seducing some from their religion and exiling others from their country. They had to choose whether to give up their religion, be mistreated at home, or flee the country, some to Abyssinia, others to Medina. Now, suddenly, all that changed.

"Permission is granted those (to take up arms) who fight because they were oppressed," verse 29 of sura 22 begins. This permission to fight, to turn from passive to active resistance to the Quraysh, was no trifling matter, as its divine sanction shows. The Quraysh's commercial enterprises were protected by their own religiously sanctioned prohibitions against violence and bloodshed during the months of pilgrimage and the annual fairs that were connected to it. Now God had in effect withdrawn that protection: the enemies of Islam would find no shelter under sacramentalism.

The Migration

The arrangements at Medina were now complete and the *hijra*, the migration of Muslims to Mecca, began, though gradually and with great caution, beginning with Muhammad's followers. The Quraysh became aware that the Muslims were slipping away and decided to assassinate the cause of their discontent. But the plan misfired. Warned of the plot by the Angel Gabriel, Muhammad slipped away with Abu Bakr while Ali pretended to sleep in his stead, before he too successfully escaped and joined the others at Medina. The Prophet had escaped an almost certain death.

Afterthoughts: Two Versions of the Good News

The "Good News" announced by Jesus and Muhammad was identical up to a point: repent/change your life—the Kingdom/Judgment is at hand. But that message resonated differently in the two different milieus. Jesus positioned himself in the footsteps of a contemporary predecessor, John the Baptist, so closely in fact that his followers had to go to some lengths to separate them. Muhammad had no John the Baptist—he was novel in his context, though not in the form of his message, which resembled the mantic pronouncements of the Bedouin poets.

Jesus' listeners could look behind Jesus and readily identify, with only the slightest prompting, both Moses and Elijah as prophetic prototypes. Muhammad had instead to recall or construct his own context as a "warner" by frequent and detailed references to the prophets, chiefly biblical, of the monotheistic tradition. Nor did Muhammad have an apocalyptic literary tradition to provide him and his listeners with a repertoire of images and motives to undergird the message of the Last Days. In the Quran these images of the End Time are as vivid as those in the Gospels, but as far as we can tell, Muhammad's audience was hearing them for the first time. Jesus' descriptions are embedded in a deep and rich Jewish environment, indeed, a Scriptural environment.

Muhammad was speaking to pagan idolaters from whom he had made a profound break—"my way is not your way." His words have a discernible context, a biblical one that we can see quite clearly behind the lines of the Quran. There is an enigma here: his listeners seem perfectly familiar with that same biblical context that Muhammad refers to without much explanation. We have no idea how either he or they came by such information. It should be remarked, Muhammad's warnings were prophetic but not apocalyptic. In the Gospels and Paul, the End Time is onrushing; in the Quran it is merely inevitable.

The Christian message was one of anticipation, at the same time of blazing hope and fearful dread. The Kingdom was breaking in, and Jesus' followers were bidden to rejoice at the presence of the bridegroom; but at the same time the full arrival of God's Kingdom would also signal the end of days, a time of fearsome torment before the triumph of Jesus' return. There is no similar sense of anticipation in the Quran, neither of the breaking in of a new age nor of a cataclysmic final hour. The Quran speaks often of the judgment, of the reward of the virtuous and the punishment of the wicked; but though the language is eschatological, it is not apocalyptic. The judgment is no closer and no farther than it has been for any human being. Indeed, the Quran barely recognizes the distinction between past, present, and future; it is cast in what has been called the "eternal present" of God's own perspective.

7

Act Two: Tragedy and Triumph

SCOTT FITZGERALD'S LOGION that there are no second acts in American lives may be more entertaining than true, and it was certainly not true of the lives of the two Middle Eastern holy men under consideration here. Jesus and Muhammad each made an abrupt entrance upon the familiar stage of his own homeland and each had a public career as a not altogether successful preacher. And each eventually ran into serious, even mortal opposition that threatened his life and that of his followers. With that the stage cleared and each protagonist entered into the second and final act of his dramatic life.

Jesus in Jerusalem

There is a pastoral quality to the Galilean chapters of the Gospels. The fields, in sowing and growth and harvest, the plains, hills, and sea are all on display, as are the people who work in them. We see fishermen and farmers, tax gatherers, the Roman military and prostitutes, whether in the flesh or as figures in Jesus' parables drawn from Galilean life. When the action is moved to Jerusalem, the focus is still on Jesus, but it is now so intensely centered on events that we get little sense of the ordinary life of this city at the heart of the Jewish world. We now stand in the midst of a drama whose principal characters, like Pilate and Caiaphas, are portrayed in bold relief, while others are deftly thumbnailed: Peter, Judas, the Temple priest's maidservant, the thieves executed with Jesus, and Simon of Cyrene, the hapless tourist who is forced to carry Jesus' cross through Jerusalem's streets. But of the larger Jerusalem background there is little: we are in an enclosed space.

A Two-Part Gospel

Jesus' biographies fall into two main sections (with a variety of epigraphs and conclusions). The first is what is being called here "Jesus in Galilee," which is followed by a quite distinct "Jesus in Jerusalem." It is in this latter that the generalized landscape and chronological vagueness of Jesus' public ministry, which serve chiefly to provide a backdrop for the originally unembedded Q logia and similar teaching material, is replaced by the urgent facticity of what is known in the Christian tradition as the "Passion and Death of Jesus."

If Q and what we may assume was a similar collection of sayings/teachings that lay behind Jesus' words in Mark were the original "Galilean" form of the Jesus tradition, then what produced our current Gospels with their heavily weighted "Passion" narratives? Was it those very events, Jesus' arrest, his arraignment before the Jewish authorities of Jerusalem, his trial before the Roman procurator, and his public execution as a criminal, that created the need for some form of explanation? The Markan prototype provided just such an explanation by adding to the older logoi a detailed account of the last days of the Jesus and then framing them both in a species of biographical narrative that came to be called "The Good News."[1]

"Jesus in Jerusalem" is not, then, an arbitrary division in a narrative of the life of Jesus. All four of the Gospels fall into this two-act scenario: Jesus in Galilee (with a "Nativity Prologue" in Matthew and Luke and an "Overture in Heaven" in John) and Jesus in Jerusalem (with appendices on the risen Jesus). The second act has a clear-cut beginning with the arrival in Jerusalem of Jesus and his inner group of supporters. There follow his increasingly portentous remarks and the equally portentous events that precede Jesus' celebration of Passover. Here the four Gospels come together to describe his arrest outside the city, a late-night hearing before the high priest, a trial the next morning before Pilate, and his final execution by crucifixion outside what was then the western wall of the city, all of which constitutes the largest single part of all of the Gospel narratives.

A Common Account?

Chronologically, the earliest view we have of the final week in Jesus' life is found in two lines of the first of Paul's letters to the Corinthians (15:3–4). There we are told simply that the "tradition" received by Paul and now passed on—surely not for the first time—to the believers in Corinth was that "Christ died for our sins, in accordance with the Scriptures, and that he was buried . . ." The plain, undetailed facts—"died" and "was buried"—are here quite noticeably wrapped in the now familiar argument "in accordance with the Scriptures" and already freighted with a profound theological significance, "for our sins." Jesus' immolation as a sin-offering to God had thus entered the

Christian repertoire of explanations of this extraordinary event and, if the traditional chronology is accurate, even before our Gospels were written.

For their part, the slightly later Gospel accounts of Jesus' death are all very conscious of the argument for Jesus' claims based on the fulfillment of Scripture, and they provide an ongoing biblical gloss on the events of Jesus' last days. But they are also interested, as Paul obviously was not, though he must have heard it repeated many times, in precisely what happened when Jesus came to Jerusalem for the last time. All four Gospels speak of these events, which are many and varied, but what is chiefly noteworthy about their accounts is that, though John and the Synoptics go their own way in the incidents leading up to Jesus' arrest, from that point onward (Mk 14: 43–52; Jn 18:2–11) Mark and John have the same schematic presentation of the same events in the same order. This extraordinary agreement of the two—Q, it will be recalled, has no Passion Narrative—at the very least suggests that early on there was, if not a common literary source, then a basic common account of Jesus' arrest, trial, and execution, an account later filled out with the varying details that become obvious by comparing Mark 11–15 with its parallel in Matthew 21–27.

A Triumphal Entry

Jesus comes to Jerusalem to celebrate the Passover under a sky darkened by his own predictions. "We are now going to Jerusalem," he tells the Twelve. And then, invoking his messianic title, "The Son of Man will be handed over to the chief priests and scribes; they will condemn him to death and hand him over to the Gentiles. He will be mocked and spat upon and flogged and killed, and three days afterwards he will rise again" (Mk 10:33–34). The prediction is detailed and precise, too precise indeed to have won much credence from critics who regard it as an attribution after the fact, a case of the authors rather than Jesus fulfilling Scripture.

But despite the grim predictions, the week begins in apparent triumph. On the very day of his arrival, Jesus enters the Holy City in what appears to be a carefully staged procession from Bethpage where he and the Twelve are lodging. The royal detail of the progress to Jerusalem—the requisitioned mount, the cloths spread on the ground before him, the waving palm fronds, his acclamation as the "son of David"—all fulfill a prophecy, as Matthew is once again careful to tell the reader (21:4). Everyone in the city must have been aware of this very public demonstration. "The city was wild with excitement," Matthew says. "'This is that prophet Jesus from Nazareth in Galilee'"

(21:10–11). It was certainly noted by the Romans who were habitually on high alert in Jerusalem during Passover and who did not take public demonstrations lightly.

The Temple Incident

Mark inserts a homely detail in his otherwise tense narrative: Jesus spends the following day sightseeing in Jerusalem: "He went into the Temple and looked around at everything" (11:11). He must not have liked what he saw since the next day he returned and angrily drove out of the Temple precincts—he whipped them with a homemade lash, according to John (2:15)—the sellers of the kosher animals prescribed for Temple offerings and overturned the tables of those who changed Roman coinage into the Temple shekels used to pay the religious tithes (Mk 11:15–17). This time it is Jesus himself who quotes the prophets, Isaiah and Jeremiah: "You have turned His house of prayer into a den of thieves" (Mk 11:17).

What first arises off the Gospel text is Jesus' disgust at the commercial goings-on in the Temple precincts. But his objection could only have been aesthetic; there was nothing patently illegal or immoral about either of those activities. Mark immediately moves on to something deeper and darker however. "The chief priests and the scribes heard of this and looked for a way to bring about his death" (11:18). We are somewhat baffled. The incident was clearly too minor to provoke any immediate police response either by the Romans, who did not hesitate to intervene in the Temple, or by the Temple authorities: Jesus simply walked off and then returned to the Temple the next day, when all he got was a question: "By what authority are you doing this?" (11:28).

A Priestly Plot

Jesus was put to death effectively by the Romans, all the Gospels agree, through the machinations of the principals among the Temple priests. Why? The Jerusalem Temple priesthood, whose integrity had been compromised under both the Maccabees and Herod, was a provocative issue for many Jews in Jesus' day, but Jesus himself appears to have had no problems with either the institution or the individuals who comprised it. Rather he reserved his scorn and his polemic for the Pharisees, the advocates of a meticulous—in Jesus' eyes an overmeticulous—observance of the Torah. Thus Mark draws our attention to the Temple incident as a possible cause of the priestly plot, and some modern critics have read Jesus' act of measured violence—and they assume the priests read it that way as well—as a highly charged symbolic gesture by which he signaled the end of the old spiritual order and the initiation of the new. Thus, the argument concludes, the high priest understood both the action of Jesus and its intent and reacted accordingly.

John locates the Temple incident early in Jesus' career (2:13–22) and so effectively disconnects it from a priestly plot. But for John there was indeed such a plot and he seems to have had privileged information about its hatching, of a very different sort from the Synoptics' and possibly due to Nicodemus, a member of the ruling Sanhedrin and a secret follower of Jesus (Jn 3:1–2). Jesus had performed the famous, and for some notorious, act of raising a certain Lazarus from the dead in a suburb of Jerusalem (Jn 11:1–44). The news spread and an alarmed Sanhedrin was convened in Jerusalem:

> "What action are we taking?" they said. "This man is performing many signs. If we leave him alone like this the whole populace will believe in him. Then the Romans will come and sweep away our Temple and our nation." But one of them, Caiaphas, who was high priest that year, said, "You know nothing whatever; you do not use your judgment; it is more to your interest that one man should die for the people than that the whole nation should be destroyed." . . . So from that day on they plotted his death. (Jn 11:47–53)

In John's account what the priests feared was that another popular demonstration of the type Jesus had already provoked—Josephus provides abundant evidence that the fear was well grounded—would lead to a Roman reaction against the entire Jewish enterprise in Palestine. They decided that Jesus would have to be sacrificed not only to abort this particular threat but to demonstrate that the Jewish authorities were capable of protecting their own—and the Romans'—interests.

Challenges

To return to the Synoptics' thread, Mark's narration does not proceed in a straight line. Jesus is challenged, apparently in Jerusalem, since that is where the developing story has placed him, by three different groups. The first comes from the Pharisees, who pose Jesus what is described as a trap-question on the legitimacy of paying tax to the Romans, which he elegantly and famously sidesteps: "Pay to Caesar what belongs to Caesar and to God what is God's"

(Mk 12:15–17). Next to confront him are the Sadducees, the priestly party. They do not ask him about the priesthood, however, nor about the incident of the Temple that had immediately preceded. Rather, it is bodily resurrection, which they denied in principle since it had no scriptural warrant, that interests them. Jesus derisively dismisses them: "You understand nothing about Scripture or the power of God" (12:19–27). Finally, one of Israel's rising class of canon lawyers, a scribe, comes forward and asks the classroom question: which of God's commandments is the greatest? Jesus gives him the classroom answer straight from Deuteronomy (6:4–5). Jesus is congratulated, and in turn bestows his own, perhaps ironic, reward on the scribe: "You are not far from the Kingdom of God" (12:28–34).

The Last Days

All the Synoptics at this point insert into their account Jesus' own version of an apocalypse, an unfolding or unveiling of the Last Days (Mk 13 and parr.), texts in which, as already noted, many have seen clear enough references to Jerusalem's own destruction in AD 70 to enable them to date the Gospels to after that watershed event. Then in Mark 14 (= Mt 26–27; Lk 22–23; Jn 12–19) begins an account of Jesus' own end. The time is set precisely: "Two days before the festival of Passover and Unleavened Bread," the priests begin devising a scheme to do away with Jesus, but not, they agree, during the holy days, "else there would be rioting among the people" (Mk 14:1–2). Jesus meanwhile is at a friend's house in Bethany. And it was then and there that Judas, one of the Twelve, resolved to betray Jesus. The motive, we are told, was money (Mk 14:10–11).

The Last Supper

The next day, Passover eve, which turns out to be a Thursday—by Jewish reckoning, Passover will begin at sunset on that Thursday—there takes place what the Christians came to call the Last Supper or, when it began to be reenacted as a Christian liturgy, the Eucharist (Mk 14:12–26). It was a formal evening meal celebrated within the walls of Jerusalem as prescribed by Jewish law, and it seems in some ways like a traditional Passover Seder and yet in other ways not: the meal is not eaten standing or in haste and there is no sign of a Passover lamb. Matthew, Luke, and John all have Jesus wash the feet of his followers; Mark does not. At the meal Jesus predicts his betrayal by one of the Twelve present, and John (13:30) has Judas leave soon after.

At some point Jesus takes bread, blesses it—the Greek word for "blessing" is *eucharistia*—and distributes it to the Apostles with the extraordinary words, extraordinary in any Jewish context known to us, "This is my body" (Mk 14:22 and parr.; 1 Cor 11:24). He does the same with a cup of wine: "This is my blood," and ends, "the blood of the new covenant, shed for many (Mk 14:24 and parr.; 1 Cor 11:25), and Paul's account adds to both the bread and the wine, "Do this in remembrance of me." Whether Jesus said it or the early Christians deduced it, the reenactment of the ritual of the bread and wine had become in fact, on Paul's own testimony, a central act of worship among Christians two decades after Jesus' death.

The Arrest in the Garden

Jesus and the Twelve, now eleven, leave their rented hall and go out into the Jerusalem night, an extraordinary act at that time and in that place. They go to a private olive garden on the near slope of the Mount of Olives east of the city. We are not told why, except that Jesus decides to pray (Mk 14:26–32). It is an anguished prayer, almost in desperation (Mk 14:33–36). Judas appears with the Temple police and identifies Jesus. There is a scuffle, a bit of swordplay—Luke for some reason insists that there were two swords among the Jesus party (22:35–38)—and Jesus is put under arrest. His followers flee (Mk 14:43–50), among them—noted only in Mark—an odd young man "wearing nothing but a linen cloth" (14:51–52).

The Sanhedrin Trial

By all accounts, Jesus is taken directly back into the city, this time to the house of the high priest Caiaphas, where there is a species of trial (Mk 14:53–72), though it seems to lack all formality: it is being held at night, on the first day of Passover, and in a private house.[2] Peter is tagging along in the shadows, and when he is identified by his Galilean accent, he denies any association with Jesus, not once but three times, as Jesus had earlier predicted he would (Mk 14:30). Witnesses are summoned; they lied, the Gospels aver, when they testified that Jesus threatened to destroy the Temple. The defendant is silent. The high priest then poses the question direct: "Are you the Messiah, the Son of God?" "Yes," Jesus responds. "I am. And you will see the Son of Man seated at the right hand of God and coming in the clouds of heaven" (Mk 14:61–62). "Blasphemy!" the high priest cries.[3]

The Trial before Pilate

Jesus must have spent the night in custody at the high priest's house, much of it while being abused by the servants (Mk 14:66). Matthew alone (27:3–10) reports the end of Judas: he hanged himself in remorse.[4] Early the next morning, which is Friday and the first day of Passover, the Jewish authorities of the previous evening bind Jesus over to the Roman procurator of Judea, Pontius Pilate, who hears the case in his headquarters, probably in Herod's former palace near the Western Gate. Pilate has no interest in messiahs. "Are you the king of the Jews?" he asks (Mk 15:2). Jesus declines to answer. Pilate, who is portrayed in the Gospels as a very reluctant prosecutor and judge—the authors of the Gospels were careful not to antagonize the Romans—tries another approach. He offers to the crowd outside the praetorium a Passover amnesty: he will release either Jesus or the imprisoned political terrorist Barabbas. But "the chief priests incited the crowd" (Mk 15:11) and they call for the release of Barabbas and the execution of Jesus.

Jesus is stripped, a purple robe thrown around his shoulders, a crown of thorns placed on his head and he is mocked and roughed-up by the Roman soldiers. He is once again shown to the crowd, who are growing increasingly restless and violent. "I find no criminal fault in him," Pilate is made to say, and he washes his hands in a formal gesture of disavowal. It is Matthew alone who supplies the bloodcurdling finis that has so fatally echoed down the centuries. "I am innocent of this man's blood," Pilate says. "It is now your business." "And all the people answered, 'His blood be upon us and upon our children'" (Mt 27:24–26).

The Crucifixion

Roman criminals were humanely flogged into a state of weakness before they were crucified. So it was with Jesus, who was then taken outside the western wall of the city to a place that is specifically remembered as being called Golgotha, the "Place of the Skull" (Mt 27:33). He is nailed to a cross to which is attached his indictment, "The King of the Jews." Two "brigands"—the contemporary codeword for political terrorists—are crucified with him and they join with the bystanders in mocking Jesus. "If you are the Messiah of Israel, come down from the cross so we can see and believe" (Mk 15:32).

Jesus is crucified at nine in the morning (Mk 15:25) and hangs on the cross until three in the afternoon, when he finally expires: "Jesus gave a loud cry and died" (Mk 15:37). There were omens and prodigies. Darkness is said to cover the earth from noon on, and at the moment of Jesus' death the veil that shields the Holy of Holies in the Temple is reportedly rent in two. And the Roman centurion who stood guard at the foot of the cross is heard to say, "Truly this man was God's Son" (Mk 15:39). All who remain to witness the end are "Mary Magdalene and Mary the mother of James the younger and of Joses and Salome.[5] These used to follow him and provided for him when he was in Galilee" (Mk 15:40–41).

The Burial

The Jewish Sabbath would have begun at sunset on that Passover Friday and so there is some haste in removing the body from the cross and interring it. The arrangements are taken care of by one Joseph of Arimathea, "a respected member of the Sanhedrin who was also himself awaiting expectantly for the Kingdom of God" (Mk 15:43). John adds (19:39) that Nicodemus, Jesus' other follower on the Sanhedrin, was involved. Pilate is asked to release the body, which Pilate, once determining from the Roman guard on the site that Jesus is actually dead, does. Joseph wraps the body in a linen cloth—a more elaborate washing and anointing will take place once the Sabbath has passed—and places it in a tomb newly hewn out of the rock face in a garden nearby (Mk 15:46; Jn 19:40–42).

So ended the public career of Jesus of Nazareth, the Galilean charismatic and preacher who some thought might be the Jewish Messiah. He died, like many other claimants to power or authority in that day, as a condemned criminal at the hands of the Romans in whom resided all power and authority. We are not too surprised at that. But unlike most of those others, Jesus was not seized in an open act of revolt or disobedience but, it would seem, proleptically, in anticipation of what he might do. Likewise, and this is far more puzzling, it was not to the Romans that he was principally the concern, but to the Jewish authorities, which still meant in first-century Judea, as it had for many centuries before, the Temple priesthood. Did he threaten Judaism or did he threaten the priests and the Temple, which was not only the spiritual center of Israelite identity but the dominant economic institution in Israel? The Gospels do not seem to care. This is a theological passion play and the villains of the piece represent religious, not economic or even political, forces.

Muhammad at Medina

In the early 620s, after ten years of public preaching at Mecca, the future was bright for neither the message of Islam nor its messenger. Muhammad's wife Khadija was dead, his clan protector Abu Talib was dead, and the surrounding tribes and settlements to whom Muhammad had offered himself showed little interest in Muhammad's message and even less inclination to anger the

Quraysh by granting him asylum. Salvation, we have seen, came in an unexpected form from a not entirely unexpected source. Among those who had come to Mecca for the commercial fairs were some men of Medina, an oasis 275 miles northeast over rough terrain from Mecca. They had heard the Prophet more than once and were impressed; they were ready to "submit." But they had another idea. The two paramount Arab tribes of the oasis and their associated Jewish clients had been locked in a destructive civil war for over a decade. Mistrust and violence had turned the oasis into an armed camp, each extended family living within its own heavily fortified plantation. Muhammad, it was thought, as a recognized holy man, might perform one of the traditional duties of such Arabian charismatics and arbitrate the differences that were destroying an otherwise prosperous agricultural settlement.

The Medina Accords

Most of the oasis dwellers agreed to the proposal, and in 622 Muhammad and his Muslim followers completed the gradual and stealthy "migration" (*hijra*; Hegira) from Mecca to Medina, an event Muslims later thought to be of such importance that they used it to mark the beginning of the Muslim or "Hijri" era.[6] Some of his followers who had earlier been sent to Christian Abyssinia for their protection also rejoined the community at Medina. And in the spirit of reconciliation, or desperation, that had prompted the invitation, there was drawn up what might be called the "Medina Accords." It is a multipart document—some clauses may in fact have been added later—which constituted *all* the population of Medina—Muslims, pagans, and Jews—a single community.[7] All parties agreed to accept Muhammad's judgment as final in the affairs of the oasis.

There were problems, of course. Muhammad's Meccan followers, whom history was to dub the "Migrants," had to be integrated and supported inside the tight oasis society, and the Jews of Medina—there were none apparently at Mecca—who were arrayed on both Arab sides of the conflict in the oasis, almost certainly had qualms about this new "prophet" who was now their sovereign and whose message and practices, which he continued to declaim in his self-styled Quran, were uncomfortably like their own.

The Medina Quran

In our bondage to written texts, we must constantly remind ourselves that, when it comes to the Quran, there can be no question of an "original." The

original of the Quran is the recitation or performance that Muhammad chose
to have his followers memorize, and which is very unlikely to have been its
first utterance. Thus, the "original" of our Quran is the finished sura that
either Muhammad or someone else had edited and that had then become
fixed by social memorization. In neither instance was there any concern to
preserve what we might think of as the original revelation in the sense of the
first (and only) words to issue from the Prophet's mouth on a given subject.
As we have seen, that notion, though theologically a cornerstone of belief—
the Quran is God's unchanging Word—defies every convention of oral poetry
and performance. Our Quran, like the *Iliad*, is a fixed product standing at the
end of a complex and fluid process.

But if the Quran represents a collection of oral poems, poems, that is,
composed in performance, the Quran is *not* the Iliad: it was regarded by the
one who pronounced it and by those who memorized it as the words of God.
In addition, the speech that issued from the Prophet's mouth had the not
inconsiderable safeguard of careful and frequent repetition by the faithful in
what we shall see was a liturgical setting, and with what we may assume was
the direct supervision of the Prophet. But with the turn in Muhammad's
career at Medina, the suras grow ever longer and more proselike. With the
loss of the mnemonic aids represented by insistent rhyme and assonance, they
would also have become more difficult for all to retain and repeat with any
degree of accuracy. Hence, it is argued, the increasing need for a more stable
and fixed written text. Was, then, Muhammad editing a (dictated?) written
text at Medina, one he could not himself read? Was it then that the shorter
Meccan units began to be inserted in, or perhaps added to the end of, the
dictated Medina suras?

We have enough experience of oral literature and its passage into writing,
even in quite modern times, to understand that when an oral poet or storyteller is performing for or in the presence of one who will commit that performance to writing, there are considerable changes that will take place, changes
that emanate from both the performer's self-consciousness (altered speed,
pace, deliberateness, emphasis) coupled with a desire to impress, and the tran-
scriber's willingness to "improve" what he is hearing. If Muhammad's recitations were really transcribed, as the tradition tells us they were, even as he was
"reciting" them, in short, in performance, then those same conditions might
have occurred. And perhaps they did. We are told the story of Abdullah ibn
Abi Sarh, one of the Prophet's reported amanuenses, who took it upon himself to "improve" the endings of two verses, one at 4:148 and the other
unknown. Even more boldly, he finished a verse the Prophet was dictating

(12:14), at which Muhammad was reported to have said in effect, "Keep it in. That's it exactly!"

But the Quran itself cautions another look. We note a marked change in the suras after we have arranged them in something approximating their chronological order. The revelations delivered at Medina are quite different from the earlier Meccan ones. The high emotion, richly affective images, the rhymes and powerful rhythms of the Meccan poetry have all yielded at Medina to something that is not only longer but far more didactic and prosaic. The high poetic style of the Meccan suras disappears, along with their insistent rhymes and assonances. The oaths, the bold imagery, and the intense fervor of the early poems—we may even call them songs, as we have seen—have yielded to a flatter diction and a lower and more level emotional pitch.

Writing Down the Quran?

The change is generally explained by the Prophet's preaching at Medina to a new audience of believers who needed the more commonplace instruction and encouragement in the new faith rather than urgent exhortations to leave off their idolatry and worship God alone. The change of audience, and so of purpose, from Mecca to Medina is true and important, but is it not equally plausible to think that Muhammad may have found a scribe at Medina? The Medina suras do indeed show some of the signs of a *dictated* text, in circumstances perhaps where the Prophet could no longer *recite* in the earlier bardic style but now had to *pronounce*, and slowly and clearly enough for an unskilled scribe to catch and record it. It is the same man preaching the same message—there were not two Muhammads—but where he once "recited," he now dictates.

This is a hypothesis based mostly on stylistic criteria; more specifically, it is a construct to explain a noticeable change in styles within the same collection, and it is supported in part by the Muslim tradition that parts of the Quran were written down in the Prophet's lifetime, though without suggesting that such took place only at Medina. Nor is there any reference to such a dictation in the Quran itself. It is a plausible explanation of the change in style—the study of early Islam floats on a raft of such surmises, whether medieval Muslim or modern non-Muslim—but the dictation hypothesis also has an adamantine implausibility built into it: the profound unlikelihood of a professional scribe among the date farmers of Medina.

Our surmise about the process of Quranic transcription may be correct, that our present Quran gives indications in its stylistic variations of the transfer of an oral text into written form, but the identification of the time and the place—Medina in the lifetime of the Prophet—is almost certainly wrong. Everything we know about that time and place makes it highly unlikely that there should be in Medina in Muhammad's day a scribe skilled enough to have taken down the suras as dictation. The integration of the oral and memorized Meccan suras into a written text of the later revelations, which have now been divided, quite artificially or mechanically, into suras like the earlier ones, must have taken place later, possibly under the caliph Uthman circa 650, if we give credence to the Muslims' own traditions on the subject.

Whether the Quran was first written down under Uthman or at an even later date, both scenarios carry the alleged dictation of suras into writing away from Muhammad's Medina; they remove the process from Muhammad's own mouth and put it into the ink-stained hands of editor-scribes like the *soferim* who worked on the written text of the Bible in the Second Temple and following centuries. On this hypothesis, it was these later *katibs* who would have composed the Medina suras out of remembered Muhammad material in something approximating the Prophet's diction and style.

Muhammad and the Jews of Medina

We are sometimes referred to the Jews of Medina—there were apparently none living at Mecca—to explain the possibility that there might have been scribes there. The Medina Jews were said by the Muslim tradition to have had a "book"—we must think it was The Book—which Muhammad saw (read?) and accused the Jews of distorting. Such a discussion may well have taken place, but if it did, it had to do with the "Book," that is, Scripture, and not a Hebrew book which neither the local Jews nor Muhammad could read. And if there were "rabbis" at Medina, as is also sometimes said, the normal assumption would be that they were literate. But there is no contemporary trace of such anywhere outside the Yemen and no trace of anything they might have read in either Hebrew or Arabic. It is easier to believe there was an actual Jewish book at Medina than that there was anyone there to read it.

With his own doubtless sincere conviction that he stood in the line of Abraham and Moses, Muhammad may well have expected those Medinese Jews with their *Tawrat* to accept his prophetic claims as willingly as they had his new political charge. They did not, and quickly. Though we are not given the details of what passed between them, the Quran unmistakably reflects Muhammad's reaction to the Jews' rejection of Islam.[8] Certain Muslim practices are changed: no longer would the Submitters pray facing Jerusalem, as all the Jews did; rather, Muslims would henceforth direct their prayers toward the Arabs' own Ka'ba at Mecca (2:142–50). More, the Quran's tone noticeably darkens in references, if not to the still-revered "Israelites" of old, then certainly to the contemporary "Jews" (*Yahud*) who are accused of religious deception, like changing the Scripture to give the lie to Muhammad, and, more consequentially, of political treason. Muhammad was convinced that the Jews of Medina were taking back-channel counsel with his Quraysh enemies at Mecca to unseat and destroy him. The charge is neither impossible nor implausible, and its effects are unmistakable: over the next decade Muhammad first dislodged the Jewish tribes from their properties at Medina, which in the long run solved the problem of the Migrants' insolvency (Q. 33:26–27), and then exiled and finally destroyed the remnant there.

Muhammad's attitude toward the Jews of Medina affected his politics but not his theology. The Quran continued to preach Islam as the natural born successor and heir to both Judaism and Christianity. Moses and Abraham, who was neither an Israelite nor a Jew in Muhammad's regard (3:67), were still prophets of the highest rank, and the Jews never ceased being, like the Christians, "People of the Book," the recipients of an authentic earlier revelation and so eligible for special treatment under Muslim sovereignty. Unless they converted to Islam, pagans were threatened with death wherever they were found. Jews and Christians had only to signal political submission; once surrendered, they were to be permitted to continue in their now distorted but undoubtedly genuine religious beliefs (9:29, 47:4).

Badr Wells

Before there could be political submission, there had to be conquest. That grave step—God had permitted Muslims to take up arms against oppression only during the final dark days at Mecca—was taken two years after the Migration. And not for conquest but as simple revenge and perhaps from desperation. In 624 Muhammad led his Meccan Migrants, not all of them enthusiastic for the venture (Q. 8:5), to the ambush of a Quraysh caravan returning from the north; the encounter took place at a watering hole called Badr Wells.[9] The ambush was a bold and aggressive act of retaliation against the Quraysh, obviously, but it may also have been intended to ease the uncertain economic situation of the Migrants at Medina: in that marginal society one does not simply take in a hundred or so indigent guests for an unlimited stay. Whatever its motive, the venture was an unexpected success against great odds and made an enormous impression on the Medinese, whose wide eyes were taking measure of the loot, one suspects.[10]

The raid at Badr Wells was the *peripateia* in the dramatic life of the Prophet and it changed the fortunes of Islam as well. Muhammad, the preacher of Mecca, had won few souls and had generated a near-fatal animosity there. The Muhammad of Medina, whose mind was clearly still on Mecca and the Quraysh, would likely have done equally poorly in the oasis settlement as a public administrator with a prophetic agenda. But Badr Wells put him in a new light. Were the still-pagan Medinese impressed by the theology of Badr— God was clearly on the Muslims' side, the Quran claimed (8:9–10, 3:123)—or by the size and ease of the spoils? And the dawning prospect of more?

A Failed Response

The Badr Wells attack stirred the Quraysh at Mecca. There were two retalia-tory attacks on Medina. Both of them failed. The first was a serious assault on the oasis, when the Prophet was wounded (3:102–79);[11] the latter a somewhat ineffectual siege (33:9–25).[12] The Arabs of the settlements were unaccustomed to warfare—it was chiefly the Bedouin who entertained and honored them-selves with armed battle—but there seems a singular failure of will on the part of the Quraysh when it came to Muhammad. In any event, they lacked Muhammad's own iron resolve, and it comes almost as an unsurprising anti-climax when in 630 Muhammad and the Muslims interrupt their rolling wave of Arabian conquests to accept the peaceful submission of Mecca.[13] What is perhaps more surprising is that the Prophet then turned his back on his birth-place, with its "House of God," one of the holiest places on earth, and returned to Medina to rule from there rather than from Mecca, just as his successors were to do after him.[14]

The Wives of the Prophet

Neither the Quran, whose intense gaze is generally more elevated, nor even the *Sira*, whose organizing principle is the "Raids of the Prophet," tell us much about the private or personal life of Muhammad. The hadith, on the other hand, are crammed with the most circumstantial details: recollections, leg-ends, and gossip, and perhaps some of it even true. All of it became the grist for the fashioning of a Muslim ethic and a Muslim lifestyle modeled on Muhammad's own behavior. Later biographies of the Prophet, medieval or modern, Muslim or not, have had perforce to lean rather heavily, and rather uncritically, on those Prophetic reports when it comes to Muhammad's private life, which was more easily omitted by the classical *Sira* authors than it was by those who came after them.

There are, however, moments of crisis when the personal does break into the Quran, and most of them have to do with Muhammad's wives. Those latter were, of course, rich fodder for Christian polemicists: the sheer number of them was an obvious witness to Muhammad's unbridled *luxuria*, as was, for the celibacy-riveted Christians, the mere fact that there were wives to begin with. Their number may have troubled some of Muhammad's contemporaries as well. The Quran had specifically permitted the Muslim man as many as four wives, though with conditions (4:3).[15] But Muhammad assuredly had more than four wives, and that fact must have troubled some in Medina since it was addressed by a revelation: if the ladies were agreeable, the Prophet might have as many wives as he wished, "a privilege for you alone and not the rest of the believers."[16]

Two specific incidents were more pointed in the pain they caused the Prophet. The first was his planned marriage at Medina to Zaynab, the wife of Zayd, Muhammad's manumitted slave and then adopted son. Adoption was thought to create a blood tie, and so for Muhammad to marry Zaynab, who had first to be divorced by Zayd, was a breach of the prohibited degree of consanguinity. It was a messy business all round, both the somewhat peremptory divorce and the remarriage, even though later accounts of how ill-suited Zayd and Zaynab were for one another attempted to neaten it up. In the end it took a revelation to end the matter. It was forthcoming in Quran 33:36–37, which told the Medinese in effect to mind their own business and Muhammad to keep Zaynab. The Quran then proceeded to abrogate the taboo against marrying the wives of adopted sons.

A second incident had to do with Muhammad's wife Aisha, the daughter of the early and revered Submitter Abu Bakr. They were betrothed at Mecca when she was six and the union was consummated at Medina when she was nine. Modern critics are here more bothered by the girl's age than were their medieval predecessors and far more than the Muslim reporters, who were not bothered at all. In many societies marriages can be contracted—for that is what they are, contracts—at any time by the principals' agents, and desirable spouses of either gender are spoken for early, sometimes, with royalty, in the womb. And in many societies too the age of puberty is the de facto age of consent. Aisha we assume reached puberty, not altogether unusually, at nine, just as we assume that Jesus' mother Mary was perhaps about twelve— betrothed at ten?—when her pregnancy was announced.

L'Affaire Aisha that is commented on in the Quran—her name is not mentioned—had nothing to do with her age, which never comes up, but concerns a scandal that spread among the believers and for which the Quran chastises them at length (24:11–20), without going into the details. The details are supplied by the *Sira* tradition, as reported by Aisha herself.[17] Aisha had been taken on one of the Prophet's raids. On the return she had by mischance become separated from the main group and was discovered by one of the other troopers who escorted her back to Medina. At their late arrival together tongues began to wag. When questioned Aisha swore to the Prophet that nothing untoward had occurred, but the business was not ended until Quran 24:11 was sent down in exoneration. And in a postscript, the Quran tightened the rules for evidence.

The Establishment of Islam

From Badr Wells to his death in 632, Muhammad was engaged in two major enterprises, the unfolding of the religious culture of Islam through Quranic revelation and his own personal instruction and counsel, and the construction and consolidation of the community of Muslims, the shaping of a political culture. The two are kept relatively separate in our sources. The Medina chapters of the Quran are devoted entirely to the first; the storms and stress of the Muslims' military adventures find only the faintest of echoes there. For the latter, one must turn to the later literary sources, the standard *Life* of the Prophet and the triumphant genre called "The Raids." We may be interested in other things, but for the Muslim historians, these "raids" were in fact the chief matter of Muhammad's life at Medina.

It was at Medina surely that the cult practices of Islam first began to be publicly deployed: the often clandestine prayer at Mecca now became the prescribed daily prayers, including the noon prayer on Friday when the entire community crowded into Muhammad's courtyard—the prototype of the later mosque—to hear his instructions and exhortation;[18] the payment of the tithe (*zakat*) for the support of the needy (9:29); the fast during the lunar month of Ramadan (2:185); and, belatedly, the hajj or ritual pilgrimage to the holy places in and around Mecca which Muhammad made as a Muslim—it was a long-established pre-Islamic ritual at Mecca adapted into Islam—for the first and last time just before his death (2:196–99, 22:27–32).[19] The Quran, meanwhile, continued to answer questions, resolve doubts and disputes, stiffen resolve.

Submission

The Muslims at Medina were, in a phrase used to describe the Christians of Spain during the Reconquista, a "society in arms." For the eight years of Muhammad's life after Badr Wells, the unprovoked military forays called raids were almost continuous. And almost always successful. The surrounding settlements were approached and submission demanded. In the case of pagans, the submission was both political and religious: they had to accept the sovereignty both of the Muslims who stood poised before them and of Islam, or else be destroyed. And once Muslims, they had to pay the religious tithe into the Muslim treasury at Medina. If they were Jews or Christians, they had, as has already been noted, to accept only Muslim political sovereignty and, of course, pay the tributary poll-tax (*jizya*) that accompanied it.

Imperium Islamicum

In such circumstances, there is little talk of, and obviously little time for, date-palm cultivation at Medina. The oasis was becoming an imperial city, and if the Muslim imperium was still, during Muhammad's lifetime, limited to Arabia and the southern reaches of what is today Jordan, it soon passed extravagantly beyond those frontiers. The Prophet, whether he intended it or not, and he seemingly had not, had created not merely a church, to use more modern terms, but also a state; and he stood, without competition from either a pretender or a priesthood, at the head of both. The Frankish Christians had to counterfeit a document to pass temporal authority from the hands of an emperor into those of a pope. The Muslims had no need. In this sense Muhammad was his own Constantine and his own Sylvester, an emperor and a pope who did not require two swords but only the sharp two-edged scimitar he had forged himself.

Death

Muhammad died in 632 and, according to her own account, it was at Medina in the apartment and arms of his wife Aisha.[20] He was at the height of his spiritual and political power, and though he would have been sixty-two years old by the traditional chronology, he may very well have been somewhat younger than that. He was carried off by an unspecified illness whose onset was unattended but which permitted him to linger for two weeks before expiring. So his death, though unexpected, was not surprising. He was buried in his own compound at Medina.

Afterthoughts: Politics and Piety

At Medina Muhammad became the head of a functioning community, at first an apparently civil one as envisioned in the Medina Accords, but soon, with the expulsion of the Jews and the rapid conversion of the Medinese, there emerged the *umma*, a community that was at the same time, and inextricably, religious and political and that recognized him as its leader. During the last ten years of his life Muhammad was, in short, both prophet and statesman, pope and emperor. Jesus, on the other hand, showed no interest in politics— "My kingdom is not of this world" (Jn 18:36). For someone to show no interest in politics in first-century Palestine was no simple matter,[21] and the Gospels seem to go out of their way to show how Jesus avoided the political traps that his hostile questioners often set for him. And yet, for all that, Jesus was executed by a political authority on what appear to be political charges. "Kingdom," it is clear, was a term that could cut many ways in Roman Palestine, some of them fatal.

If we cannot always come to term with Jesus' political views, it is clear he wielded no political power. While he was undoubtedly regarded as a leader by his disciples—that latter term already suggests they were after all more like the students of a teacher rather than militants in an Army of God—it is difficult to recognize in that band of itinerants a society, or even a movement, in any ordinary sense. In any event, it was effectively ended with Jesus' death and the fellowship had to be reconstituted by his followers afterward. Jesus had no personal role in the shaping of his community, his *ekklesia*. That was the work of his heirs, including some, like Paul, who had never even known him in the flesh.

8

A New Dawn: The Aftermath, the Legacy

Jesus was dead in Jerusalem at thirty-four, the victim of a disgraceful execution at the hands of Judea's foreign oppressors. Muhammad, who had earlier escaped a death threat from far more familiar enemies, died in his bed at Medina of natural causes at the age of sixty-two, it was said, though he was more likely in his fifties. The only symmetry between the two men is that they may have begun their careers at roughly the same age, in their early thirties. Jesus' public life lasted only a scant two or three years, however, while Muhammad's stretched over twenty-two or twenty-three.

Jesus, the Aftermath

The New Testament Gospels, which are our principal source for his life, end their account of Jesus in Jerusalem with his corpse being taken down from the cross on which he died and being placed in a nearby rock-hewn tomb chamber. A stone was rolled across the entry to protect the body from animal scavengers and, just possibly, tomb robbers with either political or theological intent on their minds. Matthew introduces exactly that notion. He has the priests and the Pharisees go to Pilate and request a guard for the tomb to prevent Jesus' followers from stealing the body and claiming that "he has risen from the dead" (27:62–66). There is a narrative follow-up (28:11–14). When the empty tomb is discovered, Matthew tells us, the same priests bribe the Roman guard to tell Pilate that that was exactly what happened. They do so, and then we reach the point of Matthew's tale and at the same time are given a rare glimpse of contemporary Jewish reaction to Jesus. "The story became widely known and is current in Jewish circles to this day," the author instructs us (28:15).

It was not an entirely glorious end to the very short and not terribly successful career of Jesus of Nazareth, an itinerant Galilean charismatic who claimed to be Daniel's messianic "Son of Man." He had managed to stir some local waters and even make a small splash in Jerusalem. He had attracted some followers, not very many apparently, and had somewhat inexplicably made enemies in high places, and it was they who did him in. The leader was dead and his followers dispersed, though none of them was either arrested or pursued at this point. But then, on the Sunday following Jesus' Friday Passover execution, a new story began to circulate, or so the Gospel accounts tell us: Jesus of Nazareth had risen from the dead!

It is at this point, where Jesus' followers become most engaged, that the modern historian loses control of the Jesus story: the risen Christ is not an appropriate or even a viable subject of historical inquiry. But there is in fact historical matter here, not least in the nature of the construction and obviously successful presentation of this critical element in his followers' case for Jesus.

The Empty Tomb

If we draw a line through the other two Synoptics at the point where the original version of Mark's Gospel seems to end or to be broken off (Mk 16:8 = Mt 28:8; Lk 24:9), we are left with the unanimously attested fact of Jesus' empty tomb and the problematic detail of the large stone that had to be used to close it. We can assume that when this story was first told, everyone was aware that the empty tomb was discovered on Sunday at dawn—again there is agreement of this detail—by the women who were quite plausibly going to complete the formal service of washing and anointing the corpse.[1] If everyone knew that the women were the first on the scene, the closure of the tomb would represent a problem, not perhaps for his male followers if they had been the first to arrive, but certainly for the women.

The problem is solved supernaturally. Mark does not say exactly how, but when the women arrive the tomb is open and there is a young man dressed in a dazzlingly supernatural white robe inside who tells them that Jesus has risen and gone ahead to Galilee (16:5). And he makes a special point of underlining the fact that the tomb is *empty*. Who took care of the large stone? Matthew alone spells out the implication of the young man in dazzling white: "There was a great earthquake. An angel of the Lord descended from heaven and rolled back the stone and then sat upon it" (28:2).

So, the witnesses agree, it was some of Jesus' women followers who discovered Jesus' empty tomb that Sunday outside the walls of Jerusalem. And, it was further agreed, one of them, indeed, the chief of them and the only constant in all the accounts, is Mary Magdelene, Mary from Migdal, a Galilean fishing village, "from whom Jesus had cast out seven demons" (Mk 16:9).[2]

All four Gospels agree, it was Mary Magdalene, together with the two other women who had stood by the cross at the end, who went to the tomb that Sunday morning.[3] They found the stone moved back from its entry and the chamber empty. They are greeted by an angel, in Matthew the same who had rolled back the stone. He tells them not to be afraid, that Jesus has risen from the dead and returned to Galilee. "Tell the disciples," they are instructed (Mt 28:7; Lk 24:9). The Apostles are skeptical of the story (Lk 24:10–11), but in the end Peter, and perhaps John (20:3), go to investigate. The tomb is indeed empty, they discover. The Fourth Gospel has a more circumstantial account (Jn 20:1–10). The two men enter the tomb, Peter explicitly the first, and they find the discarded shroud lying there. They leave but Mary Magdalene remains in the garden. Jesus suddenly appears to her. She at first mistakes him for the gardener, but when she finally recognizes him and attempts to embrace him, she is somewhat mysteriously told, "Do not touch me for I am not yet ascended to the Father" (Jn 20:11–18).[4] He instructs her to go and tell his disciples that he is "ascending to my Father and your Father, to my God and your God."

These are the accounts in sum of what was remembered to have occurred immediately after Jesus' crucifixion. When we look more closely at the evidence, we note that, if the angel is removed, the testimony is relatively straightforward: some women among Jesus' followers discover, near dawn on Sunday and thus some forty hours after his burial, that Jesus' tomb is empty. This much information, which was easily verifiable, is not likely to have been invented. Attached to it is a further piece of information from the angelic young man seated, or standing, inside the tomb: "He is risen. He is not here" (Mk 16:6). Stop, the historian says. It may be granted, on the face of it, that he was not there; that he had risen from the dead is an entirely different matter.

The Resurrection Accounts

Of our four chief sources on Jesus, one, the sayings source Q, appears to be unaware of—or ignores—both the death and the resurrection of Jesus, while another, the Gospel of Mark, knows about the empty tomb but seems almost oblivious of the reports of the resurrected Jesus.[5] Almost, but not quite, as we have seen. Mark 16:7 has that "young man ... wearing a white robe" and seated at the right of the burial place say to the faithful women who found Jesus' tomb open and empty that Sunday morning, "He has been raised; he is not here. . . . Go and say to his disciples and Peter, 'He is going ahead of you into Galilee; there you will see him, as he told you.'" But the story ends there in its original Markan version: we are not taken to Galilee; we do not see the risen Jesus. The only source to put the risen Jesus at the tomb itself is John, who, as we just saw, had Jesus appear to Mary Magdalene in the burial garden even before he presented himself to the Twelve.

Paul

Our fourth source, Paul—and indeed the authors of all the other documents in the New Testament—takes the resurrection of Jesus of Nazareth from the dead very much for granted. Paul, who is almost certainly the earliest of all our sources on Jesus and his movement, wrote to his fellow believers in Corinth in the late 50s concerning what he had passed on to them even earlier, namely, "the tradition I had received . . . that he [Jesus] was buried and raised to life on the third day, in accordance with the Scripture" (1 Cor 15:4). This is, like the angel's pronouncement to the women at the tomb, an assertion, not a descriptive narrative.

But Paul is not finished. Belief in the resurrection of Jesus was the cornerstone of the new faith. Without the resurrection, Paul tells the believers, "my preaching is in vain and your faith is empty" (1 Cor 15:17). This crucial event must be verified, and for Paul and everyone else, the reality of Jesus' resurrection from the dead was unassailably demonstrated by his postcrucifixion and postburial appearance to a number of people. According to Paul, and we must assume he was repeating what had become by then a Christian formula, the risen Jesus had appeared "to Cephas [Peter] and then to the Twelve," as well as to other witnesses—no mention of Mary Magdalene here—"to 500 of the Brethren at one time, most of whom are still alive, though some have passed away. Then he appeared to James and then to all the Apostles" (1 Cor 15:3–8).

This oddly constructed collection of witnesses concludes on a note of special pleading that does not add to our (modern) confidence: "Last of all," Paul says, "he appeared to me too" (15:9). By his own testimony, Paul, who had never met or seen Jesus in the flesh, had had a very personal "experience" of him—to keep the term open—on the road to Damascus (Gal 1:15–16). It is described three times by Luke, in Acts 9:3–9, 22:6–11, and 26:12–18, and each time as an aural/oral encounter. Paul hears and speaks with Jesus; he does not, apparently, see him. Is this when Jesus "appeared" to Paul? Whatever the circumstance, this encounter is most probably the basis of Paul's authority as an "Apostle": "No one taught me (the Gospel) . . . I received it through a revelation of Jesus Christ" (Gal 1:12).

His own "experience" apart, Paul's "tradition" of resurrection appearances seems to go back to an even earlier time, most likely to his first two-week meeting with Peter and James in Jerusalem (Gal 1:18–19), which occurred perhaps as early as AD 37. Earlier too is likely the formulation in the opening of Romans (1:4), that "he [Jesus] was proclaimed Son of God by an act of power that raised him from the dead."

Uncertainties

If the resurrection was the cornerstone of the new Christian movement, "new" in the sense that it was not part of Jesus' own "Good News," why was it not mentioned in Q and only uncertainly included as an afterthought in Mark? The simplest solution is that Q was collected or composed as a record—whatever its purpose—of Jesus' sayings, perhaps during his lifetime, or perhaps immediately after his death since that event seems to be only faintly reflected in the collection, and certainly before the resurrection stories began to circulate. Mark's Gospel presents a more difficult problem. It is a composition one of whose purposes, and perhaps its chief purpose, was, on the face of it, to explain Jesus' death by execution. It does this in detail, and while it mentions, almost in passing, the fact of his resurrection (16:7), it seems unaware of the importance of the appearance witnesses who in Paul stand so central to the proof that the resurrection in fact occurred.

As already noted, fixing the date of Mark, the earliest of the Gospels, hangs solely on the ability to find convincing mention of the actual siege and destruction of Jerusalem in chapter 13 of that Gospel. To the few who are unable to find it there, the date of Mark must inevitably be moved back to somewhere before AD 70, though exactly where is an open question. It is conceivable, then, that, given the absence of an address to the resurrection, Mark was written even earlier than Paul, at a time and a place that saw the crucifixion of the Messiah as the central issue. The alternative explanation is keep the traditional dating of circa AD 70 and think rather that the original ending, with the resurrection appearances already predicted in 16:7, was lost from Mark's Gospel, which would explain the grammatical awkwardness of verse 8—and that someone later tried to correct the loss by adding the so-called Markan Appendix (vv. 9–20), which is substantially the same as Matthew's post-resurrection account (Mt 28:8–20).

All three of the Synoptics betray odd pre-Pauline characteristics. They know the *story* of Jesus—and Paul shows he knows it too, even though he is not about to tell it—but their understanding of Jesus is essentially messianic.

Jesus is the Jewish Messiah, as proved by his fulfillment of all the biblical prophecies of the Anointed. Though the commonly held opinion is that the Gospels were composed after Paul's letters of the 50s, they are very un-Pauline documents. They share very few of Paul's theological and ecclesiastical concerns. Could Matthew's and Luke's Gospels be pre-Pauline as well? The only thing certain about the dating of Matthew and Luke is that they are later than Mark. And if most think that the Roman destruction of Jerusalem is even clearer here than in Mark—Luke 21:20 is often cited in evidence—it should be remembered that volume 2 of Luke's work, the Acts of the Apostles, breaks off at about AD 60. If that is the *terminus ante quem* of Acts, then Luke's Gospel must have been composed even earlier, perhaps in the late 50s, and apparently before Paul's letters were in general circulation.

The Witnesses

All four of the New Testament Gospels tell us what happened after the crucifixion, though all of them appear, as documents, to have been the subject of some second thoughts, that is, pieces of text may have been added at their endings.[6] These are not particularly noticeable in Matthew (28:16–20) nor in Luke (24:44–53), but in both instances appearances of Jesus are linked, and become secondary, to his instructions to the Apostles, which are, in effect, to go forth and spread the Good News, which is now no longer simply his own teaching but the meaning of his death and resurrection, and to "make disciples of all nations."

Appended Thoughts

In the case of Mark we have, as already noted, a full-fledged appendix (16:9–20) attached to the text, which we cannot be certain was the near-contemporary completion of a broken-off text or a later addition to a text already in circulation. But in the final instance, the appendix to John's Gospel (21:1–25), after its quite formal conclusion at 20:30–31, makes it certain that we are dealing with an addition to an already complete Gospel. It is, however, not so much an afterthought as an interpolation. It retells a story of the Apostles making a miraculous catch while fishing—in John, at night—in the Sea of Galilee. In Luke the same story is positioned early on in the ministry to lead into the call of those fishermen to be his chosen disciples; in John, it serves as a miraculous appearance of the risen Jesus—rather precisely, the third to his disciples after his resurrection—and so Jesus also shares in a fish meal with the Apostles.

But John's account does not end where Luke's does. It continues (15–25), "when they had finished breakfast," with the focus now on Peter, whom Jesus empowers—"feed my sheep"—and then predicts Peter's death, which likely occurred in Rome in the mid- or late 60s. Jesus then turns to "the disciple whom Jesus loved" (21:20), later (v. 24) identified as the author of the Gospel. "He will remain until I come," Jesus mysteriously says (v. 22). The Christian tradition stretched the life of this John for as far as it would go, but when he died in Ephesus, perhaps sometime about AD 100, it was said, the Lord had still not come.

Authenticating

These various quite jumbled accounts of Jesus' appearances after his death—some point to Jerusalem, others toward Galilee—seem to have two objectives in the Gospels. The first is to verify that Jesus was indeed resurrected, but neither as a ghost or wraith, nor yet as simply resuscitated. The recognition scenes have an odd quality to them: the witnesses seem to be struggling with the otherness and the sameness of what they had seen. Jesus, we have just remarked, warned Mary Magdalene, who had trouble recognizing him, not to touch him since he had "not yet ascended to the Father." Two disciples who randomly encounter him on their way to Emmaus do not recognize him either, but soon a very substantial Jesus is sitting down to a meal with them (Lk 24:13–35). On another occasion Jesus seems to pass through a closed door to join the Apostles (Jn 20:26). He eats with them—eating seems to be a guarantee of genuine corporeality—and invites a doubting Thomas, who had been absent on an earlier occasion, to touch his wounds (Jn 20:27).

Empowerment and Commission

The post-resurrection texts are equally or perhaps more interested in another project: validating the authority and the mission of the Apostles. "Go and make disciples of all nations," Jesus solemnly intones, "baptizing them in the name of the Father and the Son and the Holy Spirit.... Yes, and I am with you always, even to the end of the world" (Mt 28:18–20). "He who believes and is baptized will be saved," Jesus promises in the Markan Appendix. "He who does not believe will be condemned. These signs will accompany the believers: in my name they will cast out demons; they will speak in new tongues; they will lift up serpents and if they drink any deadly thing, it will not hurt them; they will lay their hands on the sick, who will then recover" (Mk 16:15–18).

It is clear, then, that the communities that stood behind the Gospels believed that the Twelve, and perhaps others as well, had been commissioned by Jesus to carry his message not only to their fellow Jews but to "all nations." Those "nations" were, under the same name (Greek *ethne* > Latin *gentes)*, the familiar "Gentiles" or *goyyim,* all those who were not Jews. That is not what we witness, however. The Acts of the Apostles shows the earliest believers preaching the risen Jesus inside Jewish synagogues of the eastern Mediterranean Diaspora (Acts 13:26, 43, 48, etc.), where in that era Gentiles constituted a small but welcome audience of interested parties, and even occasionally in more public non-Jewish venues (Acts 17:17, 19:9–10).

The mission to Gentiles as such was a more complex and difficult business. Paul and his companion Barnabas made a rather strong impression on many of their Gentile listeners, strong enough, at any rate, to make the local Jews uncomfortable. Paul responded that he had in fact a divinely appointed mission to be "a light for the Gentiles." He had had to preach the Good News to the Jews first, of course, "but since you reject it, we now turn to the Gentiles" (Acts 13:46–47). This was not a casual cultural brush in a provincial Anatolian town. The issue had arisen earlier when Peter, who was most certainly the most authoritative of the Twelve, had first associated with and then baptized a Roman centurion and his family (Acts 10:48). The other Apostles in Jerusalem were upset at this violation of Jewish purity statutes. Peter had managed to pacify them (11:18), but Paul's activities raised the question anew. Could one be a follower of Jesus without being a Jew? Without being circumcised?

The question was answered pragmatically and without a great deal of conviction at a meeting of the mother assembly in Jerusalem, perhaps in AD 49. Preaching and baptizing could go on among the Gentiles, it was ruled; these latter had merely to observe a few basic rules—to avoid unkosher meat, which would allow the new Gentile converts to share in the presumably still-kosher community meals with their Jewish brethren, and to refrain from various, though unspecified, sexual practices common among the pagans (Acts 15). Whether observed or ignored, the stipulations are never heard of again and Paul's mission to the Gentiles went on with new energy and growing success.

The question, then, is whether Jesus himself had commissioned, or even envisioned, a mission to the Gentiles as he is portrayed doing in his postresurrection appearance. Had Jesus in fact said, "Go then to all nations and make them my disciples . . ." (Mt 28:19)? The reports from his own lifetime are quite different, however. At one point Jesus is made to say quite specifically to the

Twelve, "Do not take the road to Gentile lands. . . . Go rather to the lost sheep of Israel" (Mt 10:5–6), and on another occasion, when confronted by a local Gentile woman begging a cure, Jesus remarks, "I was sent to the lost sheep of the house of Israel and to them alone" (Mt 15:24), though in the end he grants her request and cleanses and heals her daughter.

Equally telling is Jesus' address to the Torah's purity laws. He was not as strict in his observance as the contemporary Pharisees (Mk 2:15–28), and there is common testimony in the Gospels that he envisioned some modification, if not of the purity laws themselves, then in the way Jews ought to understand them. "Nothing that goes into a person from the outside can defile him," Jesus says, "because it does not go into his heart but into his stomach" (Mk 7:18). But what is suspect is Mark's own conclusion that immediately follows: "By saying this he declared all foods clean" (7:19). The remark is not only contradicted by Jesus' own reported behavior but by the clear evidence that none of his followers thought he had done any such thing.

In Acts, Peter, who cries out to God, "I have never eaten anything that is unclean!" (10:14), has to be reassured by a vision from on high that it is permissible to associate with Gentiles, even a God-fearer like Cornelius (10:28). And later he is publicly accused of transgression by his fellow Christians: "You have been visiting men who are uncircumcised, sitting at table with them" (11:3). And Paul too, as we have seen, encountered the same kind of opposition from Jesus' immediate followers. It seems, then, highly unlikely that Jesus thought of his message as intended for Gentiles or that he instructed his followers to carry it to any but Jews.

The End

John ends his Gospel with a literary flourish: "Jesus did many other signs in the presence of the Apostles and the disciples, which are not written in this book. But these are written that you might believe that Jesus is the Messiah, the Son of God, and that believing you may have life in his name" (20:30–31).[7] But Mark and then Luke look elsewhere to write finis to the history of Jesus. "And then the Lord Jesus, after he had spoken to them, was taken up into heaven and sat down at the right hand of God," says the Markan Appendix (16:19). Luke writes, "Then he led them out as far as Bethany, and lifting up his hands he blessed them. While he blessed them, he parted from them and was carried up to heaven" (24:50–51).[8] That final trip to Bethany is, however, another one that the historian must decline making.

Muhammad, the Legacy

The Jesus story ends with the historian attempting, not terribly successfully, to pick his way among six, perhaps even eight, different narrative patches on the events that followed Jesus' death and burial. The documentation of Muhammad's end is quite different. The Quran had of course fallen silent at some unknown point before the Prophet's death, and the *sira* tradition's account of Muhammad's death, which derived from his wife Aisha, is quiet and relatively free of special pleading.[9]

A Prophet without Miracles

Muhammad made no specific or personal claims for himself. The point was the message, not the messenger. The authority of the messenger was in play, of course, and Muhammad had trouble positioning himself on the spectrum of charismatics available to his audience. They put him, and with some justification, among the familiar mantic poets; he urged a different model, that of a messenger-prophet (*nabi, rasul*) of the familiar Arabian type like Hud (Q. 7:65–72, etc.) or Salih (7:73–79, etc.) or, what Muhammad preferred, that of the presumably less well-known biblical prophets, who are invoked often and length in the Quran: an entire sura (21) is devoted to them.

One pervasive feature of the Quran's stories of the prophets is the miracles they performed as signs of their calling. Moses and Jesus both produced such "signs" (*ayat*),[10] and so it is not unexpected that Muhammad's audience should expect just such a "sign" from the prophet who stood before them in the Haram (6:37, 13:7, 21:5). Muhammad stoutly refused to perform any of what the Gospels call "deeds of power"; the Quran was the only miracle required to demonstrate that he was the envoy of God, and the notion became so embedded that the verses of the Quran eventually came themselves to be called *ayat* or "signs" (cf. 24:1, 31:2).

There is no reason, then, that either we or his contemporaries should expect that Muhammad's career be capped with some divine vindication. He had made no claim to function as a *mahdi* or eschatological guide; indeed, such a messiahlike figure appears nowhere in the Quran's various scenarios of the End Time.[11] Nor did Muhammad require a miracle to repair the damage of a catastrophic end: he died of natural causes at the height of what had turned out to be a successful career as both prophet and statesman.

The Miracle of Badr Wells

If there was a miracle in the Prophet's life, it occurred earlier. Muslim tradition tends to regard as miraculous Muhammad's safe escape from Mecca, as perhaps it was. But what had an even greater claim to the marvelous was what had occurred at the watering hole of Badr Wells two years after the Prophet's danger-fraught arrival in Medina. He had been brought to the oasis to resolve its growing civil strife. Instead, his arrival provoked new strife, this between himself and the Jews of Medina who, to all appearances, were living in relative peace, albeit as clients, with the paramount Arab tribes there. There may have been other problems as well, the integration of the new Meccan "Migrants" and their families into the pinched economy of the agricultural settlement.

Muhammad dealt with the recusant Jews quickly and fiercely, as we have seen. Some of the Medinese Arabs were discomforted at the treatment of their Jewish clients, but if they intended to take action against Muhammad, which seems unlikely, they were soon presented with another, more consuming event. Muhammad's attack and looting of the Meccan caravan traveling homeward through Badr Wells may have been intended to remedy the financial plight of the Migrants, but it was a casus belli for the not terribly bellicose date farmers of Medina. The *bellum* came and the Meccans turned out to be as unbellicose as the Medinese and militarily inept in the bargain.

Badr Wells had the making of a disaster for both Muhammad and the Medinese, but it turned out to be something considerably more rewarding. The unexpected and enriching success of what must have appeared a foolhardy venture was not lost on the Medinese. Muhammad told all who would listen that it was God's inevitable victory against daunting odds (Q. 3:121–27). We cannot say how impressed the Medinese oasis farmers were by the theological argument, but there was no gainsaying the results. The Migrants had left the oasis poor and returned rich.

Muhammad's fortunes began to change immediately after Badr Wells. The Medinese embraced Islam—the Prophet was not always sure of the sincerity of what the Quran calls "the hypocrites" (3:167–68, etc.)—and they joined what became annual raids against an ever-widening arc of neighboring settlements. The results were tallied in plunder from those foolish enough to resist and tribute or tithe from those wise enough to read the new writing on the Arabian sands. It was a mighty triumph for a man who had only recently been begging for asylum from his murderously vengeful enemies.

The Death of the Prophet

Muhammad died of an indeterminate illness in AD 632, aged sixty-two by the traditional chronology but somewhat younger than that by our own informed guess. He had been ill for a while, so his death could not have been unexpected. Yet his companions in faith and arms appear mildly surprised. What is more surprising to us perhaps is that he made no provision whatsoever for his successor. The Quran already describes Muhammad as "the seal" or the last of the prophets (33:40) so in that sense there could be no successor, nor was there for Muslims.[12] But this charismatic "warner" was also the head of a political society that he and the Quran had created, and yet he made no move to signal who should govern it in his place or, indeed, how. His followers were left to answer both questions as best they could.[13]

As we have seen, Muhammad's Meccan audience had demanded miracles of him (17:90–92). He refused. He was, he insisted, merely a mortal (18:110). The Islamic tradition continues to affirm his mortality, particularly in the face of what are in Muslim eyes the extraordinary Christian claims of divinity for Jesus, who was a prophet—and mortal—as the Quran insists (3:59) and as Muslims freely recognize. And yet, with the passage of time, the stature of Muhammad has grown in its own extraordinary fashion. The once unmiraculous Muhammad has been provided with many miracles in the hadith or Prophetic reports that fill the pages of Bukhari's *Sahih*, and the earthbound mortal, who had been taught by God to resist the notion of a "ladder to heaven" (17:93), mounted to heaven as surely as Jesus was thought to have, Jesus to remain there until his distant Second Coming, Muhammad to return to Mecca and his prophetic career on the very same night that his journey began.

A Man without Sin

Muslim traditionalists may continue to resist, with diminishing success, the annual celebration of the Prophet's birthday,[14] but Muslim theologians have granted Muhammad, without demur, the gift of impeccability (*'isma*) or freedom from the possibility of either sin or error. If Mary's virginity *a parte post* has spread quite remarkably among Christians, so too has the Prophet's impeccability *a parte ante* among Muslims. Despite many indications to the contrary, including a reference in the Quran—"Did we not find you wandering and give you the Guidance?" (93:7)[15]—that Muhammad before his call to prophecy participated in the ordinary ritual life of Mecca, including the cults in and around the Ka'ba and most specifically the complex called the *'umra* and the hajj, the subsequent Muslim tradition would keep him prophylactically remote from all such pagan-tainted practices. It appears as dogma for the first time in the so-called *Fikh Akbar II*, a tenth-century Muslim creed that states, in Article 8, "All prophets are exempt from sins, both light and grave, from unbelief and sordid deeds. Yet stumbling and mistakes may happen on their part." And Article 9 adds, "Muhammad is His beloved, His Apostle, His Prophet, His chosen and elect. He did not serve idols, nor was he at any time a polytheist, even for a single moment. And he never committed a grave or light sin."[16]

"A Beautiful Pattern"

It is an easy step from being free of every sin to being the possessor of every virtue, and soon this was the status granted to the Prophet. Muhammad was not only the cosmic Perfect Man of Islamic esotericism; he was also the human embodiment of perfect "submission," the Muslim par excellence—the Quran has God Himself refer to His prophet as "a beautiful pattern" (33:21)—and as such, a paradigm of human, and particularly Muslim, behavior.

Like his monotheistic coreligionists, the Muslim derives from the revealed Word of God general precepts of morality as well as both counsels and detailed prescriptions on behavior. The Quran is addressed in the first instance to all humankind, calling them to goodness, to justice, equity, and particularly righteousness. The message of the Meccan Quran in particular was intended for all who were willing to listen, but as the message and the mission proceeded, the Quran's instruction was increasingly directed, without any formal change in address, to the Muslims who make up the community. Hence, the Quran is both the "Guidance"—a frequent self-characterization—for all humanity and, more precisely, a manual of behavior for the Muslim believer.

The Prophetic Reports

Muhammad himself lies well concealed behind the Quran, which was delivered through him but is only occasionally about him. But outside the Quran, there is no such reticence. There was in early circulation an enormous body of hadith, Prophetic reports, that professed to give the Prophet's own moral instruction on almost every conceivable subject and provided, moreover, vivid vignettes of Muhammad at prayer and at meals, on campaign and *en famille*, as husband, father, judge, statesman, and military strategist. Both the private Muhammad and the public Prophet are on full display in the hadith.

Though there are some personal details in the classical biographical tradition, the works that applied vivid flesh and lively blood to the portrait of the Prophet belong to a somewhat different Muslim literary genre. These latter, called either "The Proofs of Prophecy" or "The Good Qualities (of the Prophet)," are essentially collections of anecdotes, and as such they stand much closer to hagiography than to biography. Like the apocryphal Gospels of the Christian tradition, they present the life of their subject after a fashion, but their chief interest is in the Prophet's personality, character, appearance, and miracles. The earliest example of the type dates from the late ninth century, and though the genre has had a long history in Islam, most of the later works merely expand and elaborate the earlier glowing portraits of the traits, human and more than human, of the Prophet of Islam.

The *Adab* of the Prophet

Tradition provides, then, a fully fleshed-out if at times self-contradictory portrait of the Prophet, and it has served from the time of its construction in the eighth century down to the present as the template and measure of the ideal Muslim life. And not merely in matters of moral choice. The hadith offer a broad and varied menu of preferred social behavior, of etiquette rather than morality, and that latter notion of etiquette (*adab*) was later integrated into Islamic moral thinking generally. At the outset *adab* was a conservative term in a tribal society: the appropriate behavior was the traditional behavior, and *adab* stood at not too great a remove from *sunna*, "customary behavior." And as it did with sunna, the "sending down" of the Quran affected a revolution in adab. Tribal etiquette no longer sufficed; in Islam only a Muhammad adab would do.

That personal adab of the Prophet was handed down to future generations of Muslims through the great body of hadith testifying to the sayings and doings of Muhammad. Very many of those sayings have to do with what the Jews call *halakha* or regulated behavior: they provide prescriptive guidance in moral matters and as such have been built into the foundations of Islamic law. But a great many more are simply the Prophet's "table talk," or perhaps better, domestic conversations, since the majority of them come down to us on the testimony of his wife Aisha. In them, and in the many anecdotes passed on through the hadith, Islam received a rich and detailed portrait of the Prophet's adab.

The sketch of Jesus' lifestyle in the Gospels is limited by the brevity of Jesus' public life, the evangelists' staying carefully on message and, in the end, straitened by the believers' understanding that Jesus was, after all, the Son of

God. Muhammad's humanity was visible to all, however, and more, he was in the public eye for twenty-two years in the most varied of circumstances. The reports on Muhammad, if the authenticity of some of them is doubtful, are nonetheless full and plentiful, full enough, in any event, to provide the believer with a life-scaled and complex model of a Muslim manner of living.

One result of this profusion of information about the personal adab of the Prophet is that Islamic behavior has, in addition to an internal moral code and prescriptive regulations regarding behavior, a sense of a particular lifestyle not immediately present in either Judaism or Christianity, both of which prefer epigone models, a Francis of Assisi—whose own appropriation of the Jesus adab proved unsustainable—or one of the Eastern European *rebbes* who stand behind the Hasidic movement. This Muslim lifestyle is psychologically reinforced, doubtless, by the residual Arabism that rests at the bottom of Muslim identity, but the pervasiveness of the Prophetic adab is real enough and apparent in the relentlessly male Muslim society. It is visible in everything from dress and dining to the manner of prayer, particularly the Friday community prayer which is so obviously a common exercise performed in the most exquisite unison and at the same time an unmistakably individual, almost solipsistic, communion with the divine.

Muhammad the Man

The historian may make his own assessment. Muhammad was, on the face of it, a religious and political genius in that he fashioned, as single-handedly as history allows any individual, both a religious culture and a political society, both of them of enormous scope, that not only have persisted to this day but are still vital and growing. And the stamp of his personality remains on both. The pacific Jesus has often disappeared behind an exceedingly militant Christianity, but the militant, flexible Muhammad still is at the helm of Islam, and his powerfully vigorous yet controlled personality, his personal piety and heroic perseverance remain at the center of Muslim character.

If we narrow the focus somewhat, a distinct and complex personality emerges, a man who is neither the devil of Christian polemic nor the saint of Muslim hagiography. Politically Muhammad was relentless, even ruthless; pragmatic rather than an ideologue, but unbending on the core values of Islam; thin-skinned to a fault, quick to blame and equally quick to forgive; possessed of piety but the very antithesis of pious; famously uxorious yet married, monogamously, to the same woman for twenty-four years: she the mother of all his surviving children and their only daughters in a society that valued male heirs above all else; excessive in little besides energy and profound conviction; and generous, always generous.

There is far too much evidence on Muhammad: the "Prophetic reports" are a limitless sea of information, all of it professing to have come down from reliable eyewitnesses, but much if not most of it doubtlessly invented. From them the interested party may fashion whatever portrait suits the occasion or one's own persuasion. It was probably so from the very beginning and it will doubtless continue to be so for as long as the extraordinary edifice that he fathered stands.

Afterthoughts: Portraits from Life

Jesus is a more clearly defined figure in Christendom than Muhammad in Islam, not because the evidence for Jesus is better or more plentiful or more detailed—it is not—but by reason of the artistic tradition of the cultures in which each is embedded. With his followers' separation from the Judaism out of which he and they had sprung, Jesus escaped the strictures of Jewish iconophobia.[17] The face and figure of Jesus, "the "image of the invisible God," as Paul called him (Col 1:15), became, with the spread of Christianity, one of the dominant images in the Greco-Roman figurative art tradition. Jesus Enthroned, the Pantocrator, and Jesus Crucified became endlessly displayed paradigm images in Eastern and Western spirituality respectively, while the "everyday Jesus" of the Galilean ministry sat and stood and preached and cured and blessed through countless images in countless churches, and then in countless books, throughout Christendom.

In addition to the pleasure and enlightenment that was conferred by the visualization of literarily familiar scenes, there was also, and particularly in the Eastern Churches, a theological message that was being conveyed by these images: the faithful were in the presence of Christ the God-man, majestically divine, yet persuasively human. That same message is on display in Western portrayals of Jesus, but generally only when it is the *Jesus Triumphans* of the resurrection or the ascended Jesus who is being portrayed. When the image is that of *Jesus servus et humilis* the message is more likely to be affective—the humble, the caring, the loving Good Shepherd—or, later, even sentimental.

After the conversion of Constantine, depictions of Jesus and the Christian saints moved easily into the domain of religious art. In the Eastern Roman Empire religious art evolved toward the formal, static, and hieratic and so the Jesus portraiture tended to be the same, a Jesus who was "aloof and timeless," as he has been described.[18] In the West, however, religious themes migrated as well into a more secular artistic tradition that delighted in treating New Testament themes generally and Jesus in particular in a more realistic, personal, and even adventuresome manner.

None of this widespread portrayal of Jesus passed without comment and, occasionally, strenuous Christian objection, particularly in the East. The *veneration* of images, their *sacramentalization*, struck many theologians as blasphemous, as they later did some of the Protestant Reformers in the West. In his defense of the use of religious images against the eighth-century Christian iconoclasts, John of Damascus called them "books for the illiterate" that differed from what was in Scripture only in that they pictured in line and color what the Bible had painted in words.[19] Islam too had its illiterates, but they had no need of books, either written or drawn, since their Scripture was—and, even in an age of print, broadly continues to be—a "Recitation."

But there was more than that at work. Islam shared with Judaism, or perhaps derived from it, a repugnance for the graven image. Allah was, like Yahweh, an aniconic deity to begin with and so there was never a question of His representation. Bold Western artists might try their hands, with very indifferent success, granted, at picturing even the Trinity;[20] their Muslim counterparts have had to rest content with artfully inscribing God's name, a step that traditional Jews still shrink from.

At its severest, the Islamic figuration prohibition extends perhaps to all human portrayal. As a result, Muslims have from the outset preferred decoration to representation, and for the former they have devised a striking repertoire of geometrical, floral, vegetal, and, most notably, calligraphic designs for the exterior and interior walls of their public and private buildings as well as for the headers, footers, margins, and even entire ornate carpet pages in their books.

Aniconic art was the Muslim juristic ideal; the artistic reality is that there has been a good deal of representational art created under Muslim auspices, generally as book paintings and usually with seigneurial patronage. Genre and court scenes filled with human figures abound at different times and in different places in the Abode of Islam. Religious themes were illustrated as well, including incidents from the life of the Prophet. Muhammad's "Night Journey and Ascension," with first its Meccan and then its cosmic setting, was a particular favorite. The Prophet is indeed portrayed in these vignettes, sometimes full-faced but more often veiled or with his head enveloped in an obscuring oriflamme halo.[21]

Such illustrations were not for public consumption, however; they were the valuable commissioned property of wealthy connoisseurs. Ordinary

Muslims had simply to imagine the Prophet. But they had help. Not from the Quran, of course, where Muhammad is only an occasional—and nameless—addressee, but in the mostly pietistic literature that began to appear after his death. Early Muslims, like the first generations of Christians who produced the apocryphal gospels out of much the same impulse, attempted to fill in the spaces in the remembered life of the Prophet of Islam, including his physical appearance and his everyday behavior.

The Arabic name that was later applied to these literary efforts was *hilya*, literally "adornment." These began as a literary description of the Prophet's traits, physical, psychological, and spiritual. Such material was first transmitted as hadith, the purported eyewitness accounts that originated with Muhammad's contemporaries and were passed down, often orally, in the form of discrete pieces of information. While the Prophet's traditional biographers hewed fairly closely to the *events* in his life, the hadiths' more personal details of face, form, and manner were eventually bundled into the freewheeling and imaginative genre called "Tales of the Prophets" or, if centered exclusively on Muhammad, "Grace-Notes of the Prophet."

This was popular literature and it was recited altogether more often than it was read. In either form it provided the ordinary believer with at least a verbal sketch of the face and form of the Prophet, albeit in effusive rather than precise terms.[22] Abbreviated versions of these descriptive/encomiastic texts may have earlier been carried about on the person as an act of piety or as an amulet, but they veered toward actual portraiture at the end of the seventeenth century when the Ottoman calligrapher Hafiz Osman (d. 1698) began to enclose the truncated texts in an attractively formal design that rapidly became standard. Thus was born the Turkish *hilye*, a literary portrait of the Prophet framed in the manner of a figurative cameo and, quite literally, a calligraphic icon that could adorn any surface and was hung on Turkish walls quite in the manner that a Christian might a portrait of Jesus the Good Shepherd.[23]

In Christendom portraits of Jesus *en large*, together with the parallel image of Jesus crucified, painted, or figured in the round as a crucifix, adorned the walls of cathedrals, churches, chapels, and oratories and even passed from hand to hand on coins, medallions, and rosaries. They appeared on the pages of the earliest printed New Testaments and eventually were hung for pious recollection on the walls of kitchens and bedrooms. And as is plain even to the untrained eye, the Jesus facial likeness of the European tradition, after an initial period of uncertainty, settles into a remarkably consistent portrayal through the centuries.[24] And, since Western pictorialism was for long stretches realistic in its intent and execution, the portrait was understood to be the "real" or, in our context, the historical Jesus.[25]

For Christians, Jesus, who is represented to them by a repertoire of images literally from the cradle to the grave, is something like a fully realized film star, every trait etched in the public's shared visual memory. The figuration of Muhammad more resembles that of a radio personality, a voice heard from afar whose features each can only imagine for oneself. Muslims must individually picture the Prophet as the voice behind the Quran or as a figure emerging from between the lines of the *Sira* or from the concrete but often generic traits—"neither too tall nor too short"—described but never portrayed in the *hilyeler* or elsewhere.

9

Epilogue: Spreading the Word

AT THE END OF THEIR PUBLIC CAREERS Jesus and Muhammad had each left to his followers a body of teaching and the recollection of a series of acts. The teaching had begun to be memorized and collected during the lifetime of each, but the events continued to unfold to the very end and their full import could be understood and acted upon only in the sequel. There was no doubt that each holy man had laid down an imperative: it was urgent that all be brought to belief. Though for Jesus himself "all" seems to have meant what it did for most Jews, the Children of Israel, his followers soon extended it to the larger world of the Gentiles, as we have seen. Muhammad, who lived in a smaller and far more parochial society, may have had in fact the larger vision, one unfettered by any notion of a "Chosen People." "All" meant all.[1]

What gave urgency to the message was the looming menace of the End Time. What that notion meant was not terribly different for either man; both may in fact have been working with the same Jewish apocalyptic scenario: there would be a cosmic upheaval followed by the Great Judgment with its deserved eternal punishment for the wicked in Gehenna and a merited reward in Paradise of Eden for the just. Jesus' version includes, however, his own personal parsing of the End Time as the coming of "the Kingdom," with undertones of the traditional religio-political motif of the vindication of Israel, the "People of God." The Islamic End Time is missing the vindication motif—there is no indication that the Muslims were the New Israel—but where the two apocalyptic visions chiefly differ is in their imminence. What Jesus communicates, and it is verified by the reaction of his followers, is that the End Time—which is tied to the notion of *kairos*, or "the opportune time," and to the course of Israel's contemporary politics—is very near and, indeed, that he himself would have a prominent role in it as the messianic "Son of Man." That note is absent from the Quran: the Judgment, which has no connection with either Mecca or the Arabs, is inevitable, but it is not around the corner. Nor is any role in it assigned to Muhammad or the umma, the community of believers: the Day of Judgment will be preeminently a day of personal accounting.

Without the Lord

There is no need to speculate on what happened to the Good News in the days immediately following Jesus' death, his reported appearances, and his final disappearance from Jerusalem and human history; the contemporary Paul and Acts instruct us. First, the content of the Good News was transformed. What had first been described as "Repent. The Kingdom of God draws near" (Mk 1:15) is now proclaimed as "Let all Israel accept as certain that God has made this same Jesus whom you crucified both Lord (*Kyrios*) and Messiah" (Acts 2:36). And what had simply been the exhortation to "Repent" or "Change your life" is now "Repent and be baptized in the name of Jesus the Messiah. Then your sins will be forgiven and you will receive the gift of the Holy Spirit" (Acts 2:38). John's ritual baptism was now incorporated into the movement's initiation ceremony, a sign that the believer had received "the gift of the Holy Spirit."

What is notable here is that Jesus' own message, his personal teachings that are set out in his own words in the Gospels, play no part in the Apostles' "proclamation" of their Lord. Nor do they in Paul's version of the "Good News," which occurred perhaps twenty years later than what is being described in Acts though it is reported somewhat earlier. In both instances the content of the "Good News" has shifted from Jesus' *teaching* to the Jesus *event*, his death and resurrection "according to Scripture." What is equally remarkable is that here, and even earlier in Paul, Jesus is being called by his Jewish followers *Kyrios*, or "Lord," the Judeo-Greek title par excellence for the deity. Indeed, the practice even antedates Paul since the Aramaic cry *Marana tha*, "Our Lord come!" (1 Cor 16:22) and the hymn to Christ in Philippians—"God raised him to the height and bestowed on him the name above all names . . . Jesus Christ is Lord" (2:6–11)—were apparently both in circulation well before Paul quoted them.

Early on, then, the Jesus movement was shaped by a new dynamic. During his life Jesus seems to have pointed to his fulfillment of biblical prophecy in support of messianic claims; now, after his death and resurrection, that latter was being adduced by his followers as proof of his Lordship (= divinity). His resurrection too was a "proof" of that divine status as well as a guarantee of resurrection to eternal life for all who were baptized in his name (1 Cor 15:3–7,

12–15). Paul explained it in the traditional Jewish terms of atonement: Jesus' death was the buyback ("redemption") for humankind's liberation from sin/death, a benefit in which anyone might share, not by observance of the Torah, as had been the Jewish conviction, but by putting his or her trust in Jesus (Rom 4:2–4).

Jesus' resurrection is boldly advanced in Acts (4:2), though atonement and redemption are not mentioned in Luke's description of the earliest preaching of the Jesus movement in Acts 2. Paul's reflection of those early years communicates a powerful sense of unfinished business, that the expected cosmic conclusion of the inbreaking of the Kingdom was hard upon them all (1 Thes 4–5), a sense that also seeps out from between the lines of Acts, where the slowly increasing numbers of the believers (Acts 1:15; 2:41, 47; 6:7) chose the eschatological step of pooling their possessions and electing "to share the common life, to break bread and to pray" (2:42).

What seems to have advanced the publicly preached Jesus movement in its earliest post-Jesus stage was chiefly the conviction that the Twelve, and perhaps others who stood before them, had actually seen the recently dead and buried Jesus alive, that this man who had claimed to be the Messiah had been really and truly resurrected from the dead. That conviction was bolstered by various "signs" like the cures and other wonders that his followers were capable of performing in his name (Acts 3:16, 14:8). And the convinced believers, the "Brethren," in turn convinced others, now assisted by a developing soteriology: Jesus indeed saved, saved the sinner from God's eternal wrath and, perhaps even more movingly, saved the believer from the oblivion of death.

How the Message Spread

As we have seen, Jesus probably did not envision or intend that his message be heard by any but the Children of Israel. But it was nonetheless, almost by accident, and it changed the fortune of the movement. This epoch-making "mission to the Gentiles" occurred neither by Jesus' command nor by apostolic plan but because there were already Gentiles on the margins of Jewish society, and particularly in the cities and towns of the broad Mediterranean Diaspora, the "Dispersal" outside the Land of Israel where there were many Jewish communities. The Jesus message came to those communities in the first instance because it was a Jewish message and they were Jews living in an open and syncretistic society. More immediately, many of Jesus' followers were forced out of Jerusalem in the backlash following upon Stephen's scandalous preaching and equally scandalous death by public stoning (Acts 8:1). The preconversion

Paul knew this very well, and when he set out on his lethally minded pursuit of members of the Jesus movement, he headed directly to their new "congregation" (*ekklesia*) in Damascus (Acts 9:2).

There is no mystery in how Christianity spread in its initial stages. It was spread by charismatic and enthusiastic preachers like the now converted Paul working through the dense network of Jewish congregations around the Mediterranean. Every good-sized Greco-Roman city had its Jewish community, and each community had its synagogue or assembly place, whether a dedicated building or simply someone's home, where the local Jews gathered to pray, to study Torah, or to conduct community business. The synagogue was open to all, to residents and transients, to proselytes and even to Gentile sympathizers. And it was here that Jesus' energetic Jewish followers, invited to the bema for the Sabbath service, found their weekly audiences (Acts 13:13, 17:2–3, 19:8).

At first conversions to the Jesus fellowship would likely have spread along existing social networks, principally families and friends, as they did among the earliest Muslims and still do in parallel circumstances. After that, the next most likely group to switch allegiances would seem to be those with weak religious affiliations of their own and, predictably, the alienated and discontented, and again we must think of Muhammad's earliest Meccan converts. There are no clear-cut signs of who these first wave of Christian converts might be—the earlier proposals that they were chiefly slaves has been abandoned in the face of an almost total lack of evidence—but it seems highly plausible that the Jesus movement made deep inroads in the Jewish communities of the Diaspora. Those Jews would be the most assimilated to the Greco-Roman "civil religion" of their environment. In the face of the disastrous destruction of the Jewish cult and political base in Palestine in AD 70 and the consequent Roman mistrust of Jews everywhere, they would also likely be the most drawn to what has been described as a form of "accommodated Judaism." Some later European Jews in somewhat the same circumstances made their own "accommodation" in the form of Reform Judaism, but here an alternative, a familiar yet new and different take on Judaism, readily presented itself in those Diaspora synagogues.

Making Christians

With Constantine's conversion, Christianity passed rapidly from being a *tolerated*, to a *favored*, and then finally in 381 CE, to the *official* religion of the Roman Empire, a movement that in the end brought it into a long-standing and often uneasy relationship with the political and legal institutions of a powerful, venerable, and highly conservative state. It also carried the Christians into a new relationship with their religious rivals, the Jews on one hand, and the whole spectrum of pagan cults on the other. The Christians, as they were now called, had a well-defined set of beliefs and the energy and conviction to attempt to convince others of the truth of those beliefs. They did just that, with considerable success among the *pagani*, those last lingering Gentiles in the outback, though with rapidly diminishing returns among Jews and almost none later among the Muslims.

By the fourth century the Jesus movement had already become an institutionalized "Church" but it had few means to *coerce* either belief or conformity save by calling on the state. In the case of the pagans, there was little hesitation to do so: imperial legislation was enacted—in the later Roman Empire only the emperor made law—making illegal the worship of all but the Christians' God. In AD 453 an imperial constitution declared pagans enemies of the state, and that those convicted of such should have their goods confiscated and suffer execution. Pagan temples were destroyed, as often by mobs as by the state, and in 529 the emperor Justinian closed down not only the last tolerated pagan temple in the empire—it was at Aswan, where Nubians came across the frontier to trade and, formerly, to worship—but also the last bastion of intellectual paganism, Plato's Academy, still in operation at Athens after nearly a millennium.

Christian missionaries, meanwhile, many of them from the monastic communities of the Church, pushed beyond the imperial frontiers. They clambered over Hadrian's wall in Britain to evangelize the Picts, sailed the Irish Sea to convert the wild Celts on the thither shore, and crossed the Rhine and the Danube to bring first the Germanic tribes and then the Slavs into the Christian fold. Eastern Christians, merchants and monks, traveled the silk routes eastward to China and India and planted the cross there.

New worlds discovered meant new worlds to be conquered both for Christ and the king. Jesuits, Dominicans, and Franciscans rode Portuguese and Spanish caravels and men-of-war to the farthest realms of Asia and America, where the banner of the faith and the crown were planted, often on the same stanchion. With the Reformation and the Enlightenment that followed, Christians began to turn to the perhaps less fruitful but certainly equally satisfying task of converting one another to a particular confessional version of the faith. The overseas ventures among the heathen continued, but now without government subsidy or support, though the role of the churches in the progress of colonialism should not be discounted. And increasingly the evangelizing Christians encountered their other missionary rivals for the souls of the pagans, the Muslims.

Without the Prophet

The Quran ends, of course, with Muhammad's death, but the *Sira* or *Life* goes on. It follows the consequences of the Prophet's death, through the somewhat tangled events of the succession and thence into the first *Islamic* issue. The Bedouin of Arabia, on whom the demands of religion sat lightly indeed, as the Quran itself testifies (9:97–98, 49:14), took the occasion of Muhammad's death to discontinue the religious tithe owed by them as Muslims to the coffers of the Muslim community at Medina. What the Muslims had now to decide, in the person of their newly chosen caliph (*khalifa*) Abu Bakr, was whether it was permissible to secede from the umma, as the opportunistic Bedouin were now doing. The answer was no: secession was apostasy. At Abu Bakr's direction the misapprised Bedouin were coerced by arms to remain tithe-paying Muslims.

Not many others were subsequently inclined to make the same mistake. Muslim troopers, long skilled in the arts of rapid, long-distance warfare, resumed the highly successful and highly profitable "raids" that in his biographers' eyes largely characterized the Prophet's career in Medina. His successors now turned away from Arabia and back to where Muhammad himself had been leading them, into the rich provinces of the Eastern Roman Empire and the Sasanian Empire of Iraq and Iran. Their long-unbroken string of military successes stretched for over a century and by the centennial anniversary of the Prophet's death, Muslim armies stood in southern France and on the borders of China. There were, however, no missionaries among those warriors, no holy, learned, or inspired men charged with the conversion of Islam's new subjects.

The Missionary Impulse

From the beginning Christianity has been possessed by a missionary impulse, that is, by the imperative, enunciated by Jesus himself, to preach the Good News, to follow in his footsteps and attempt to persuade others, including, as his followers came to believe, even non-Jews. Muhammad's missionary preaching at Mecca was, like Jesus' own, only modestly successful and his divinely inspired warnings to the Quraysh nearly cost him his life. It was only at Medina, and only after the military experience of Badr Wells, when spiritual submission to God began to follow upon political submission to Muslim arms, that the movement we call Islam began to spread.

The Prophet sent forth armies, but he never sent his disciples to preach to the Bedouin; it was the tribes who sent delegations to him requesting conversion. During Muhammad's lifetime, and for very long thereafter, conversion to Islam followed upon conquest; it never preceded it. Christians, on the other hand, had converted anywhere from 10 percent to 20 percent of the Roman Empire before Constantine became a Christian. Christian missionaries often preceded armies; they leaped across frontiers, worked behind the enemy lines deep in Germany, Central Asia, India, and China.

That Christian missionary impulse, with Roman authority behind it but only rarely ahead of it, had converted all of the Mediterranean basin by the mid-seventh century, when Muslim armies tore the southern half away, most of it forever. Now Christian Europe faced a new religious and political rival across the Mediterranean in the "Abode of Islam," as Muslims called their ideologically unified but already rapidly diversifying polity. Unlike the Europeans, who as yet ruled no Muslims, the Muslims had Christian subjects; indeed, the overwhelming number of the conquered from Iraq to Morocco were at least nominally Christian. They had not been forced to convert when they had submitted to Muslim arms, but within two centuries, the majority of these Christians (and Jews), who had a religiously protected but politically and socially degraded status under Islam, had become Muslims.

Conversion and Assimilation

In its earliest manifestation, Islam was the faith of Arabs revealed by an Arab prophet whose message was, it boasted, "in a manifest Arabic." In the first conversions Arabs passed from tribe to umma, losing their tribal identity (though only briefly), but not, as it turned out, any of the cultural markers of language, dress, food, and the like. Islam was at first measured by prayer, which could not be monitored always and everywhere, and by payment of the alms-tithe, which could. But when the call to Islam passed among other peoples, the Greek- and Aramaic-speaking people of Syria-Palestine, the Greek- and Coptic-speaking peoples of Egypt, the Greek-, Aramaic-, and Pahlevi-speaking peoples of Iraq and Iran, it sounded theologically familiar, but culturally it remained Arab. It continued to be such for a very long time—the anchor of the Arabic Quran secured it—so that Muslim converts had to assimilate to a new culture as well as assert a new faith.

The converts' cultural assimilation to Arabism was astonishingly rapid—within thirty or forty years the language of the Bedouin was being used as the language of state—and so thoroughly that it transformed the entire North African–Near Eastern landmass into an Arab cultural *oikoumenê*. There were survivors—Persian culture held its breath long enough under the Arab flood that it finally drew breath again after a century or so, though with strong Arab overtones—but the transformation was sufficiently complete that even those Christians, Jews, and others who declined to embrace Islam were in the end content to speak its language and adopt many Arab ways.

Whether to Christianity or to Islam, we do not and cannot know for certain why conversion takes place, save perhaps where a shaykh or sovereign moves and his people perforce must follow him into a new faith, as seems to have occurred in the passage of the Slavic people of the Balkans into Christianity, or that of the Arabian Bedouin and the North African Berbers into Islam.

Though we can broadly calculate and weigh some of the social and economic incentives to conversion, we can take no measure of the spiritual ones, except in the rare individual cases where someone undertakes to explain. We do know that Muslims were at first a very small minority in the lands they so rapidly conquered and that eventually, after two or three centuries perhaps, they were the majority. We know too that the people who became Muslims from Spain to Iraq were originally Christians and some Jews, and farther east, Zoroastrians. Muslims were the rulers of those people, their sovereigns in power and in wealth, if not in sophistication and learning. Surely it was the attraction of the first two qualities and not the latter, the possibility, that is, of sharing in the Muslims' power or wealth (or at least in not suffering the liability of being excluded from the perquisites of the new order) that prompted those other People of the Book to leave their home communities and join the triumphalist Muslim umma.

Making Muslims

Muhammad was a missionary: his primary goal was to convert the pagans of Mecca to the cult of the One True God. While at Medina, and with the growing success of his mission, he turned from conversion to catechesis, the instruction of those who were already Muslims. The earliest Christians felt they had been commissioned to spread the "Good News." Their successors began by working *within* the Roman Empire; later, they followed in the tracks of the military as the borders of the empire expanded, and outran the emperor's troops in their zeal to carry the Word to the unredeemed. In Islam, the troops *were* the missionaries in the first instance: soldiers and evangelists were one.

"Submission" meant to accept the political sovereignty of the Muslims and, if you were a pagan, to submit, without preliminaries, to the absolute sovereignty of the Muslims' God. Christians and Jews, however, and latterly the Zoroastrians, who together were soon the overwhelming majority of the vanquished peoples, had only to accept the political authority of the conquistador since they already worshiped, however imperfectly, the True God who was Allah. Thus the Abode of Islam expanded politically, and as it grew, it had within it large numbers of those protected People of the Book who could not be coerced but could certainly be converted. And they were: not all, but most, of the Jews and Christians of the Abode of Islam, at first slowly and then with increasing rapidity, became Muslims. It was conversion from within, effected not by Muslim proselytizing but by Muslim example and Muslim inducements. The process went on for as long as the political borders of the Abode of Islam expanded, and, when they no longer did so, after nearly a thousand years, other Muslims, Sufis in the main, went abroad to preach the word of God among the people to the east—to the west lay only Christians and Jews, who showed themselves little inclined to convert if they were not Muslim subjects, as little as Muslims did except when they were under Christian sovereignty.

Notes

Introduction

1. On these and similar assertions, see the Guide to Further Reading below.
2. The Muslim tradition soon began its long file of prophets with Adam, but as far as the economy of salvation is concerned, the line begins with Abraham. As the Quran itself testifies, Islam is the "religion of Abraham" (2:135).
3. "Yeshua" or "Jesus" suffered a not terribly surprising decline in popularity as a name among Jews with the spread of Christianity. Among Christians, "Jesus" is not a common name except among Spanish-speaking Catholics, who alone lived for centuries in the close company of Muslims who delighted in calling their sons "Muhammad."
4. Quran 5:110, for example, has the infant Jesus preaching from the cradle and breathing life into clay birds.
5. Or, as it has appeared to more than one modern critic, a Jewish sect, biblical in its inspiration, Zionist in its aspiration.
6. Muslims waste no time on the aesthetics of the Gospels, which are in any event irretrievably corrupted by Christian tampering. It should be noted that the Christians' own aesthetic admiration of the New Testament is almost entirely limited to the seventeenth-century King James English translation; very few have praised the beauty of either the Koine Greek of the original or Jerome's Latin Vulgate version.

Chapter 1

1. It was once thought, however, that a portrait of Jesus—perhaps painted by the evangelist Luke—was preserved at Edessa, in what is today Turkey, and some few still think that the winding sheet called the "Shroud of Turin" has impressed upon it a "negative" of the dead Jesus whom it once enfolded. See Robin Margaret Jensen, *Face to Face: Portraits of the Divine in Early Christianity* (Minneapolis: Fortress Press, 2005), 134–39.
2. Or perhaps it was in Samaritan Shechem, as these latter angrily insisted.
3. It was precisely these notices that explain why so much of Josephus' work is preserved from antiquity. Christians found both these confirmations of their own past, which

Christian scribes occasionally "improved" by doctoring them (see chapter 2), as well as Josephus' primer on Bible history in the *Antiquities* extremely valuable, and his histories were assiduously copied and carefully preserved.

4. The Bible, like the New Testament, represents a *canon*, a yardstick against which genuine revelation or genuine prophecy is measured. More realistically, the biblical canon represents all those books regarded by a later generation of Jews—or the authority among them; the process, like the grounds for the choices, is not entirely clear—as somehow appropriate for the designation of Sacred Scripture.

5. Both the texts and the archaeological remains of the settlement at Qumran point to beginnings in the mid-third century BC and a rather precise end in AD 68, when the community was destroyed or violently dispersed in the course of the insurrection against Rome.

6. A comparison of the Qumran finds with what Josephus and others say about the Essenes quickly reveals that there was more than one type of Essene.

7. The often-styled "Constitution of Medina" included in the Ibn Ishaq–Ibn Hisham biography of Muhammad is an example of what is perhaps an authentic preserved document, while the extensive correspondence conducted by Muhammad and various world leaders and reproduced in other biographies is almost certainly all invented.

8. Even if such were undertaken, there is little expectation that much would be found, particularly at Mecca, where the principal buildings sit in the midst of a wadi bottom often scoured, down to the mid-twentieth century, by the flash floods common in that treeless land.

9. What should have been the chief signpost, Jesus' claim to the Jewish title of Messiah, was blunted by its rapid transformation into the Greek title-name *Christos*. *Iesus Christos* sets off very different echoes from *Yeshua haMashiah*.

10. Unlike the New Testament, however, where Jesus' voice is but one in a large chorus, the Quranic logoi proceed from a single source, the Prophet Muhammad.

11. *Sura* is also the name given to the present "chapters" of the Quran, which may or may not represent the original units of composition. Many of the present suras are transparently composites.

12. There appear to be Quranic references (7:74, 27:52) to the Nabatean ruins at what is today called Mada'in Salih in the northern Hijaz.

Chapter 2

1. For all the non-Western nonbelievers, the Christians seem to have preferred the term "heathen," though it is almost certainly a distinction without a difference.

2. The followers of "Christus" or "Chrestos" are the focus of the remarks of Suetonius' *Life of Claudius* (25.4) and *Nero* (16.2), written in the opening decades of the second century, and of the query of Pliny the Younger, Roman governor of Bithynia 109–11, addressed to Trajan and the emperor's answer (*Letters*, 10, 96, 97).

3. Translated by Shlomo Pines, *An Arabic Version of the Testimonium Flavianum and Its Implications* (Jerusalem: Israel Academy of Sciences and Humanities, 1971), 16.

4. Rabbi, "my master," is a loosely used term of respect in Second Temple times—Jesus is often so called (Lk 7:40, etc.)—but it subsequently becomes a technical term to describe the sages named and quoted in the Mishna (ca. AD 200) and the Talmud (ca. AD 400–600). Thereafter the "rabbi" is a Torah scholar, generally authorized by certification or "ordination" (*semikha*).

5. It was once thought that the Gospels might be even later than this span, but now the sense is that, if the chronology is going to be altered, it is going to be moved back, not forward.

6. Finding the destruction of Jerusalem and particularly of the Temple in any of the above cited Synoptic chapters is no easy matter. In the eyes of some, the Gospel versions of the End Time seem more like boiler-plate apocalypse than graphic eyewitness memories. If that is so, all three of the Synoptics might well have been written before AD 70. To this must be added the fact that the action of the Acts of the Apostles, volume 2 of Luke's Gospel, ends with Paul still apparently alive very early in the 60s.

7. It is clear from the continuation of the same passage that the Christians of Corinth (and presumably elsewhere) were doing just that in the early 50s.

8. Thomas apart, the apocrypha debate centers primarily on the "Gospel of Peter" and the "Secret Gospel of Mark," though most find the case for the first unconvincing and that for the second incredible.

9. The Muslim calendar differs from the Christian system used in most parts of the world. To supply the Muslim dates for events, which are not readily convertible into the more familiar Gregorian calendar, would simply baffle most readers. I use the familiar BC and AD throughout.

10. A brief pause over "inspired." The historian is in no position to judge the validity of claims to inspiration, but it is important to understand what their followers thought on the subject. Jesus was thought by his followers not so much inspired as speaking in his own voice with the authority of God Himself, his "Father in heaven." The Gospels, on the other hand, were regarded as inspired, written as they were by human hands under the guidance of the Holy Spirit, though how precisely that worked is not clear. Muhammad was regarded as inspired in the sense that what issued from his mouth in the identifiable "revelational mode," probably signaled by some form of cantillation on Muhammad's part, had come word for word from God through the Angel Gabriel. There was no human agency or conditioning involved in Muhammad's utterances, and though our Quran, the "copy" (*mushaf*), is the product of human editing, its contents share the same divine guarantee as the words uttered by the Prophet.

11. Or, more accurately, a written *consonantal* text. Semitic alphabets normally do not sign vowel sounds, which the reader must supply. "B," for example, may be read "ba" or "bi" or "bu" and often is. So the text of Uthman, while it supplied a sturdy skeleton of the Quranic text, left many uncertainties about the vocalic tendons and muscles originally attached to it.

12. We have no clue as to why this particular order was chosen. The closest analogue is in the authentic letters of Paul, which are arranged in the New Testament canon in the same order of descending length, though here the chief consideration was fitting them economically on a standard papyrus roll, a mechanical element that does not appear to have been in play in the ordering of the Quran.

13. By manipulating biblical descending genealogies and ascending Arab tribal genealogies, the later Muslim tradition made Muhammad out to be a descendant of Abraham through Ishmael. There is no evidence whatsoever that either Muhammad or his contemporaries were aware of this connection. Islam was the "religion of Abraham" in the spiritual sense, not in the (Jewish) kinship sense.

14. Ibn Ishaq, *Life*, 691, from Ibn Hisham's Introduction; see n. 15 below.

15. Ibn Hisham's version of Ibn Ishaq is available in an English translation by Alfred Guillaume, *The Life of Muhammad* (London: Oxford University Press, 1955), and it will be cited here in that edition. Guillaume has spliced into the narrative segments of the original that are preserved in Tabari's *History*.

16. It was once thought that Waqidi lifted most of his material from Ibn Ishaq, though without mentioning him. Closer inspection, however, has led Waqidi's latest editor to conclude that both authors, Ibn Ishaq and Waqidi, were drawing on a common "Raids" tradition that had already taken shape by the mid-eighth century, and whose strengths and weaknesses they both presumably share.

17. It is conceivable that there were some documents, official written records, that were available and possibly seen and used by Ibn Ishaq and others.

18. The actual literary testimony of the Muslim counterparts of the second-century "Apostolic Fathers" of Christianity has critically disappeared: the Quran apart, there are no substantial literary remains from the first century of Islam, no Muslim Clement or Ignatius or Barnabas or Didache.

19. Notably important is his *Itqan* or "Perfection (in the Sciences of the Quran)."

Chapter 3

1. A later, more sentimental generation of Christians added members of the animal kingdom to the choir of worshipers.

2. There is, of course, no historical evidence for the date of Jesus' birth. The celebration of the Nativity on December 25 was decreed by the Christian emperor Constantine to replace an important imperial holy day, the birthday of the Invincible Sun on the winter solstice.

3. There is occasionally some confusion here. Virginal conception has to do with Jesus' conception without benefit of human sexual intercourse. "Virgin birth," which will soon follow as an issue for Christians, has to do with his mother Mary's remaining physically intact, with an unruptured hymen, through the otherwise natural birth of Jesus. The

"Immaculate Conception" is a much later development in the Church. It is a declaration that Mary, alone among humankind, was conceived without the very tainted spiritual DNA called Original Sin.

4. Matthew 13:35 has the Nazarenes identify Jesus "the son of the carpenter." What he read in Mark, however, was that it was Jesus who was the carpenter (Mk 6:3), with no mention of his father. We cannot tell if Matthew was correcting Mark or if there was a confusion arising from the fact that both men were carpenters in Nazareth.

5. One of the most famous of Jesus' encounters with a woman, the pericope often called "The Woman Taken in Adultery" (Jn 8:1–11), is generally thought to be a later insertion into John's original Gospel, which does not necessarily mean, of course, that it was an invention.

6. In marked polemical contrast, of course, with the uxorious Muhammad.

7. Not all would agree. Many read Q not simply as a quondam assemblage but as an *edited collection* and that changing intent—and so the evolving history of the "Q community"— can be read off the successive "editions" (Q^2 and Q^3) of the core original (Q^1); see chapter 4 below.

8. Since the texts regarding Muhammad may not be as readily available, or familiar, as the New Testament ones, I reproduce some of the chief ones here. As stated above, all the translations from Ibn Hisham's version of Ibn Ishaq's *Sira* are taken from Guillaume's *Life of Muhammad*.

9. *Munahhemana* in Syriac means, like the Hebrew Menachem, "comforter," and seems linguistically unrelated to either "Ahmad" or "Muhammad," whose root meaning (H-M-D) is "praise." Another possibility is that the Quran, or someone, was familiar with a Gospel text that read at John 14:16, instead of the more usual *parakletos*, the variant *periklytos*, which does stand in some manuscripts and might reasonably be rendered as "Ahmad" in Arabic. In any event, Quran 61:6 caused later Muslims, and Ibn Ishaq was not the first, to search out, first in the Gospels and eventually in the entire Bible, predictions of the coming of Muhammad, the "seal of the prophets."

10. There may be a faint echo of something similar in Mark. When Jesus is led out by the Romans to be crucified, "a man called Simon of Cyrene," we are told (15:21 and parr.), "the father of Rufus and Alexander, was passing by on his way in from the countryside and they pressed him into service to carry his cross." Simon and his story must have quickly become popular fare in early Christian circles to merit such notice, and it is likewise safe to assume that Simon's sons, Rufus and Alexander, both unremarked in Matthew and Luke, were well-known figures in the (Roman? Cf. Rom 16:13) community to which Mark was addressing his Gospel.

11. Ibn Ishaq, *Life*, 79, 90–98.

12. Ibn Ishaq, *Life*, 82.

13. Joseph A. Fitzmyer, "The Virginal Conception of Jesus in the New Testament," in *To Advance the Gospel: New Testament Studies*, 2nd ed. (Grand Rapids: William B. Eerdmans, 1998), 45.

Chapter 4

1. The Quran also calls itself "The Book" (19:16, etc.), "The Admonition" (7:63, etc.), "The Guidance" (2:185, etc.), and "The Criterion" (25:1, etc.).

2. But not our earliest extant source. Paul's letters are exhortatory and instructive rather than narrative or dramatic. But the Jesus events clearly lie behind them, most obviously in 1 Corinthians 15:3–7.

3. The logic of this reconstruction points to the possible existence of an Aramaic Q as well, though no trace of such now exists. But the Greek Q has disappeared as well, save for its ghostly footprints in Matthew and Luke.

4. It is this kind of allusion that has suggested to critics that such passages represent a later rewriting of the text when relations between Jesus' followers and their fellow Jews had grown much more tense. Whatever its explanation, its presence here in what may be our oldest source on Jesus must give pause.

5. This is not to say that Jesus' sayings in the Gospels are all totally decontextualized. The Gospels' miracle stories and the words uttered in them, for example, are usually preceded by quite specific and concrete "occasions." On two such this context is so deep that it remembers some of Jesus' actual Aramaic words on those occasions: *Talitha, qumi*, "Young girl, arise," Jesus says to the maiden he raises from a death state (Mk 5:41), and *Ephphatha*, "Be opened," is his healing Aramaic word to a man he cures of deafness (Mk 7:34).

6. The same question may be posed, of course, if in a somewhat lesser degree, to our own Gospels, and most notably that of Luke, who was reputedly one of Paul's own followers.

7. Or, more precisely, a *written* copy. The implication is clear: a recited Quran is the genuine Quran; the written version is merely a copy.

8. E.g., the story of Lot and Sodom (Q. 11:77–83, 15:51–84) and of the Arabian prophet Salih and the Thamud people (7:73–79, 26:141–58, etc.).

9. See chapter 6 below.

10. So, for example, the entire sura (12) devoted to Joseph and the Pharaoh's wife and the oft-repeated tale of Moses and the Pharaoh's wizards (7:103–36, 10:75–89, 20:24–76, etc.).

11. The Quran devotes an entire sura (72) to them.

12. Or so Caedmon seemed to suggest. It is generally thought, however, that Caedmon's "inspired" skill came from listening to the learned monks in whose company he was. Something similar may have occurred in Muhammad's case.

13. And to compound the curiosity, the other Jesus sayings source, the Gospel of Thomas, has 114 logoi, the same number as the suras of the Quran.

Chapter 5

1. *Antiquities* 18:116–19 on Herod Antipas' execution of the Baptist; cf. Mark 6:17–28.

2. The Church did not much favor such uncertainties in Scripture. It attempted to harmonize the lists by positing two names for some individuals. Thus Mark's "Thaddeus" was reckoned identical with Luke's "Jude" and John's "Nathanael" with the others' "Bartholomew."

3. Though the notion is generally absent from the biblical books and later generations of Jews had their doubts, many Jews of Jesus' day, including both Jesus and his followers, early and late—and Muhammad and the Muslims in their wake—had a firm conviction that there was a life after death, complete with rewards in a restored Garden of Eden ("Paradise") and hellish punishments in a place imagined as the garbage dump of Jerusalem, Ge Hinnom or Gehenna.

4. Marcus J. Borg, "The Palestinian Background for a Life of Jesus," in Herschel Shanks et al., eds., *The Search for Jesus: Modern Scholarship Looks at the Gospels* (Washington, D.C.: Biblical Archaeology Society, 1995), 44.

5. And in Arabic *bushra*, one of the names the Quran gives to itself (2:97). In 25:34 Muhammad is called a *bashir*, a "bringer of good news."

6. "Trust in" is preferable to "believe in" or "have faith in." Both "belief" and "faith" have been too heavily conceptualized to do justice to the more basic notion of the Greek *pistis* and its cognates. *Pistis* is both the quality in the object that inspires confidence and the subjective reaction, trust.

7. Matthew's preferred variant, "Kingdom of Heaven," may be a reflection of the author's very Jewish desire to avoid mentioning God's name.

8. This latter notion of the community as a "nation of priests" appealed, however, to a later generation of Christians; see 1 Peter 2:5.

9. Mark 10:2–12 is quite explicit, and theological, on the matter of divorce:

> And Pharisees came up and in order to test him asked, "Is it lawful for a man to divorce his wife?" He answered them, "What did Moses command you?" They said, "Moses allowed a man to write a certificate of divorce, and to put her away." But Jesus said to them, "For your hardness of heart he wrote you this commandment. But from the beginning of creation, 'God made them male and female.' 'For this reason a man shall leave his father and mother and be joined to his wife, and the two shall become one flesh.' So they are no longer two but one flesh. What therefore God has joined together, let not man put asunder." And in the house the disciples asked him again about this matter. And he said to them, "Whoever divorces his wife and marries another, commits adultery against her; and if she divorces her husband and marries another, she commits adultery."

The parallel passage in Matthew (5:32) comes to the same conclusion, but permits divorce on what seems to be a somewhat more specific version of the Torah grounds of "something unseemly" (Dt 24:1): "anyone who divorces his wife, except for lewdness (*porneia*). . ." Luke 16:18 stands closer to Mark, but without underlining the theology: "Anyone who divorces his wife and marries another woman commits adultery."

Chapter 6

1. Interrupted rhymes within the sura point to interpolations, while abrupt shifts in the rhyme scheme often, though not always, suggest a new pronouncement.

2. The Meccan eras of the Quran, each arranged in a highly speculative chronological order, are comprised as follows:

    Early Meccan: suras 96, 74, 111, 106, 108, 104, 107, 102, 105, 92, 90, 94, 93, 97, 86, 91, 80, 68, 87, 95, 103, 85, 73, 101, 99, 82, 81, 53, 84, 100, 79, 77, 78, 88, 89, 75, 83, 69, 51, 52, 56, 70, 55, 112, 109, 113, 114, 1.

      Middle Meccan: suras 54, 37, 71, 76, 44, 50, 20, 26, 15, 19, 38, 36, 43, 72, 67, 23, 21, 25, 17, 27, 18.

      Late Meccan: suras 32, 41, 45, 16, 30, 11, 14, 12, 40, 28, 39, 29, 31, 42, 10, 34, 35, 7, 46, 6, 13.

    The lengthy chapters that are reckoned to be Medinan are suras 2, 98, 64, 62, 8, 47, 3, 61, 57, 4, 65, 59, 33, 63, 24, 58, 22, 48, 66, 60, 110, 49, 9, 5.

3. Ibn Ishaq, *Life*, 82–83.

4. See chapter 3.

5. Ibn Ishaq, *Life*, 98–103.

6. Or rather, and perhaps more likely, "I have nothing to recite."

7. Ibn Ishaq, *Life*, 104–6.

8. The Quran also seems to indicate (2:185) that it was sent down in its entirety during the month of Ramadan, on the "night of destiny" (97:1), which was reckoned to be the twenty-seventh of that lunar month.

9. Night Journey: Ibn Ishaq, *Life*, 181–84; Ascension to heaven: 184–87.

10. Ibid., 181.

11. Ibid., 107.

12. Recognitions: Ibid., 90–95; Bahira: 79–82.

13. Ibid., 117.

14. Another appellative that appears, then disappears, from the Quran is "The Merciful One" (*al-Rahman*), which seems at times to be used as a proper name, as in fact it appears in South Arabian inscriptions. Verse 17:110 seems to put that possibility to rest: "Call upon Allah or call upon al-Rahman, whoever you call, His are the beautiful names."

15. Like the Jewish custom, three times daily according to the Quran (24:58): at dawn, noon, and night. A later, more self-conscious tradition extended it to five.

16. Ibn Ishaq, *Life*, 114–17; 155–59 (Umar).

17. Ibid., 165–67.

18. The pre-Islamic prophets are listed at 6:83–89, Muhammad as the "seal of the prophets" at 33:40.

19. There are stories of Muhammad's debate with South Arabian Christians in the *Sira* (Ibn Ishaq, *Life*, 270–77), but there are serious doubts as to their historicity.

20. Ibn Ishaq, *Life*, 133–34; cf. Mark 3:20–21, where his mother and brothers attempt to restrain Jesus. " 'He is out of his mind,' they said."

21. Ibn Ishaq, *Life*, 146–53.

22. Ibid., 191–97.

Chapter 7

1. That Mark's Gospel was not about Jesus' resurrection is clear from the manuscript tradition which shows that the original version of Mark ended not with the appearances of the risen Jesus but at what is now Mark 16:8, the discovery of Jesus' empty tomb. After Mark, Jesus' post-resurrection appearances begin to take on an added importance; see chapter 8 below.

2. There are indications of a more formal Sanhedrin trial on Friday morning, most explicitly in Luke 22:66–71; cf. Mark 15:1 and Matthew 27:1. This may represent the historical reality, while the detailed and dramatic hearing at Caiaphas' house is a later Christian imagining of what might have happened immediately after Jesus' arrest.

3. Blasphemy is a somewhat problematic charge in Jewish law. According to its narrow definition, it is simply pronouncing the divine name (Lv 24:10–16), but more broadly it is never quite defined. Claims to be the Messiah, or indeed "Son of God" (without all the trailing Christian theology!), seem hardly to constitute this crime whose penalty was, in any event, death by stoning.

4. Luke saves his account of Judas' end for Acts (1:18–20), where he says merely that Judas "fell headlong so that all his entrails spilled out."

5. Some naturally wish to identify this "Mary the mother of James the younger and of Joses" as Jesus' mother. John after all puts her there, together with her sister, "Mary, the wife of Clopas," as well as Mary Magdalene (19:25). It is almost impossible to say whether Mark and John are here speaking of the same person.

6. Ibn Ishaq, *Life*, 221–27. This starting event in the Muslim reckoning of time can be dated to July 16, 622 (cf. Ibn Ishaq, *Life*, 281), and with this chronological anchor the dating of many subsequent events can be established more firmly—the battle at Badr Wells in 624, for example, the fall of Mecca in 630, and the death of the Prophet in 632. It is only in proceeding backward from the Hegira that the chronological ground becomes slippery underfoot.

7. Ibid., 231–34.

8. Ibid., 247–70, attempts to integrate the scattered verses on the subject in the long sura 2 into a coherent account of what was happening.

9. Ibid., 289–360.

10. The spoils of Badr were large enough at any rate to provoke a dispute about their division among the raiders: Quran 8, 1 ff.; cf. Ibn Ishaq, *Life*, 321–27.

11. The verses here seem almost irretrievably jumbled in their sequence; Ibn Ishaq, *Life*, 370–404, and particularly the attempted integration of the Quran, 391–401.

12. Ibn Ishaq, *Life*, 456–601.

13. Unremarked in the Quran; Ibn Ishaq, *Life*, 540–61.

14. But not for very long. In 661 sovereignty over the umma passed to the Umayyad family who chose to rule from the old Syrian metropolis of Damascus. Thereafter Medina, and indeed Mecca as well, for all their religious allure, became political backwaters of the Abode of Islam.

15. We do not know why exactly that was an issue in a society where polygamy was not un-usual, except perhaps among those shadowy "natural" monotheists that hover behind the Quran. Would *they* have made objection to polygamy, an objection answered in Q. 4:3?

16. Their exact number is uncertain because they go unnamed and uncounted in the Quran, and the later tradition was not quite sure whether some of the names that had come down were those of wives or concubines, on whose number there was no limit.

17. Ibn Ishaq, *Life*, 493–99.

18. Ibid., 228–31.

19. Ibid., 649–52.

20. Ibid., 678–83.

21. And for some, so implausible as to suggest a deliberate, albeit imperfect, deception on the part of the evangelists and/or Jesus' earliest followers.

Chapter 8

1. Not exactly so in the usually well-informed John (19:38–42), where Joseph of Arimathea and Nicodemus perform what seems to be this ritual on Friday before the tomb is sealed.

2. Luke had introduced her earlier—her exorcism is also noted—with two named others, "Joanna, the wife of Chuza, Herod's steward, and Susanna," together with "many others who provided for them (Jesus and his circle) out of their resources" (8:2–3). Somewhat later, the Christian tradition, which was from the outset invested in harmonizing the Gospel evidence, identified Mary from Migdal with the unnamed sinful woman—later still, the sin became, inevitably, prostitution—who anoints Jesus' feet and wipes them with her hair (Lk 7:36–50) as well as with the Mary who lived in Bethany with her bustling sister Martha and her brother Lazarus, whom Jesus raised from the dead (Lk 19:38–42; Jn 11:1–40). John identifies Martha's sister and the anonymous sinner (11:2).

3. Except for Mary Magdalene, about whom there is no doubt, the names of these women at the crucifixion and the empty tomb are hopelessly confused in the sources and no amount of effort has succeeded in straightening them out. Mary Magdalene's prominence at these crucial Gospel junctures, and so arguably her importance to the earliest Christians, is surely not accidental, and Magdalene's career has been spectacular in both the later apocrypha—she had her own gospel—and the modern imagination.

4. In Scriptural traditions no crucial stone is left unturned, but centuries of Christian exegetical ingenuity have not succeeded in satisfactorily rolling back "Do not touch me . . ."

5. By nearly unanimous consent, Mark's Gospel originally ended somewhat awkwardly at 16:8 with the women's discovery of Jesus' empty tomb. Verses 9–19 of that same chapter, which describe Jesus' post-resurrection appearances, may then be an addition by a later hand.

6. The collectors of the New Testament were careful about authenticity—witness all the contemporary writings that were not included—but not when it had to do with textual

matters. They were not text critics: they accepted and included texts as they were in circulation in the second century.

7. This sounds like it might have been the conclusion of John's putative source, a "Book of Signs" (see chapter 3 above).

8. Luke describes the final scene with the Twelve once again, and with added details, in the Acts of the Apostles: " . . . he was lifted up before their very eyes, and a cloud took him from their sight. They were gazing intently into the sky as he went, and all at once there stood beside them two men robed in white, who said, 'Men of Galilee, why do you stand there looking up into the sky? This Jesus who was taken from you up to heaven will come in the same way as you have seen him go" (1:9–11).

9. Ibn Ishaq, *Life*, 682–83.

10. The classic instance is Moses' confrontation with the Pharaoh: Q. 7:103–36, etc. On Jesus: 3:49, 5:112–15 (the Eucharist as a heavenly table?).

11. The expression "the messiah" (*al-masih*) does appear there, but only as a denominative title of Jesus (e.g., 3:45), which is the way Christians had come to use it, and without eschatological implication.

12. This is not to say that there were not later Muslims who claimed they were in fact prophetic successors of Muhammad. Their claims and followers have littered the Islamic landscape with sectarian groups from the eighth century down to the present. Some, like the Baha'i, have parted company with the umma while others, like the Ahmadiyya, have clung fiercely to their Islamic identity.

13. Two of the principal responses are represented by Sunni and Shiite Islam.

14. It is in part the improper exaltation of the mortal Muhammad that is being fought, in part the parallel to the Christians' Christmas. Where there has been greater success is in discouraging Westerners from calling Islam "Muhammadanism" on the analogy of Christianity.

15. The Arabic word *dallan* here translated as "wandering" usually refers, like the Latin *errare*, to being wrong or mistaken.

16. A. J. Wensinck, *The Muslim Creed: Its Genesis and Historical Development* (London: Frank Cass, 1968), 192.

17. Jews too, as they were drawn into Greco-Roman culture, were rethinking the biblical prohibitions against graven images; witness the programmatic paintings on the walls of the Dura Europos synagogue and the floor mosaics of the synagogues of Byzantine Palestine.

18. André Grabar, cited in Jaroslav Pelikan, *Jesus through the Centuries: His Place in the History of Culture* (New Haven: Yale University Press, 1985), 93.

19. Ibid., 91. Pelikan (83–94) gives a succinct summary of the Christian struggle over images.

20. Jesus' familiar characterization of the formerly aniconic Yahweh as his "father" is the controlling image in His Christian imaging, where He is inevitably portrayed as an elderly patriarchal figure, while Mark's description of the Holy Spirit as descending on

the newly baptized Jesus "like a dove" (1:10) sealed the latter's unhappy iconic fate forever. The problem, of course, was getting the three to sit for a group portrait.

21. Examples of this and of other Muslim depictions of Muhammad are available online at
www.religionfacts.com/islam/things/depictions-of-muhammad-examples.htm

22. An altogether typical example, this on the authority of the Prophet's cousin Ali:
"Muhammad was middle-sized, did not have lank or crisp hair, was not fat, had a wide
circular face, wide black eyes and long eyelashes. . . . He was taller than middling stature
but taller than conspicuous shortness. . . . His complexion was bright. Muhammad had a
wide forehead and fine, long-arched eyebrows that did not meet. . . . The upper part of
his nose was hooked; he was thick bearded, had smooth cheeks, a strong mouth and his
teeth were set apart." Cited in Annemarie Schimmel, *And Muhammad Is His Messenger:
The Veneration of the Prophet in Islamic Piety* (Chapel Hill: University of North Carolina
Press, 1985), 34; Schimmel provides a good idea of Muslim literary portraits of Muhammad's
appearance (34–39).

23. In the standard form there is at the top an important horizontal panel enclosing the
introductory *bismillah* formula, "In the name of God. . .," while the main descriptive text
is contained within a circle, often with a surrounding crescent. Four disks at the corners
of the central circle bear the names of the first four caliphs of Islam. Below is a horizontal
panel with a verse from the Quran (usually 21:107 or 64:8) in its own distinctive calligraphy. The lowest horizontal panel, which may be divided vertically, contains the rest of
the descriptive text, if necessary, encomia, and finally the name of the calligrapher. See
M. Uğur Derman, *Letters in Gold: Ottoman Calligraphy from the Sakip Sabanci Collection, Istanbul* (New York: Metropolitan Museum of Art, 1998), 34–37. I owe this citation
to the kindness of Professor Ulku Bates of Hunter College of the City University of New
York.

24. See Jensen, *Face to Face*, 142, and 131–73 generally on portraits of Jesus.

25. Though the "realistic" Jesus of the West looks far more like a European than a Palestinian
Jew, the portrait is not immutable. The Jesus of African and Asian Christians, who had
generally arrived there from European shores, often looks like neither a European nor a
Palestinian Jew but bears all the "realistic" physical markers of the local ethnic culture.

Chapter 9

1. Islam was tied to social tribalism by its past and to cultural Arabism by the fact that its
revelation was "a manifest Arabic Quran" (Q. 39:28, 41:3, etc.), and while both elements
can be illustrated from its history, neither the theology nor the dynamic of Islam has
been much affected by these links to the past.

A Guide to Further Reading

Jesus and Muhammad are two figures, two dominant figures, in a broad landscape that also features, as their peer and indeed their quite explicit prototype, the biblical Moses. The landscape is, of course, that of the three great monotheistic siblings—Judaism, Christianity, and Islam—whose genesis, evolution, and confrontations I have spelled out in *The Monotheists: Judaism, Christianity, and Islam in Conflict and Competition*, 2 vols. (Princeton: Princeton University Press, 2002). Earlier I had collected the pertinent textual evidence regarding all three in *Judaism, Christianity, and Islam: The Classical Texts and Their Interpretation*, 3 vols. (Princeton: Princeton University Press, 1990). Finally, the matter of both works is resumed more briefly, with supplementary reading, in my *Children of Abraham: A New Edition* (Princeton: Princeton University Press, 2004).

The Quests

The long quests for Jesus and Muhammad have been recorded in some detail, particularly that for Jesus since it has been the subject of considerable argument. It can be joined in high-volume rivalrous progress in Marcus Borg, *Jesus in Contemporary Scholarship* (Valley Forge: Trinity Press International, 1994); Ben Witherington, *The Jesus Quest: The Third Search for the Jew of Nazareth* (Downers Grove: Intervarsity Press, 1995); Luke Timothy Johnson, *The True Jesus: The Misguided Quest for the Historical Jesus and the Truth of the Traditional Gospels* (San Francisco: HarperSanFrancisco, 1996); William E. Arnal and Michael Desjardins, eds., *Whose Historical Jesus?* (Waterloo: Wilfrid Laurier University Press, 1997), particularly the contribution there of Larry W. Hurtado, "A Taxonomy of Recent Historical-Jesus Work," 272–95; and finally, James D. G. Dunn, *A New Perspective on Jesus: What the Quest for the Historical Jesus Missed* (Grand Rapids: Baker Academic, 2005). The Muhammad quest, which is considerably less high-spirited, is also less caught up in reports of its own progress, perhaps because there has been so little; see, however, Clinton Bennett, *In Search of Muhammad* (London: Cassell, 1998), 93–138, "Non-Muslim Lives: From the Renaissance to Today."

The Respective Roles of the Two Men

The position of Jesus in Christianity as Messiah, Lord, and Savior was already fixed before Paul; see Larry W. Hurtado, *How on Earth Did Jesus Become a God? Historical Questions about Earliest Devotion to Jesus* (Grand Rapids: William B. Eerdmans, 2005). All that remained was to work out its liturgical expression in worship and fashion an explanation in theology. For the first, Dom Gregory Dix, *The Shape of the Liturgy* (1945; rpt. with additional notes by Paul V. Marshall, New York: Seabury Press, 1985), remains the classic treatment, though with the progress noted in Paul F. Bradshaw, *The Search for the Origins of Christian Worship: Sources and Methods for the Study of the Early Liturgy* (New York: Oxford University Press, 1992); and for the second, Alois Grillmeier, *Christ in Christian Tradition*, rev. ed. (Atlanta: John Knox Press, 1975), is a reliable guide to the theology, and Jaroslav Pelikan, *Jesus through the Centuries: His Place in the History of Culture* (New Haven: Yale University Press, 1985), sketches the broader cultural picture.

The role of Muhammad in the less institutionalized Islam is more complex, but Uri Rubin, *The Eye of the Beholder: The Life of Muhammad as Viewed by the Early Muslims* (Princeton: Darwin Press, 1995), and Annemarie Schimmel, *And Muhammad Is His Messenger: The Veneration of the Prophet in Islamic Piety* (Chapel Hill: University of North Carolina Press, 1985), cover the ground fully and well.

Looking across the Divide

The evolving, and highly polemical, Christian view of Muhammad is traced in detail in Norman Daniel, *Islam and the West: The Making of an Image*, rev. ed. (Oxford: Oneworld, 1993), and, more analytically and with an emphasis on more modern approaches, Maxime Rodinson, "A Critical Survey of Modern Studies on Muhammad," in Merlin Swartz, ed., *Studies on Islam* (Oxford: Oxford University Press, 1981), 23–85. In addition to Georges Anawati's article "'Isa" in the *Encyclopaedia of Islam* (Leiden: E. J. Brill, 1961–) and its parallel by Neal Robinson, "Jesus" in the *Encyclopedia of the Qur'an* (Leiden: E. J. Brill, 2001–2006), 3:7–20, the comparative treatment by Robinson, *Christ in Islam and Christianity* (Albany: SUNY Press, 1991), is highly useful for the present purpose. And the surprisingly rich trove of Jesus' sayings, which are revealing of Muslim attitudes though of no demonstrable historical value for Jesus himself, is presented by Tarif Khalidi, *The Muslim Jesus: Sayings and Stories in Islamic Literature* (Cambridge: Harvard University Press, 2001).

Galilee and Palestine

There is a brief but richly detailed portrait of the Galilean political and social milieu in John S. Kloppenborg, *Excavating Q: The History and Setting of the Sayings Gospel* (Edinburgh: T. & T. Clarke, 2000), 214–61, with a full review of earlier work. See in particular Sean Freyne, *Jesus, a Jewish Galilean: A New Reading of the Jesus Story* (New York: Continuum, 2004), and his survey of Galilean scholarship in *Galilee and Gospel: Selected Essays* (Tübingen: J. C. C. Mohr, 2000), 1–26. Also useful are the papers collected in Lee I. Levine, *The Galilee of Late Antiquity* (New York: Jewish Theological Seminary of America, 1992), and Richard Horsley, *Archaeology, History, and Society in Galilee: The Social Context of Jesus and the Rabbis* (Valley Forge: Trinity Press International, 1996).

The archaeological evidence from Palestine as it pertains to Jesus' world is authoritatively collected and reviewed in Jack Finegan, *The Archaeology of the New Testament* (Princeton: Princeton University Press, 1992), and in the papers more recently published in James Charlesworth, ed., *Jesus and Archeology* (Grand Rapids:William B. Eerdmans, 2006).

Jesus' Background

The literary sources that serve to fill in the background on Jesus' time and place are set out in detail in Emil Schürer, *The History of the Jewish People in the Age of Jesus Christ, 175 B.C.– A.D. 135*, revised and edited by Geza Vermes and Fergus Millar, vol. 1 (Edinburgh: T. & T. Clarke, 1973), 17–124, "The Sources." The biblical apocrypha are available in English in James H. Charlesworth, ed., *The Old Testament Pseudepigrapha*, 2 vols. (Garden City: Doubleday New York, 1983), and H. D. F. Sparks, ed., *The Apocryphal Old Testament* (Oxford: Clarendon Press, 1984). On the notion of a Scriptural canon for Jews and Christians, see my own *The Voice, the Word, the Books: The Sacred Scriptures of the Jews, Christians, and Muslims* (Princeton: Princeton University Press, 2007), 39–67.

There is a full appreciation of Roman powers and practices and Jewish restrictions and privileges in Roman Judea between AD 6 and 41 in Schürer, *History of the Jewish People*, 1:359–98.

The portrait of first-century Jews and Judaism that emerges from Josephus and our other sources is displayed in Schürer, *History of the Jewish People*, 1:125–560 for the history, and vol. 2 (1979) for the religious background, with special attention to "Messianism" (488–554) and the Essenes of Qumran (555–90). For another illuminating perspective on the Jewish enterprise of that era, see Shaye J. D. Cohen, *From the Maccabees to the Mishnah*, 2nd ed. (Louisville: Westminster John Knox Press, 2006), and for the range of opinions, Robert Kraft and George W. E. Nickelsburg, eds., *Early Judaism and Its Modern Interpreters* (Philadelphia: Fortress Press, 1996).

Two presentations by scholars in the forefront of the quest for the historical Jesus are worthy of particular note. E. P. Sanders, *Judaism, Practice, and Belief, 63 BCE–66 CE* (Philadelphia: Trinity Press International, 1992), is a full-scale portrait of a religious culture (and Jesus is moved convincingly into it in Sanders' *Jesus and Judaism* [Philadelphia: Fortress Press, 1985]); briefer but no less substantial and illuminating are the pages devoted to "First Century Judaism within the Greco-Roman World" in N. T. Wright's *The New Testament and the People of God* (Minneapolis: Fortress Press, 1992), 145–338.

For the apocalyptic background of the New Testament, there are John J. Collins, *The Apocalyptic Imagination: An Introduction to the Jewish Matrix of Christianity* (New York:

Crossroad, 1985), and Adela Yarbro Collins, *Cosmology and Eschatology in Jewish and Christian Apocalypticism* (Leiden: E. J. Brill, 1996).

The Dead Sea Scrolls are readily available in English in Geza Vermes, *The Complete Dead Sea Scrolls* (New York: Penguin, 2004).

On the issue of messianism, the symposium papers edited by James H. Charlesworth, *The Messiah: Developments in Earliest Christianity and Judaism* (Minneapolis: Fortress Press, 1992), cover all the ground, but see too John J. Collins, *The Scepter and the Star: The Messiahs of the Dead Sea Scrolls and Other Ancient Literatures* (New York: Doubleday, 1995), and Stanley E. Porter, *The Messiah in the Old and New Testaments* (Grand Rapids: William B. Eerdmans, 2007), which survey the whole field. On Qumran messianism, see, more precisely, Lawrence H. Schiffman, *Reclaiming the Dead Sea Scrolls* (New York: Doubleday, 1995), 315–68; Vermes, *Complete Dead Sea Scrolls*, 84–90.

Muhammad's Arab and Arabian Background

The classic studies on Muhammad's background are those of Julius Wellhausen, *Reste arabischen Heidentums* (Berlin, 1897), relying heavily on Ibn al-Kalbi; the first volume of Leone Caetani's monumental *Annali dell'Islam* (Milan: Hoepli, 1905); and, among the works of Henri Lammens, *La Mecque à la Veille de l'Hégire* (Beyrouth: Imprimerie Catholique, 1924). It is their work, particularly the extensive studies of Lammens, that provides the background for the influential analyses of E. Wolf, "The Social Organization of Mecca and the Origins of Islam," *Southwestern Journal of Anthropology* (1951): 329–56; W. Montgomery Watt, *Muhammad at Mecca* (Oxford: Clarendon Press, 1953); and the discussion in Maxime Rodinson, *Islam and Capitalism* (Austin: University of Texas Press, 1978), 254 n. 3.

For the pre-Islamic Arabs on the broad canvas of Arabia and the Middle East, there is Robert G. Hoyland, *Arabia and the Arabs from the Bronze Age to the Coming of Islam* (London: Routledge, 2001), and for recent work more precisely on the pre-Islamic background of Mecca and the Hijaz, see the studies reprinted in my *Arabs and Arabia on the Eve of Islam* (Aldershot: Ashgate Variorum, 1999), particularly those of Walter Dostal, Gerald Hawting, Uri Rubin, and Ugo Fabietti; and my own attempt to reconstruct something out of them in *Mecca: A Literary History of the Muslim Holy Land* (Princeton: Princeton University Press, 1994), chap. 1, "A Speculative History of Mecca in the Age of Ignorance."

For attempts at reconstructing the Arab paganism encountered by Muhammad, see the already cited Wellhausen, *Reste;* Gonzague Ryckmans, *Les religions arabes préislamiques* (Louvain, 1951); the studies by Henninger and Serjeant reprinted in my *Arabs and Arabia;* and Hoyland, *Arabia and the Arabs*, 139–45, with a bibliography, 296–98. For the evolution of many Islamic rituals out of pre-Islamic practice, see the articles collected in Gerald R. Hawting, ed., *The Development of Islamic Ritual* (Aldershot: Ashgate Variorum, 2006), and, on the difficulty of connecting Islam back to that past, Hawting, *The Idea of Idolatry and the Emergence of Islam: From Polemic to History* (Cambridge: Cambridge University Press, 1999). Information on the origins and development of the hajj is collected in my book *The*

Hajj: The Muslim Pilgrimage to Mecca and the Holy Places (Princeton: Princeton University Press, 1994), 3–59.

Of great importance are the pioneering efforts of M. J. Kister to sort out the various and scattered Muslim reports on the pre-Islamic era; his work was first collected in his *Studies in Jahiliyya and Early Islam* (London: Variorum Reprints, 1980), and his own and his students' subsequent writing on the same subject fill the pages of successive volumes of the journal *Jerusalem Studies in Arabic and Islam*. For the demolition of the myth of Mecca as a great pre-Islamic trading emporium, see Patricia Crone, *Meccan Trade and the Rise of Islam* (Princeton: Princeton University Press, 1987).

The Jesus Sources

The pagan and Jewish sources on Jesus are reviewed at length in Schürer, *History of the Jewish People*, 1:17–124, as well as in John P. Meier, *A Marginal Jew: Rethinking the Historical Jesus*, vol. 1, *The Roots of the Problem and the Person* (New York: Anchor Doubleday, 1991), 56–166.

JOSEPHUS

Background information on Josephus and his work are readily available in Schürer, *History of the Jewish People*, 1:56–88, and in the collection of studies edited by Louis H. Feldman and Gohei Hata, *Josephus, Judaism, and Christianity* (Detroit: Wayne State University Press, 1987). More particularly on Josephus and Jesus, there is a thorough analysis in Meier, *A Marginal Jew*, 1:56–88; cf. Schürer, *History of the Jewish People*, 1:428–41. The Arabic text's contribution to the debate about the Testimonium Flavianum (see Meier, *A Marginal Jew*, 1:78–79 n. 17) can be found at Shlomo Pines, *An Arabic Version of the Testimonium Flavianum and Its Implications* (Jerusalem: Israel Academy of Sciences and Humanities, 1971). For a more recent update on the debate, see Alice Whealey, *Josephus on Jesus: The Testimonium Flavianum Controversy from Late Antiquity to Modern Times* (New York: Peter Lang, 2003), and Whealey, "The *Testimonium Flavianum* in Syriac and Arabic," *New Testament Studies* 54 (2008): 571–90.

THE DEAD SEA SCROLLS

Two collections twenty-five years apart sample various views on the connection between Jesus and the Dead Sea Scrolls: Krister Stendahl, ed., *The Scrolls and the New Testament* (1957; rpt. with a new introduction by James H. Charlesworth, New York: Crossroad, 1992), and James H. Charlesworth, *Jesus and the Dead Sea Scrolls* (New York: Doubleday, 1992). Charlesworth's essay "The Historical Jesus" in the latter (1–74) reviews the questions raised by the Scrolls and surveys some of the answers; for a somewhat different perspective, see Murphy O'Connor, "Qumran and the New Testament," in Eldon Jay Epp and George W. MacRae, eds., *The New Testament and Its Modern Interpreters* (Philadelphia: Fortress Press,

1989), 55–74. The question of influence is still very much alive; see, most recently, James H. Charlesworth, ed., *The Bible and the Dead Sea Scrolls* (Waco: Baylor University Press, 2006), vol. 3, *The Scrolls and Christian Origins*.

THE RABBIS

The principal monument to the conviction that the rabbinic sources might add to the understanding of Jesus was H. Strack and P. Billerback, *Kommentar zum Neuen Testament aus Talmud und Midrasch*, 6 vols. (Munich: Beck, 1924–1928), and Jacob Neusner its principal sapper; see, *inter alia multa*, his *Rabbinic Literature and the New Testament: What We Cannot Show, What We Do Not Know* (Valley Forge: Trinity Press International, 1994). Now on the rabbinic sources there is also Peter Schäfer, *Jesus in the Talmud* (Princeton: Princeton University Press, 2007).

THE CHRISTIAN LITERARY SOURCES

The sources on Jesus can be approached from the direction of either their availability and content—plainly stated in James D. G. Dunn, *The Evidence for Jesus* (Louisville: Westminster Press, 1985)—or the historiographical method to be used on them—densely argued in Gerd Theissen and Dagmar Winter, *The Quest for the Plausible Jesus: The Question of Criteria* (Louisville: Westminster Press, 2002). Or, more generally, in a combination of the two.

Two of the most complete overviews and (differing) analyses of the literary sources on the historical Jesus are those in Meier, *A Marginal Jew*, 1:41–195, and John Dominic Crossan, who is much more inclined than Meier to admit the so-called apocryphal Gospels into evidence in *The Historical Jesus: The Life of a Mediterranean Jewish Peasant* (San Francisco: HarperSanFrancisco, 1991). An even wider net is cast over the Gospel genre by Helmut Koester, *Ancient Christian Gospels: Their History and Development* (Philadelphia: Trinity Press International, 1990). The effect of this latter approach, seconded by the Jesus Seminar, is visible in the broad range of "gospels" presented in Robert J. Miller, *The Complete Gospels: Annotated Scholars Version*, rev. ed. (Santa Rosa: Polebridge Press, 1994).

Particularly clear and useful on the methods of sorting out the Synoptics is Robert H. Stein, *The Synoptic Problem: An Introduction* (Grand Rapids: Baker Book House, 1987). On the special historical problems presented by John's Gospel, see C. H. Dodd, *The Historical Tradition in the Fourth Gospel* (Cambridge: Cambridge University Press, 1963); Raymond E. Brown, *The Gospel According to John*, vol. 1 (Garden City: Doubleday, 1966), xxvii–xxxii (on John's sources) and xli–li (John and the historical Jesus). For John and a sayings source, see Barnabas Lindars, "Discourse and Tradition: The Use of the Sayings of Jesus in the Discourses of the Fourth Gospel," in Stanley E. Porter and Craig A. Evans, eds., *The Johannine Writings* (Sheffield: Sheffield Academic Press, 1995), 13–30; and on the "*semeia* source," Robert Fortna, *The Gospel of Signs: A Reconstruction of the Narrative Source Underlying the Fourth Gospel* (Cambridge: Cambridge University Press, 1970).

The beginnings of the literary tradition of a gospel are examined in Lawrence Wills, *The Quest of the Historical Gospel: Mark, John, and the Origins of the Gospel Genre* (London: Routledge, 1997). For a broader approach to the canonical Gospels in the context of New Testament Studies, there is Epp and MacRae, eds., *The New Testament and Its Modern Interpreters*, part 3, "The Literature of the New Testament" (201–320). There are interesting reflections on the Christian literary sources in Wright, *The New Testament and the People of God*, 31–80 and 371–443.

On what Paul has to tell us, see Meier, *A Marginal Jew*, 1:45–47, and James D. G. Dunn, "Jesus Tradition in Paul," in Bruce Chilton and C. A. Evans, eds., *Studying the Historical Jesus* (Leiden: E. J. Brill, 1994), 155–78.

THE NEW TESTAMENT APOCRYPHA

The New Testament apocrypha are available in English in Edgar Hennecke and William Schneemelcher, eds., *New Testament Apocrypha*, 2 vols. (Philadelphia: Westminster Press, 1963–1965), and J. K. Elliott, ed., *The Apocryphal New Testament: A Collection of Apocryphal Christian Literature in an English Translation* (Oxford: Clarendon Press, 1993); cf. Ron Cameron, *The Other Gospels: Non-Canonical Gospel Texts* (Philadelphia: Westminster Press, 1982), and J. K. Elliott, *The Apocryphal Jesus: Legends of the Early Church* (New York: Oxford University Press, 1996).

The Muhammad Sources

THE QURAN

The best single introduction to the Quran as both Scripture and a document remains W. Montgomery Watt, *Bell's Introduction to the Qur'an* (Edinburgh: Edinburgh University Press, 1970), though with important considerations proposed in Neal Robinson, *Discovering the Qur'an: A Contemporary Approach to a Veiled Text*, 2nd ed. (Washington: Georgetown University Press, 2003). The most skeptical and influential statements on the entire Quranic tradition are doubtless John Wansbrough, *Quranic Studies: Sources and Methods of Scriptural Interpretation*, foreword, translations, and expanded notes by Andrew Rippin (Amherst: Prometheus Books, 2004), and John Burton, *The Collection of the Qur'an* (Cambridge: Cambridge University Press, 1977).

There are now new research tools for the study of the Quran. First and foremost is Jane Dammen McAuliffe, ed., *The Encyclopedia of the Qur'an*, 5 vols. (Leiden: E. J. Brill, 2001–2006 [hereafter *EQ*]), and the single-volume work edited by Oliver Leaman, *The Qur'an: An Encyclopedia* (New York: Routledge, 2006), both to be supplemented by McAuliffe, ed., *The Cambridge Companion to the Qur'an* (Cambridge: Cambridge University Press, 2006); Andrew Rippin, ed., *The Blackwell Companion to the Qur'an* (Chichester: Wiley-Blackwell, 2009); and Gabriel Said Reynolds, *The Qur'an in Its Historical Context* (London: Routledge, 2008).

Extracting Muhammad from the Quran is no simple matter. There have been notable attempts by W. Montgomery Watt, *Muhammad's Mecca: History in the Qur'an* (Edinburgh: Edinburgh University Press, 1988); Alford T. Welch, "Muhammad's Understanding of Himself: The Koranic Data," in Richard G. Hovannisian and Speros Vryonis, eds., *Islam's Understanding of Itself* (Malibu: Undena Publications, 1983), 15–52; Andrew Rippin, "Muhammad in the Qur'an: Reading Scripture in the 21st Century," in Harald Motzki, ed., *The Biography of Muhammad: The Issue of the Sources* (Leiden: E. J. Brill, 2000), 298–309; and now Uri Rubin, art. "Muhammad" in *EQ*, 4:440–57, but the most detailed and successful to date is Jacqueline Chabbi's extraordinary *Le Seigneur des Tribus: L'Islam de Mahomet* (Paris: Editions Noesis, 1997).

ARAB HISTORY WRITING

There are excellent introductions to Arab history writing, particularly as it applies to the life of Muhammad, by A. A. Duri, *The Rise of Historical Writing among the Arabs*, edited and translated by Lawrence I. Conrad (Princeton: Princeton University Press, 1983); R. Stephen Humphreys, *Islamic History: A Framework for Inquiry*, rev. ed. (Princeton: Princeton University Press, 1991), 69–91, "The Character of Early Islamic Historiography," who concludes, regarding the first century of Islam, "The evidence is such . . . that reasonable certainty may be beyond our grasp" (69); Chase F. Robinson, *Islamic Historiography* (Cambridge: Cambridge University Press, 2003), 18–38, "The Emergence of Genre"; and the important studies collected in Lawrence I. Conrad, ed., *History and Historiography in Early Islamic Times: Studies and Perspectives* (Princeton: Darwin Press, 1992).

THE NARRATIVE SOURCES

The nature of the narrative sources on the entire first century of Islam, which Humphreys succinctly describes as "a rather late crystallization of a fluid oral tradition" (*Islamic History*, 69), renders all attempts at a reconstruction of that era highly problematic. What is true of the era generally is also true of the career of Muhammad in particular. The critical issues in the narrative sources on Muhammad are treated in Motzki, ed., *Biography of Muhammad*, as well as in many of the articles reprinted in Uri Rubin, ed., *The Life of Muhammad* (Aldershot: Ashgate Variorum, 1998), and Ibn Warraq, ed., *The Quest for the Historical Muhammad* (Amherst: Prometheus Books, 2000). Important too is M. J. Kister, "The *Sira* Literature," in A. F. L. Beeston et al., eds., *Arabic Literature to the End of the Umayyad Period* (Cambridge: Cambridge University Press, 1983), 352–67; and John Wansbrough's skeptical look at Ibn Ishaq's *Sira* in *The Sectarian Milieu: Content and Composition of Islamic Salvation History*, foreword, translations, and expanded notes by Gerald Hawting (Amherst: Prometheus Books, 2006), a skepticism more broadly and pointedly expressed in Patricia Crone, *Slaves on Horseback: The Evolution of the Islamic Polity* (London: Cambridge University Press, 1980), 3–17, "Historiographical Introduction."

As already noted, the standard medieval biography of the Prophet is available in English in Alfred Guillaume, *The Life of Muhammad: A Translation of Ibn Ishaq's Sirat Rasul*

Allah (London: Oxford University Press, 1955). Guillaume's own introduction there to Ibn Ishaq, his predecessor, and successors (xiii–xlvii) is both useful and informative. The so-called Constitution of Medina is an example of what is perhaps an authentic preserved document (see R. B. Serjeant, "The *Sunnah Jami'ah*, Pacts with the Yathrib Jews and the *Tahrim* of Yathrib: Analysis and Translation of the . . . Constitution of Medina," *Bulletin of the School of Oriental and African Studies* 41 [1978]: 1–42; and Humphreys, *Islamic History*, 92–98), while the extensive correspondence conducted by Muhammad and various world leaders and reproduced in other biographies is almost certainly all forgeries.

On Waqidi and the "Raids" literature, J. M. B. Jones, "The *Maghazi* Literature," in Beeston et al., eds., *Arabic Literature to the End of the Umayyad Period*, 344–51, is the best beginning, with further details in Rizwi Faizer, art. "Expeditions and Battles" in *EQ*, 2:143–53. The Muhammad section of Ibn Sa'd's work is available in English in *Ibn Sa'd's Kitab al-Tabaqat al-Kabir*, translated by S. Moinul Haq assisted by H. K. Ghazanfar, 2 vols. (Karachi: Pakistan Historical Society, 1967–1972), and the pertinent sections of Bukhari in *Sahih al-Buhkari: The Early Years of Islam, Being the Historical Chapters of the Kitab Jami'i al-Sahih Compiled by Iman Abu Abd-Allah Muhammad ibn Isma'il al-Bukhari*, translated and explained by Muhammad Asad (Gibraltar: Dar al-Andalus, 1981).

The literature on the hadith is extensive. The classic treatment is Ignaz Goldziher, "On the Development of the Hadith," originally published in 1890 and then reprinted in *Muslim Studies* (London: George Allen & Unwin, 1971), edited by S. M. Stern, 2:17–254. Important contributions have been collected and reprinted in Harald Motzki, ed., *Hadith: Origins and Development* (Aldershot: Ashgate Variorum, 2004), to which should be added his own article, "Dating Muslim Traditions: A Survey," *Arabica* 52 (2005): 204–53. For a skeptical view of the results: Henri Lammens, "Qoran et tradition: Comment fut composée la vie de Mahomet," *Recherches de Science Religieuse* 1 (1910): 25–61; English trans., "Koran and Tradition—How the Life of Muhammad was Composed," in Ibn Warraq, ed., *Quest for the Historical Muhammad*, 169–87.

On the *qissas*/storyteller tradition, see H. T. Norris, "Qisas Elements in the Qur'an," in Beeston et al., eds., *Arabic Literature to the End of the Umayyad Period*, 246–59; and for Wahb's influence on the narrative sources, Duri, *Rise of Historical Writing*, 122–35; and M. J. Kister, "On the Papyrus of Wahb ibn Munabbih," *Bulletin of the School of Oriental and African Studies* 37 (1974): 545–71.

Coming of Age

Almost everything that needs saying on the subject of Jesus' Infancy Narratives has been said (or read) by Raymond E. Brown, *The Birth of the Messiah: A Commentary on the Infancy Narratives of the Gospels of Matthew and Luke*, new updated ed. (New York: Anchor Doubleday, 1993), though his relatively conservative conclusions need not always be drawn. The subject of Jesus' family and related personal issues exceeds the boundaries of the Infancy Narratives, of course, and extends in quite imaginative fashion into the New Testament apocrypha (summarized in Hennecke and Schneemelcher, eds., *New Testament Apocrypha*,

1:418–32, including material on Joseph [429–32]). All the available information has been thoroughly surveyed, and the various conclusions from it judiciously weighed, in Meier, *A Marginal Jew*, 1:253–315, "Language, Education, and Socioeconomic Status," and 1:316–71, "Family, Marital Status, and Status as a Layman."

The parallel "Infancy Narratives" in the life of Muhammad have not yet found their Raymond Brown, but one may nevertheless start by looking at the full range of the prerevelation stories in Martin Lings, *Muhammad: His Life Based on the Earliest Sources* (Rochester, VT: Inner Traditions International, 1983), 1–42; and peering behind some of them with Arthur Jeffery, "Was Muhammad a Prophet from His Infancy?" *Muslim World* 20 (1930): 226–34; and Rubin, *Eye of the Beholder*, 21–126, on "Attestation," "Preparation," and "Revelation," and particularly his "Conclusions" (217–60).

The chronology of Muhammad's life at Mecca is particularly vexed (Rubin, *Eye of the Beholder*, 189–216), and nowhere more evidently than in its tie to the Ethiopian viceroy Abraha; see M. J. Kister, "The Campaign of Hulaban: New Light on the Expedition of Abraha," *Le Muséon* 78 (1965): 425–36; rpt. Kister, *Studies*; and Lawrence I. Conrad, "Abraha and Muhammad: Some Observations a propos of Chronology and Literary *Topoi* in the Early Arabic Historical Tradition," *Bulletin of the School of Oriental and African Studies* 50 (1987): 225–40.

The complex of stories around the "Opening of Muhammad's Breast" has been analyzed by Harris Birkeland, *The Legend of the Opening of Muhammad's Breast* (Oslo: Jacob Dybwad, 1955), and Rubin, *Eye of the Beholder*, 59–74; that centering on the Prophet's involvement in the "Sinful Wars," by Ella Landau-Tasseron, "The 'Sinful Wars': Religious, Social, and Historical Aspects of *Hurub al-Fijar*," *Jerusalem Studies in Arabic and Islam* 8 (1986): 37–59; and Crone, *Meccan Trade*, 145–48.

The Living Voices

JESUS' WORDS

Intensive work on the sayings source Q has now been going on for more than twenty years and latecomers can conveniently join the dialogue with the convinced in Arland D. Jacobson, *The First Gospel: An Introduction to Q* (Sonoma: Polebridge Press, 1992), Burton L. Mack, *The Lost Gospel: The Book of Q and Christian Origins* (San Francisco: HarperSanFrancisco, 1994), or Kloppenborg, *Excavating Q*. For quite another view of Q, one should consult Meier, *A Marginal Jew*, 1:43–44, 134–37.

Authenticating the contents of the sayings sources and of Jesus' words in the Gospels is an even more complex matter, as is clear from the studies collected in Bruce Chilton and Craig A. Evans, eds., *Authenticating the Words of Jesus* (Boston: E. J. Brill, 2002), and the essay of Darrell L. Bock, "The Words of Jesus in the Gospels: Live, Jive, or Memorex?" in Michael J. Wilkins and J. P. Moreland, *Jesus Under Fire: Modern Scholarship Reinvents the Historical Jesus* (Grand Rapids: Zondervan, 1995), 73–100. The most specific, and notorious, attempt at separating the authentic from the imagined or invented is doubtless the color-coded results published in Robert W. Funk, Roy A. Hoover, and the Jesus Seminar, *The Five Gospels: The Search for the Authentic Words of Jesus; New Translation and Commentary* (New York: Maxwell Macmillan International, 1993).

The notably skeptical findings of the Jesus Seminar were not greeted with universal acclaim: see Witherington, *The Jesus Quest*, 42–57, "Jesus the Talking Head"; and Johnson, *The Real Jesus*, 1–27, "The Good News and the Nightly News."

MUHAMMAD'S WORDS

The approach to the living voice of Muhammad has paused, or stalled, on the threshold of the work that preserves and presents it, the Quran. The work can be addressed as both *text* (James Bellamy, art. "Textual Criticism of the Qur'an" in *EQ*, 5:237–52; François Déroche, "Written Transmission," in Rippin, ed., *Blackwell Companion to the Qur'an*, 2009, 172–86) and as *product* (the studies collected in Rippin, ed., *The Qur'an: Style and Contents* [Aldershot: Variorum, 2001]), but what is far more problematic is an understanding of its composition and construction; see Fred McGraw Donner, "The Qur'an in Recent Research—Challenges and Desiderata," and Gerald Böwering, "Reconstructing the Qur'an: Emerging Insights," both in Reynolds, ed., *Qur'an*, 29–50 and 70–87 respectively.

There is a major clue in the Quran's own admission that Muhammad was identified—an identification he denied—as a mantic poet, which we can further gloss as an *oral* mantic poet, a notion thoroughly unpacked by Michael Zwettler, "A Mantic Manifesto: The Sura of 'the Poets' and the Quranic Foundations of Prophetic Authority," in James L. Kugel, ed., *Poetry and Prophecy: The Beginnings of a Literary Tradition* (Ithaca: Cornell University Press, 1990), 75–119; and further resumed in Alan Jones, art. "Poetry and Poets" in *EQ*, 4:110–14.

Behind the "The Recitation"(*al-Qur'an*) lies the entire tradition of oral poetry in Arabia which has been investigated in its profane dimensions by Michael Zwettler, *The Oral Tradition of Classical Arabic Poetry* (Columbus: Ohio State University Press, 1978), but which, in the case of the Quran, spills into the notion of Scripture; see, generally, William A. Graham, *Beyond the Written Word: Oral Aspects of Scripture in the History of Religion* (Cambridge: Cambridge University Press, 1987), and, for the Quran, his *Divine Word and Prophetic Word in Early Islam* (The Hague: Mouton, 1977); "The Qur'an as Spoken Word: An Islamic Contribution to the Understanding of Scripture," in Richard Martin, ed., *Approaches to Islam in Religious Studies* (Tucson: University of Arizona Press, 1985), 19–40; and the articles "Scripture and the Qur'an" in *EQ*, 4:558–69, and "Orality," *EQ*, 3:584–87; cf. Alan Jones, art. "Orality and Writing in Arabia" in *EQ*, 3:587–93.

The path from oral poetry/pronouncements to the Quran is exceedingly ill lit, but what light there is has been largely contributed by Angelika Neuwirth in a number of different studies, most substantially in "Du texte de recitation au canon en passant par la liturgie: A propos de la genèse de la composition des sourates et de sa redissolution au cours du développement du culte islamique," *Arabica* 47 (2000): 194–229; but see also her "Structural,

Linguistic, and Literary Features," in McAuliffe, ed., *Cambridge Companion to the Qur'an*, 97–114; and the article "Form and Structure of the Qur'an" in *EQ*, 2:245–66.

Jesus in Galilee

JOHN THE BAPTIST

Jesus' important connection with John the Baptist is exhaustively treated in John P. Meier, *A Marginal Jew: Rethinking the Historical Jesus*, vol. 2, *Mentor, Message, and Miracles* (New York: Anchor Doubleday, 1994), whether the Baptist alone (19–99, with special attention to his mention in Josephus, 56–62) or the connection between the two (100–288), to which should be added Joan E. Taylor, *The Immerser: John the Baptist within Second Temple Judaism* (Grand Rapids: William B. Eerdmans, 1997).

PETER

Meier has paid equal, and equally critical, attention to the Twelve in *A Marginal Jew: Rethinking the Historical Jesus*, vol. 3, *Companions and Competitors* (New York: Anchor Doubleday, 2001), 125–288, but note should also be taken of his full address (40–124) to the larger question of discipleship and to the more precise and important issue of the Gospels' presentation of Peter (221–45), the "rock" on whom Jesus would build his "Church."

THE ITINERANT PREACHER

There is no doubt that the Jesus whose Galilean career is described in the Gospels may be accurately described as an itinerant preacher who taught by both aphorism and parable but who also possessed a strong charismatic appeal and the undoubted ability to work wonders. Most modern portraits depict him as such; Martin Hengel's *The Charismatic Leader and His Followers* (Edinburgh: T. & T. Clarke, 1996) is a classic example. Where the assessments differ, and quite radically, is on *what* Jesus was teaching. Here the great divide opens over the preferred sources. Those who lean heavily, or predominantly, or exclusively on the sayings sources Q and Thomas, regard Jesus as *essentially* an itinerant preacher with a message of social reform, though possibly with political overtones and almost certainly with political consequences. These are the views, for example, of the Jesus Seminar, which is not really certain about anything Jesus said (see *Five Gospels* above) or did (Robert Funk et al., *The Acts of Jesus: What Did Jesus Really Do?* [New York: HarperCollins, 1998]), and, with varying nuances, of Burton L. Mack, *A Myth of Innocence: Mark and Christian Origins* (Philadelphia: Fortress Press, 1988); John Dominic Crossan, *The Historical Jesus* and *Jesus: A Revolutionary Biography* (San Francisco: HarperSanFrancisco, 1994); and Marcus Borg, *Jesus: A New Vision* (San Francisco: HarperSanFrancisco, 1987) and *Meeting Jesus Again for the First Time* (San Francisco: HarperSanFrancisco, 1994). Finally, there are the contributions of both Mack and Crossan to "The Mediterranean Jesus," and Sean Freyne's engagement with

Crossan, "Galilean Questions to the Mediterranean Jesus," in Arnal and Desjardins, eds., *Whose Historical Jesus?*, 4–60 and 63–91 respectively.

All such assessments have, of course, to deal with the Gospel evidence, as particularly represented by Mark, that presents Jesus in a quite different light and in a trajectory that rises from Promised Messiah to Suffering Servant to Risen Christ to Son of God to Eschatological Savior. That narrative Gospel problem is most directly addressed by Mack, *A Myth of Innocence* and *Who Wrote the New Testament: The Making of a Christian Myth* (San Francisco: HarperSanFrancisco, 1995), and John Dominic Crossan, *The Birth of Christianity: Discovering What Happened in the Years Immediately Following the Execution of Jesus* (San Francisco: HarperSanFrancisco, 1998).

Crossan feels constrained to explain away the eschatological strain that is patently present in the sayings source (*Birth of Christianity*, 239–92), but others are inclined to take it at face value. Thus for scholars like Gerd Theissen, *The Gospels in Context: Social and Political History in the Synoptic Tradition* (Minneapolis: Augsburg Press, 1991), and Richard A. Horsley, *Jesus and the Spiral of Violence* (San Francisco: HarperSanFrancisco, 1987), Jesus was a radical social reformer, but, as the Gospels suggest, it was in the context of an approaching End Time: class warfare was simply the run-up to the Apocalypse.

PROPHET AND MESSIAH

The "Jesus in Galilee" segment of the Synoptic Gospels is, its ominous predictions aside, not very different from "The Jesus of Q," but those who continue to privilege the narrative Gospels over (the more or less exclusive use of) the sayings sources read the narrative Gospels with one eye cast forward to "Jesus in Jerusalem," which is pretty much the way their authors wrote them: the passion and the resurrection are used to illuminate and unpack all that had gone before. The Jesus that emerges from that reading of the sources is not, then, simply an ethical teacher or social reformer, but at very least—to stay within the bounds of historical analysis—a prophet of the End Time who put himself forward not as a twentieth-century social reformer or revolutionary but as the first-century Messiah of Israel. It was a claim that in the sequel was found convincing by a not insubstantial number of his contemporaries.

Such was the view of C. H. Dodd, *The Founder of Christianity* (New York: Macmillan, 1970), and that put forward by Raymond Brown in *Introduction to New Testament Christology* (New York: Paulist Press, 1994) as well as in his *Birth of the Messiah* cited above and his *Death of the Messiah* cited below; by James D. G. Dunn, *Christianity in the Making*, vol. 1, *Jesus Remembered* (Grand Rapids: William B. Eerdmans, 2003), and *A New Perspective on Jesus*; E. P. Sanders, *The Historical Figure of Jesus* (New York: Penguin, 1993); John P. Meier in the four volumes of *A Marginal Jew* (1991–2009); and N. T. Wright, *Jesus and the Victory of God* (Minneapolis: Fortress Press, 1996).

This is not of course everything that these authors believe about Jesus. Most have additional convictions about the man the Christians call the Son of God. The just-cited *Christology* by Raymond Brown carries us into that new area of Jesus' supernatural status, but he is not the only guide. There is as well Martin Hengel, *The Son of God: The Origin of Christology and the History of Jewish Hellenistic Religion* (Philadelphia: Fortress Press, 1976); James D. G. Dunn, *Christology in the Making: A New Testament Inquiry into the Origins of the Doctrine of the Incarnation*, 2nd ed. (Grand Rapids: William B. Eerdmans, 1989); and the already cited work of Hurtado, *How on Earth Did Jesus Become a God?*

KINGDOM AND MIRACLES

On the "Kingdom" of Jesus' message, there is a complete treatment of the subject in Meier, *A Marginal Jew*, 2:237–508, with a bibliography (272–73); see also Bruce Chilton, ed., *The Kingdom of God in the Teaching of Jesus* (London: SPCK, 1984), and his "The Kingdom of God in Recent Discussion," in Chilton and Evans, eds., *Studying the Historical Jesus*, 255–80. Particularly influential on modern discussions have been C. H. Dodd, *The Parables of the Kingdom* (New York: Scribner, 1961), and the works of Norman Perrin, *Jesus and the Language of the Kingdom: Symbol and Metaphor in New Testament Interpretation* (Philadelphia: Fortress Press, 1976) and *The Kingdom of God in the Teaching of Jesus* (Philadelphia: Westminster Press, 1963).

Meier has devoted a similar degree of careful detail to the miracles of Jesus in *A Marginal Jew*, 2:509–1038, with a bibliography (522–24), to which should be added the reprint of Morton Smith's classic "Prolegomena to a Discussion of Aretologies, Divine Men, the Gospels, and Jesus," in his *Studies in the Cult of Yahweh*, vol. 2, *New Testament, Early Christianity, and Magic* (Leiden: E. J. Brill, 1996), 3–27; as well as the overviews by Barry L. Blackburn, "The Miracles of Jesus," in Chilton and Evans, eds., *Studying the Historical Jesus*, 353–94; and Graham Stanton, "Message and Miracles," in Markus Bockmuehl, ed., *The Cambridge Companion to Jesus* (Cambridge: Cambridge University Press, 2001), 56–71.

Muhammad in Mecca

A useful introduction to the issues here is Wim Raven, art. "Sira and the Qur'an" in *EQ*, 5:29–51. Muhammad's teaching can be elicited from both those sources, but there are more oblique strategies. Patricia Crone and Michael Cook, *Hagarism: The Making of the Islamic World* (Cambridge: Cambridge University Press, 1977), canvassed the testimony of Islam's neighbors for their (and our!) earliest impressions of the Prophet and his message, while Sidney H. Griffith, "The Prophet Muhammad, His Scripture, and His Message According to the Christian Apologies in Arabic and Syriac from the First Abbasid Century," in *La vie du prophète Mahomet: Colloque de Strasbourg 1980* (Paris, 1983), 99–146, weighed eighth-century Christian responses to the new religion; cf. A. Saadi, "Nascent Islam in the 7th Century Syriac Sources," in Reynolds, ed., *Qur'an* 217–22. The results are more interesting than satisfying and eventually the biographer returns to the standard sources, the Quran and the various versions of the *Sira*.

THE MECCAN CAREER

Muhammad's prophetic career at Mecca is covered in considerable, if not always convincing, detail in the Ibn Hisham version of Ibn Ishaq, available in English in *The Life of Muhammad*:

A Translation of Ibn Ishaq's Sirat Rasul Allah, with introduction and notes by A. Guillaume (London: Oxford University Press, 1955), 109–218; and in Tabari's version in *The History of al-Tabari*, vol. 6, *Muhammad at Mecca*, translated and annotated by W. Montgomery Watt and M. V. McDonald (Albany: SUNY Press, 1988), 60–152. These are the materials that form the basis of modern treatments like Watt's still-standard *Muhammad at Mecca* (Oxford: Clarendon Press, 1952), in Frants Buhl and Alford T. Welch, art. "Muhammad" in the *Encyclopaedia of Islam*, vol. 5 (1968), 360–76, "The Prophet's Life and Career"; the Meccan chapters of Maxime Rodinson, *Mohammed* (London: Penguin, 1971), 69–148; and my own *Muhammad and the Origins of Islam* (Albany: SUNY Press, 1994), 133–66.

CALL TO PROPHECY

The available material on Muhammad's call to prophecy (see Lings, *Muhammad*, 43–45) has been studied by Richard Bell, "Mohammed's Call," *Moslem World* 24 (1934): 13–19, and "Muhammad's Visions," *Moslem World* 24 (1934): 145–54; and Stefan Wild, "'We have sent down to thee the book with the truth . . .': Spatial and Temporal Implications of the Qur'anic Concepts of *nazul, tanzil* and *'inzal*," in Stefan Wild, ed., *The Qur'an as Text* (Leiden: E. J. Brill, 1996), 137–56. The "Night Journey" too (Lings, *Muhammad*, 101–4) has received special attention: Geo Widengren, *Muhammad, the Apostle of God, and His Ascension* (Wiesbaden: Otto Harrassowitz, 1955); J. R. Porter, "Muhammad's Journey to Heaven," *Numen* 21 (1974): 64–80; Heribert Busse, "Jerusalem in the Story of Muhammad's Night Journey and Ascension," *Jerusalem Studies in Arabic and Islam* 14 (1991): 1–40; and, opening into its larger influence in Islam, Schimmel, *And Muhammad Is His Messenger*, 159–75.

SATANIC VERSES

The incident of the insertion of "Satanic Verses" in sura 53:20 is related by Tabari among others (*History*, 6:107–12) and was filled out by medieval Muslim commentators like Zamakhshari (Helmut Gaetje, *The Qur'an and Its Exegesis* [Berkeley: University of California Press, 1976], 53–55). It is offered as illustration of a statement elsewhere (Q. 22:52) where God avers that He has granted permission for Satan to cast verses into the Quran (see Shahab Ahmed, art. "Satanic Verses" in *EQ*, 4:531–35, and Rubin, *Eye of the Beholder*, 156–68).

THE LAST DAYS

The Meccan suras of the Quran paint a number of graphic pictures of the Judgment and the Afterlife, with its punishments and rewards—see Jane I. Smith, art. "Eschatology" in *EQ*, 2:44–54; Fazlur Rahman, *Major Themes in the Qur'an*, 2nd ed. (Minneapolis: Bibliotheca Islamica, 1994), 106–20—which had their own elaborate afterlife among the Muslim commentators (a sample in Gaetje, *The Qur'an and Its Exegesis*, 172–86). The sequence begins with the death of the believer (Jane I. Smith and Yvonne Haddad, *The Islamic Understanding of Death and Resurrection* [Albany: SUNY Press, 1981] with its development in later exegesis) and includes vivid portraits of *Jahannam* (R. Gwynne, art. "Hell and Hellfire" in *EQ*, 2:414–40; Stefan Wild, art. "Hell" in Leaman, ed., *Qur'an Encyclopedia*, 259–63) and "The Garden" or Paradise (Josef Horovitz, "Das koranische Paradies" [Jerusalem, 1923; rpt. Rudi Paret, *Der Koran* (Darmstadt: Wissenschaftliche Buchgesellschaft, 1975)], 53–73; Stefan Wild, art. "Heaven" in *Qur'an Encyclopedia*, 258–59), with its promise of virginal *houris,* "full-breasted damsels" (78:33) . . . "like rubies and pearls" (55:58) to whom the believers will be wed (52:20), which has provoked lively discussion of what "houri" actually means (Oliver Leaman, art. "Houris" in Leaman, ed., *Qur'an Encyclopedia*, 269–71) and provided Christian writers with infinite grist for their polemical mills.

THE PROPHETS OF GOD

This threatening posture as a warner is transformed—but never quite replaced—in the evolving Quran by another approach. Muhammad located himself in the history of revelation and more specifically in the line of God-sent prophets that had begun with Adam and was now coming to its climax, and its end, with him. See Rahman, *Major Themes*, 80–105, and a full treatment in Uri Rubin, "Prophets and Prophethood," in Rippin, ed., *Blackwell Companion to the Qur'an*, 234–47.

Behind this is Muhammad's understanding of God, his will and his work in the world. Like all other such larger concepts, it unfolds piecemeal in the Quran as circumstances and inclination dictate. The data have been assembled by Rahman, *Major Themes*, 1–16, and Rippin, "God," in his *Blackwell Companion to the Qur'an*, 223–33. And there is as well humans' place in the scheme of the divine economy traced, from two very different perspectives, by Rahman, *Major Themes*, 17–36, and Toshihiko Izutsu, *God and Man in the Koran* (Tokyo: Keio Institute, 1964).

"COMMAND THE RIGHT AND FORBID THE WRONG"

The individual does not stand alone before God; he has a life in society and the Quran lays down a simple but powerful imperative from which the entirety of Muslim morality depends: "Command the right and forbid the wrong" (3:104, 110; 9:71, a verse that explicitly includes women in those bound). But it does not often spell out either the modalities of the command or explicit examples of its application; see A. Kevin Reinhart, art. "Ethics in the Qur'an" in *EQ*, 2:55–78. That fell to Islam's prodigious legal tradition, as described in detail by Michael Cook, *Commanding Right and Forbidding Wrong in Islamic Thought* (Cambridge: Cambridge University Press, 2000) and more summarily in his *Forbidding Wrong in Islam: An Introduction* (Cambridge: Cambridge University Press, 2003). The ethical structures that underlie the Quran can also be approached by measuring them against their pre-Islamic counterparts, as was done by Ignaz Goldziher, "Muruwwa and Din," in *Muslim Studies*, ed. Stern, 1:11–44, 201–8; and M. M. Bravmann, *The Spiritual Background of Early Islam: Studies in Ancient Arab Concepts* (Leiden: E. J. Brill, 1972), this latter through a semantic analysis of its key terms, a method also followed by Toshihiko Izutsu in *The Structure of Ethical Terms in the Koran* (Tokyo: Keio Institute, 1959) and *Ethico-Religious Concepts in the Quran* (Montreal: McGill University Press, 1966).

The Quran does, however, descend to particulars at times, on the believers' duties toward God, like prayer, fasting, tithing, and the hajj, whose Quranic occurrences are underlined by Watt, *Bell's Introduction to the Qur'an*, 162–64. There are more earthly concerns as well in what the Quran offers not as advice but as prescriptive legislation: marriage and divorce, inheritance, food laws, wine-drinking, usury (Watt, *Bell's Introduction*, 164–66) and the regulation of a broad range of sexual practices (surveyed in Khaleel Mohammed, "Sex, Sexuality, and the Family," in Rippin, ed., *Blackwell Companion to the Qur'an*, 298–307).

A JEWISH CHRISTIAN MATRIX?

The "sources" for Muhammad and the Quran began in earnest with Abraham Geiger's 1832 doctoral thesis, "What Did Muhammad Borrow from Judaism?" which was translated into English in 1898 and reprinted as *Judaism and Islam* (New York: Ktav, 1970). (On Geiger and his work, see Jacob Lassner, "Jacob Geiger: A Nineteenth Century Jewish Reformer on the Origins of Islam," in Martin Kramer, ed., *The Jewish Discovery of Islam: Studies in Honor of Bernard Lewis* [Tel Aviv: Moshe Dayan Center, 1999], 103–36). That rather direct approach with its reductionist implications appears to have lost its momentum in more recent time, though it may have simply been reformulated as a search for possible informants; see Claude Gilliot, art. "Informants" in *EQ*, 2:512–18.

What is being proposed here is something more modest, that some form of heterodox Jewish Christianity provided an unstated religious context, along with the local Arab paganism, from which Muhammad spoke and against which his audience heard and understood him. I am not the first to suggest such. The same direction was pointed to by Hans-Joachim Schoeps in his seminal work *Jewish-Christianity: Factional Disputes in the Early Church* (Philadelphia: Fortress Press, 1969), 136–40, and reflected on by Neal Robinson, *Christ in Islam and Christianity*, 15–22.

"Jewish Christianity" is still a highly problematic term and concept, as is clear from even the most summary glance at Matt Jackson-McCabe, *Jewish Christianity Reconsidered* (Minneapolis: Fortress Press, 2007). The problem centers, however, chiefly at the beginnings of the Jesus movement and its relationship to the phenomenon later identified as "Jewish Christianity"; see Craig C. Hill, "The Jerusalem Church," in Jackson-McCabe, ed., *Jewish Christianity Reconsidered*, 39–56. But there is also no doubt that later Christians saw among their contemporaries a version of their own faith that was judged deviant by reason of its too broad Torah observance and too lowly a view of Jesus, distortions they traced back to Jewish origins. And it is equally certain that they encountered, described, and attempted to refute those of their fellow Christians who held them; see, on two of the most prominent of such, Petri Luomenen, "Ebionites and Nazarenes," in Jackson-McCabe, ed., *Jewish Christianity Reconsidered*, 81–118.

The fourth century seems to have been the high-water mark of the Jewish Christian phenomenon in the Middle East, but there is convincing evidence of its survival well into the Islamic era, as emerges from the scholarly debate described by John G. Gager, "Did Jewish Christians See the Rise of Islam?" in Adam H. Becker and Annette Yoshiko Reed, *The Ways That Never Parted: Jews and Christians in Late Antiquity and the Early Middle Ages* (Minneapolis: Fortress Press, 2007), 361–72. Early on some groups, most notably the Elkasaites, were associated with Arabia, but our knowledge of Christianity in sixth-century Arabia is so thin—what we do know has mostly to do with South Arabia and the tribes of the Syrian steppe in clientage to Byzantium and Ctesiphon (see Hoyland, *Arabia and the Arabs*, 146–50, 298–99)—that we are reduced to surmise.

Jesus in Jerusalem

Just as he covered the Infancy Narratives in all their details, Raymond Brown has devoted an even more ambitious study to a good part of Jesus' last days in Jerusalem: *The Death of the Messiah: From Gethsemane to the Grave; A Commentary on the Passion Narratives in the Four Gospels*, 2 vols. paged consecutively (New York: Doubleday, 1994), with complete sectional bibliographies on each element of the narrative. Brown's account is sober and balanced but it represents a traditional view of the proceedings of those few days. Quite other is the presentation of John Dominic Crossan, *The Cross That Spoke: The Origins of the Passion Narrative* (San Francisco: Harper and Row, 1988), written before Brown, and his *Who Killed Jesus?: Exposing the Roots of Anti-Semitism in the Gospel Story of the Death of Jesus* (San Francisco: HarperSanFrancisco, 1995). Brown deals with Crossan, or rather, Crossan's source, the Gospel of Peter, in *Death*, 1317–49; Crossan defines their difference as "history remembered" (Brown's view of the passion narrative) vs. "prophecy historicized" (his own judgment on it) in *Who Killed Jesus?*, 1–38, "History and Prophecy."

THE LAST SUPPER

Brown's work begins with the departure of Jesus and his followers from their Thursday evening Passover supper. That event is presented in one fashion or another in all our sources (analyzed in Joachim Jeremias, *The Eucharistic Words of Jesus* [Philadelphia: Trinity Press International, 1966]; Xavier Léon-Dufour, *Sharing the Eucharistic Bread* [Mahwah: Paulist Press, 1982], 182–280; and Paul F. Bradshaw, *Eucharistic Origins* [Oxford: Oxford University Press, 2004], 1–23), and it is difficult to discern which is the most reliable (Bradshaw, *Search*, 47–48), or indeed the precise connection between that meal and the Jewish Passover (Bradshaw, *Search*, 48–51; Jeremias, *Eucharistic Words*, 15–88).

THE TRIALS

After his arrest in Gethsemane (Brown, *Death of the Messiah*, 237–314), Jesus is reported to have stood two, or perhaps even three, trials: one before the high priest Caiaphas on Thursday night (Brown, *Death*, 315–560, with bibliography, 315–27), perhaps a second, more formal Sanhedrin trial on Friday morning (Lk 22:66; but see Brown, *Death*, 431–32), and a Roman trial before the procurator Pontius Pilate on Friday morning (Brown, *Death*, 665–877, with bibliography, 665–75). There is an important collection of studies devoted to all aspects of the trials: E. Bammel, ed., *The Trial of Jesus: Cambridge Studies in Honour of C.D.F. Moule* (London: SCM, 1970), as well as individual treatments by S. G. F. Brandon, *The Trial of Jesus of Nazareth* (London: Batsford, 1968); D. R. Catchpole, *The Trial of Jesus* (Leiden: E. J. Brill, 1971); and Paul Winter, *On the Trial of Jesus*, 2nd ed. (Berlin: de Gruyter, 1974). There are also more specialized approaches like H. Mantel, *Studies in the History of the Sanhedrin* (Cambridge: Harvard University Press, 1961), 254–90; A. N. Sherwin-White, *Roman Society and Roman Law in the New Testament* (Oxford: Clarendon Press, 1963), 1–47; and E. M. Smallwood, *The Jews under Roman Rule* (Leiden: E. J. Brill, 1976), 145–80.

THE CRUCIFIXION

Brown's treatment of the crucifixion of Jesus is long and detailed (*Death of the Messiah*, 884–1096, with a particularly rich bibliography, 884–99). On crucifixion generally, see E. Bammel, "Crucifixion as a Punishment in Palestine," in his *Trial of Jesus*, 162–65; Martin Hengel, *Crucifixion in the Ancient World and the Folly of the Message of the Cross* (Philadelphia: Fortress Press, 1970); and now Joel B. Green, "Crucifixion," in Bockmuehl, ed., *Cambridge Companion to Jesus*, 87–101. Finally, on Jesus' death on the cross, there is the quite remarkable study by W. D. Edwards et al., "On the Physical Death of Jesus," *Journal of the American Medical Association* 255 (1986): 1455–63.

THE BURIAL

Particular attention is drawn to the site, traditionally identified with the place where the Church of the Holy Sepulcher now sits, by V. C. Corbo, *Il Santo Sepulcro di Gerusalemme*, 3 vols. (Jerusalem: Franciscan Press, 1981–1982), and C. Coüasnon, *The Church of the Holy Sepulcher in Jerusalem* (London: Oxford University Press, 1974), and two articles in the *Biblical Archeology Review* 12 (1986): Dan Bahat, "Does the Church of the Holy Sepulcher Mark the Burial of Jesus?" (26–40) and G. Barkey, "The Garden Tomb—Was Jesus Buried There?" (40–57). Jesus' burial itself is studied by Brown, *Death of the Messiah*, 1201–1316, with a bibliography, 1201–4. Against this traditional presentation should be read the skeptical account in Crossan, *Who Killed Jesus?*, 160–88.

THE RESURRECTION

Brown's *Death of the Messiah* ends with the burial of Jesus, which may mark the limits of the historical Jesus narrative. But Brown did have his say on Jesus' resurrection, significantly coupled with another miraculous event, in *The Virginal Conception and Bodily Resurrection of Jesus* (New York: Paulist Press, 1973), 69–130. The first step in any approach to the resurrection are the narratives that purport to describe not the event itself but the circum-stances surrounding it: David Catchpole, *Resurrection People: Studies in the Resurrection Narratives of the Gospels* (London: Dartman, Longman and Todd, 2000); and Bruce Chilton, "Resurrection in the Gospels," in A. J. Avery-Peck and Jacob Neusner, eds., *Judaism in Late Antiquity*, part 4, *Death, Life-After-Death, Resurrection, and the World to Come in the Juda-isms of Antiquity* (Leiden: E. J. Brill, 2000), 215–39. This latter moves the resurrection into the context of Jewish beliefs on the subject, which is made even more specific in Pinchas Lapide, *The Resurrection of Jesus: A Jewish Perspective* (London, SPCK, 1983). Geza Vermes too has insisted on the Jewishness of Jesus, so his brief study, *The Resurrection: History and Myth* (New York: Doubleday, 2008), also belongs here. There is an excellent brief study by Markus Bockmuehl, "Resurrection," in his *Cambridge Companion to Jesus*, 102–20, but the full range of interest in the subject and the variety of opinions about it are more graphically illustrated in four collections of essays devoted to the resurrection of Jesus: Stephen T. Davis, ed., *The Resurrection: An Interdisciplinary Symposium on the Resurrection of Jesus* (Oxford: Oxford University Press, 1997); S. E. Porter et al., eds., *Resurrection* (Sheffield: Sheffield Academic Press, 1999); S. Barton and G. Stanton, eds., *Resurrection: Essays in Honor of Leslie Houlden* (London: SPCK, 1994); and Robert B. Steward, ed., *The Resurrection of Jesus: John Dominic Crossan and N. T. Wright in Dialogue* (Minneapolis: Fortress Press, 2006), where there is more to learn than merely the views of the two engaging principals.

Muhammad in Medina

Muhammad's migration cast him into a new environment, the oasis culture of Medina, and both the town and its people have been intensively studied by Michael Lecker in the studies collected in his *Muslims, Jews, and Pagans: Studies on Early Islamic Medina* (Leiden: E. J. Brill, 1995) and *People, Tribes, and Society in Arabia around the Time of Muhammad* (Aldershot: Ashgate Variorum, 2005). Initially at least, Muhammad's role there was governed by an ap-parently written document called the "Medina Accords" or, less properly, the "Constitution of Medina" and it has been studied at length by Serjeant, "*Sunnah Jami'ah*," and with empha-sis on community formation by Frederick Denny, "Ummah in the Constitution of Medina," *Journal of Near Eastern Studies* 36 (1977): 39–47.

The Medina Accords were rather quickly replaced by a new, and what turned out to be a long-lived, concept, that of the umma, or community of Muslims, whose understanding by Muhammad is analyzed by Frederick Denny, "The Meaning of *Umma* in the Qur'an," *History of Religions* 15 (1975): 34–70; and, on a broader canvas, Ella Landau-Tasseron, "From Tribal Society to Centralized Polity: An Interpretation of Events and Anecdotes in the Formative Period of Islam," *Jerusalem Studies in Arabic and Islam* 23 (1999): 180–216.

MUHAMMAD AND THE JEWS OF MEDINA

Soon after his arrival in Medina Muhammad engaged with the Jewish tribes there. Their mutual interaction, which is reflected in the Quran (Uri Rubin, art. "Jews and Judaism" in

EQ, 3:21–34), has attracted much attention, both medieval and modern. This matter was studied in detail by A. J. Wensinck, *Muhammad and the Jews of Medina* (Freiborg: Klaus Schwartz, 1975), but there are now more detailed studies like that of Michael Lecker, "A Jew with Two Side-Locks: Judaism and Literacy in Pre-Islamic Yathrib (Medina)," *Journal of Near Eastern Studies* 56 (1997): 259–73, which discusses the tradition of Jewish literacy there. Lecker has also studied the political conflict in "Did Muhammad Conclude Treaties with the Jewish Tribes Nadir, Qurayza and Qaynuqa?" *Israel Oriental Studies* 17 (1997): 29–36, as had earlier M. J. Kister, "The Massacre of the Banu Qurayza: A Re-examination of a Tradition," *Jerusalem Studies in Arabic and Islam* 8 (1986): 61–96; and see, from a Muslim perspective, Barakat Ahmad, *Muhammad and the Jews: A Re-Examination* (New Delhi: Vikas, 1980).

A COMMUNITY IN ARMS

Though later generations, Muslim and non-Muslim alike, found much else to interest them there, the authors on the Prophet's biography structured it, as we have seen, around the continuous raids (*maghazi*) he mounted from the ambush at Badr Wells down to the year of his death. The legitimacy of these, and the more general issue of the use of force, arose even before Muhammad left Mecca (Fred M. Donner, *The Early Islamic Conquests* [Princeton: Princeton University Press, 1981], 55–62; Reuven Firestone, *The Origin of Holy War in the Religious Civilization of Islam* [Oxford: Oxford University Press, 1999], 13–98), but his biographers had no problems with the spread of Muslim sovereignty through the use of arms; Donner, *Early Islamic Conquests*, 62–82; Firestone, *Origin of Holy War*, 105–26; Faizer, art. "Expeditions and Battles" in *EQ*, 2:143–53.

Muhammad, the Legacy

THE DEATH OF THE PROPHET

The description of the last illness and death of the Prophet was apparently pared down in Ibn Hisham's version of the *Sira* (Ibn Ishaq, *Life*, 678–83) since Tabari presents us with a far more complex collection of reports (*The History of al-Tabari*, vol. 9, *The Last Years of the Prophet*, translated and annotated by Ismail K. Poonawala [Albany: SUNY Press, 1990], 162–88), all of which have been harmonized by Lings, *Muhammad*, 337–41.

THE "BEAUTIFUL PATTERN," THE MAN WITHOUT SIN

What later Muslims thought of Muhammad is already expressed in the *Sira* tradition, but it is often cued in the Quran. This was certainly the case with its pointing to Muhammad as "a beautiful pattern" (33:21) or excellent exemplar of human behavior. The development of that notion from the appearance of hadith on the subject to collections of such into freestanding works devoted to the virtues of the Prophet is traced by Schimmel, *And Muhammad Is His Messenger*, 24–55. There the development was largely anecdotal, but the same or similar notion gave birth to a doctrine that soon developed, as we have seen, into a dogma, that of the impeccability (*'isma*) of the Prophet; see A. J. Wensinck, *The Muslim Creed: Its Genesis and Historical Development* (London: Frank Cass, 1968), 217–18.

The doctrine of 'isma, which has also been followed by Schimmel (*And Muhammad Is His Messenger*, 56–66), emerged not so much to exalt Muhammad, as the parallel Christian doctrine of the Immaculate Conception did for Mary, as the guarantee of the veracity of the Quranic revelation and, not insignificantly, of the hadith credited to him; see Marianna Klar, art. "'ism/'isma" in Leaman ed., *Qur'an Encyclopedia*, 318–21.

THE BIRTHDAY OF THE PROPHET

"Impeccability" was matter for the theologians, but the events, real or legendary, in the life of Muhammad were the stuff of popular piety. Nowhere is this clearer than in the celebrations, narratives, and liturgies that developed around the birth, and hence, with a clear assist from the Christians' Christmas, the birthday of the Prophet (*mawlid* or *milad al-nabi*) on the twelfth of I Rabi'.[1] Schimmel, *And Muhammad Is His Messenger*, 144–58, made a preliminary sketch of its celebration, but now there is Marion Holmes Katz, *The Birth of the Prophet Muhammad: Devotional Piety in Sunni Islam* (London: Routledge, 2007), and compare Fadwa el Guindi, art. "Mawlid" in John Esposito, ed., *The Oxford Encyclopedia of the Modern Islamic World* (New York: Oxford University Press, 1995), 3:79–82.

MIRACLES

The Quran leaves no doubt that in the past prophetic claims were accompanied by confirmatory "signs" (*ayat*) or "demonstrations" (*bayyinat*) that took the form of miracles; see A. J. Wensinck, "Muhammad and the Prophets," in Rubin, ed., *Life of Muhammad*, 319–44; Uri Rubin, "Prophets and Prophethood," in Rippin, ed., *Blackwell Companion to the Qur'an*, 243–44, "Signs and Miracles." The Quran was one such miraculous sign, but Muhammad's audience demanded that he produce something more specific, more concrete, an angel sent down (23:24), a treasure given him (11:12), or a miraculous spring (17:90). His responses are consistent: it is God who produces miracles, not the prophets, who are mere mortals (14:11, 12:109, 13:38, etc.; see Watt, *Bell's Introduction to the Qur'an*, 124–27).

What Muhammad declined to do alive, the Muslim tradition freely granted to him after his death. Already there are miracles reported in Ibn Ishaq and they are likely to have originated even earlier, as argued by Josef Horovitz, "The Growth of the Muhammad Legend," *Muslim World* 10 (1920): 49–58; rpt. in Rubin, ed., *Life of Muhammad*, 269–78.

1. Since the Muslims use an unadjusted lunar calendar that annually loses eleven days against the solar calendar, the birthday of the Prophet, unlike Christmas, will not fall on the same solar date each year.

Miracles appear early and often in the hadith; see John Burton, *An Introduction to the Hadith* (Edinburgh: Edinburgh University Press, 1994), 97–101, for a representative sample. Two of the most famous are the "Opening of the Prophet's Breast" and the "Night Journey," each of which takes its starting point from an opaque reference in the Quran (94:1, 17:1) but which the biographical tradition, and almost certainly the Prophetic reports out of which it was constructed, enlarged with miraculous detail; see Schimmel, *And Muhammad Is His Messenger*, 67–69. The same treatment was given to Quran 54:1, which says, in what seems to be an eschatological context, "the moon was split." This became, in the minds of his followers, a Prophetic miracle: the moon was split by Muhammad (Schimmel, *And Muhammad Is His Messenger*, 69–71). As it turned out, this was only the rather sober beginning. As Islam spread, so too did the legend of Muhammad, not merely as a prophet but as a wonder-worker whose *baraka*, or blessing, could produce both food and water and could of course work cures (Schimmel, *And Muhammad Is His Messenger*, 74–80).

THE ADAB OF THE PROPHET

The *Sira* represents the events of Muhammad's life formalized as a biography. But before there were biographies those events circulated as individual memories that were later thought of as "reports" (*hadith*). The biographies come to our attention before the hadith, which are chiefly represented in the great vetted collections of the ninth century (Burton, *Introduction to the Hadith*, 119–47, and Muhammad Zubayr Siddiqi, *Hadith Literature: Its Origin, Development, and Special Features* [Cambridge: Islamic Texts Society, 1993], 43–75), but the hadith are, for all that, the earliest attestations on Muhammad.

The *sira* writers took the hadith they required and sometimes integrated them and sometimes laid them whole into their texts. The hadith collectors were writing for Islam's emerging class of lawyers and so they left the reports as is but grouped them into categories useful for jurisprudence: divorce, inheritance, war, etc. But their vision was somewhat broader than merely the law; it included what is known as *adab*, which in this context is best understood as everyday conduct or quotidian morality.

In his *Sahih*, or "The Sound," Islam's most reliable collection of Prophetic reports (Siddiqi, *Hadith Literature*, 55–58), Muhammad al-Bukhari (d. 870) devotes a section to what is called *al-Adab al-Mufrad*, loosely "Behavior As Such." It is available in English in a number of versions, including *Imam Bukhari's Book of Muslim Morals and Manners*, translated by Yusuf Talal Delorenzo (Alexandria, VA: Al-Saadawi Publications, 1997). In it Bukhari has assembled under 623 widely divergent heads a total of 1329 hadith (with repetitions) to illustrate the appropriate behavior for Muslims. Somewhat fewer than half of them report the customary behavior (*sunna*) of the Prophet, however; the rest are devoted to sayings and actions of Muhammad's Companions, that first generation of Muslims whose behavior was thought by later Muslims to be equally representative of an Islamic ideal of conduct.

Bukhari's collection of hadith to illustrate a Muslim adab is typically wide-ranging: it covers everything from the treatment of parents and children to afternoon naps, games, and camel courtesy. It is filled with homely and telling anecdotes from the remembered (or, on occasion, imagined) everyday life of Muhammad to provide for all future Muslims a vivid behavioral template unrivaled by anything in the Jesus tradition.

Spreading the Word

To follow the early spread of the Word that was the "Good News" and the "Submission" is nothing less than to trace the history of Christianity and Islam and so here it can only be a question of some pointing in the appropriate direction. For Christianity, when once that direction led chiefly to Adolph Harnack, *The Mission and Expansion of Christianity in the First Three Centuries*, translated by James Moffett, 2 vols. (New York: Putnam and Sons, 1908; vol. 1 rpt. New York: Harper and Bros., 1961), there are now some more generous options. For a general orientation there is no better place to begin than with Richard Lim, "Christian Triumph and Controversy," followed by Ian N. Wood, "Conversion," both in G. W. Bowersock, Peter Brown, and Oleg Grabar, eds., *Late Antiquity: A Guide to the Postclassical World* (Harvard: Harvard University Press, 1999), 196–218 and 393–94 respectively. Another angle of approach is by way of Michele R. Salzman, "Pagans and Christians," in Susan Ashbrook Harvey and David C. Hunter, eds., *The Oxford Handbook of Early Christian Studies* (Oxford: Oxford University Press, 2008), 186–202.

Two very different works are entirely devoted to the early spread of Christianity, Ramsay MacMullen, *Christianizing the Roman Empire, A.D. 100–400* (New Haven: Yale University Press, 1984), and Rodney Stark, *The Rise of Christianity* (San Francisco: HarperSanFrancisco, 1997), and there are detailed if sidelong glances at the spread of Christianity throughout a general history like W. H. C. Frend's *The Rise of Christianity* (Philadelphia: Fortress Press, 1984), 126–31, 178–84, 285–94, 309–14, 444–52, and particularly 553–92, "From Pagan to Christian Society, 330–360 A.D." On Constantine and the new faith there is, in summary, H. A. Drake, "The Impact of Constantine on Christianity," and Mark Edwards, "The Beginnings of Christianization," in Noel Lenski, ed., *The Cambridge Companion to the Age of Constantine* (Cambridge: Cambridge University Press, 2006), 111–36 and 137–58; and, for its formal imperial ratification, Charles Freeman, *A. D. 381: Heretics, Pagans, and the Dawn of the Monotheistic State* (Woodstock: Overlook Press, 2009).

The problem of the spread of Islam is more complex and at the same time less studied since first, it generally follows upon military conquest and political absorption and second, it is accompanied or preceded by cultural assimilation. The best appreciation of those factors is Georges Anawati, "Factors and Effects of Arabization and Islamicization in Medieval Syria and Egypt," in Speros Vryonis, ed., *Islam and Cultural Change* (Malibu: Undena Publications, 1975), 17–42, and the quite different situation in Iraq is reflected in Michael G. Morony, *Iraq after the Muslim Conquest* (Princeton: Princeton University Press, 1984).

The pioneer work on the subject, and still worth consulting, is Thomas Walker Arnold, *Preaching of Islam: A History of the Propagation of the Muslim Faith*, 2nd ed. (London: Constable and Co., 1913). Two more recent works merit particular remark. There is an important and influential quantitative study of conversion to Islam by Richard W. Bulliet, *Conversion to Islam in the Medieval Period* (Cambridge: Harvard University Press, 1979). Then there is the collection of essays in Michael Gervers and Ramzi Gibran Bikhazi, eds., *Conversion and Continuity: Indigenous Christian Communities in Islamic Lands, Eighth to Eighteenth Centuries* (Toronto: Pontifical Institute of Mediaeval Studies, 1990). Among them special note should be made of Bulliet's two contributions, his programmatic "Process and Status in Conversion and Continuity" (1–14) and "Conversion Stories in Early Islam" (123–34); as well as those of Michael Morony, "The Age of Conversions: A Reassessment" (135–50); Nehemia Levtzion, "Conversion to Islam in Syria and Palestine and the Survival of Christian Communities" (289–312); and Hanna E. Kassis, "Roots of Conflict: Aspects of Christian and Muslim Confrontation in Eleventh Century Spain" (151–60).

Index

BASEMENT

200.92

BASEMENT